ISRAELI
FIGHTER ACES

BY

PETER MERSKY

ISBN: 1-883809-15-0

Library of Congress Catalog Card No. 95-72959

Text by Peter Mersky

Cartography by Stephen D. Oltmann

Terrain by Ron Melton

Color aircraft profiles by John C. Valo

Published by:
Specialty Press Publishers and Wholesalers
11481 Kost Dam Road
North Branch, MN 55056
Phone: 800-895-4585

Book Trade Distribution by:
Voyageur Press
123 North Second Street
Stillwater, MN 55082
Phone: 800-888-9653
Fax: 612-430-2211

Printed in the United States of America

Acknowledgments:

I could not have written this book without the interest and support of Brigadier General Zvi Kanor, the IDF air attache in Washington, D.C. General Kanor helped me negotiate the maze of requirements and schedules to interview aces and visit various facilities.

IAF exchange officer Lieutenant Colonel Ohad Noy was another enthusiastic supporter. I relied on him for advice and emotional support, and he became an important by-product of this project – an understanding and dependable friend.

A similar thank-you also goes to Norman Polmar, who gave valuable advice at the right times.

Other people who helped were Tami Zeevy, Uri Dromi, and the staff of the Dan Tel Aviv Hotel, site of many of my interviews. (It's impossible to overstress the importance of the proper interview atmosphere.) IDF members who provided security input, but in a plesant, and sometimes informative way were Second Lieutenant Raul, Sergeant Guy and Sergeant Danny Amir. During my visits to Israel, Lieutenant Tali Pearl of IDF Headquarters coordinated my activities. Major Dahlia, Lieutenant Colonel Moshe Bar-Lev, and Major Natan Rotenberg of the IDF Spokesman's Office also helped during various stages of the project. Ms. Sharon Evenzur guided me through the IAF Museum at Hatzerim Air Base.

Gil Arbel, a well-published photographer, himself, conducted important last-minute photo research when it really counted. I also appreciate the work of the photographers of the IDF and *Israel Air Force Magazine* whose photos appear in this book.

A special thanks to author Lon Nordeen for his encouragement. His own research in the area of military aviation in the Middle East helped flesh out my narrative. Long-time friend and fellow author Richard Shipman described his experiences ferrying a much-needed A-4 to Israel in the middle of the 1973 Yom Kippur War. Ms. Shula Friedman helped by translating several reference articles from their original Hebrew.

General Kanor's predecessors, Brigadier General Joshua Shani and Brigadier General Giora Goren, also deserve a special note of gratitude because it was to them that I broached my desire to write a book on IAF aces. Their positive responses allowed General Kanor to take up the project when he arrived in Washington in 1991.

My gratitude also goes to Brigadier General Benjamin Zin, who succeeded Zvi Kanor as Air Attache, and his assistant, Lieutenant Colonel Oron Orian, whose assistance at a late stage of the project helped sew up several loose ends.

In Israel, an energetic young man was my first contact with the IDF. Rani Rahav runs a busy public relations firm in Tel Aviv, but he found the time to help me under IDF direction.

I especially want to thank the IDF and IAF for helping me conduct interviews with several IAF aces, and for reviewing my manuscript. Obviously, I bear all responsibility for the material in this book.

Note: The identification of IAF squadrons is derived from my own research and from sources in published books and magazines as detailed in endnotes and the bibliography. In each case, I have done my best to ascertain the correct squadron number through a selection of intensely researched articles in such enthusiast publications as *The Small Air Forces Observer* (Carmel, CA), *Airforces Monthly* (UK), and *Air Enthusiast* (UK). These accounts, along with occasional extrapolation, determined the appropriate numbers. Thus, in this specific area, these designators do not indicate any IDF/IAF sanction or assistance.

Preface

What is an air ace? Legend credits the French with having first used the term in World War I. An enthusiastic newspaper reporter, after meeting a successful French fighter pilot who had dispatched five enemy aircraft, declared that he was "l'as," or the ace, the top card. The moniker stuck and down through the next eight decades has come to mean a certain level of achievement among combat aviators.

Most countries that have fielded a combat air force claim at least one ace. While the larger nations, such as the U.S., Great Britain, France, Germany, Japan and the Soviet Union naturally have lengthy lists of aces, other countries, who might not be expected to have had much success in the air, can also point to their own rolls of aerial heroes. In its 1940 war against the Soviet Union and during the so-called Continuation War as an ally of Germany, tiny Finland had several aces who claimed more than 30 aircraft destroyed. China had a few aces, as did Bulgaria, Rumania, Hungary and Yugoslavia, although the careers of those pilots are not well documented.

Among the smaller countries who can point to the successes of their air forces, only Israel clings to such tight security regarding its flight crews that only the merest whispers of their activities are allowed. Yet, time eventually discloses most secrets, and the time has come to describe the careers of some of Israel's most successful fighter pilots.

Writing a book about Israeli fighter aces did not promise to be an easy task. The legendary security that surrounds all activities of the Israel Defense Force (IDF) was a formidable obstacle. It took two years of patience and understanding from both sides to obtain even an initial positive response. However, when the first tacit approval arrived, it was clear that, within certain boundaries, the project appealed to the current generation of senior air force officers. Eventually, the centerpiece of the proposed book became one-on-one interviews with several Israeli aces.

Fighter aces the world over combine innate physical skill and courage, with generous portions of patriotism and luck. To this mixture Israeli aces add their own native *chutzpah* (a special form of daring combined with a finely tuned gambling sense), love of country and a particular—even for military fighter pilots, in general—love for the hunt and the kill, although I seldom uncovered any malice toward their adversaries.

Occasionally, there was real empathy for the Egyptian and Syrian pilots who formed the majority of kills scored by IAF aces. The emotion was not a feeling of "There but for the grace of God go I," but sympathy for someone who might have the courage but not the training nor understanding to use his tools (his aircraft) well.

Most IAF aces ran up their scores in one of two specific aircraft: the French Mirage III (and its derivitives) and the American F-4E Phantom II. (One F-4 ace also became the first ace in the F-16 Fighting Falcon.) And most of them flew in at least three major conflicts: the 1967 Six Day War, the 1969-71 War of Attrition, and the 1973 Yom Kippur War. A select few even fought in a fourth conflict, the 1982 Lebanon war.

The first Israeli ace did not appear until the 1967 war—and he was the *only* ace of that war—even though IAF pilots had been engaging their Arab counterparts since 1948 with fairly impressive results.

Many of the first generation of aces came from the *kibbutzim*, the uniquely Jewish settlements that were the initial fabric of the modern state, which had their beginning in the 1880s. The members of these communes were the heart of the post-1948 population and the defense force. Although kibbutzniks were only three percent of the overall Israeli population, they made up 40-50 percent of IAF pilots through the 1970s.

The IAF pilots of the late 1950s and early 1960s who came from the settlements were used to hard work, appreciated machinery, and exuded the youthful confidence and drive so important to a military pilot. Even today, these successful pilots, some of whom are in their late 50s and early 60s, still exhibit these qualities; indeed, sometimes they still border on arrogance. They talk with their hands, in the manner of all pilots, but throw in the occasional shrug and out-stretched palms, a typically Jewish gesture of *ennui*, resignation, or...confidence.

There is also an underplayed, but deep-seated love of Israel, and a deep feeling of being part of the team, fostered by intense indoctrination and training. But there are still the great individual personalities of fighter pilots who trace their genealogy back to the German pilot Baron von Richthofen, the top-scoring ace of World War I.

Readers will also realize that most of each IAF ace's kills were fighters (with a scattering of helicopters and occasional odd types, such as air-to-ground missiles). The small bomber squadrons of the individual Arab air forces were seldom used, and then with little or no success. Most Arab aerial missions were flown by single-seat fighters and fighter-bombers – MiG-17s, MiG-19s, and MiG-21s, and Sukhoi Su-7s and Su-20s.

Until 1973, the majority of Israeli kills was made with guns, not missiles. Israeli aces, who underwent a difficult gunnery course, seem to have relied more on their carefully aimed cannon than on their Sidewinder and Shafrir missiles. The performance of the early air-to-air missiles did little to inspire confidence, and probably created the mindset of guns first—especially close in—then missiles. By the end of the 1973 war, a new generation of missiles was operational, however, and although the cannon was still useful, the IAF employed the highly capable, late-model Sidewinders and Shafrir IIs with greater frequency and confidence, to good effect.

IAF aces preferred the Mirage III for air-to-air combat, but they certainly learned to appreciate the heavier, more powerful twin-engined F-4 Phantom for overall efficiency, reliability, and available power. Many Mirage pilots who transitioned to the two-seat Phantom also had to overcome their "single-seat" mentality. One ace who had flown Mirages said that initially he told his navigator (as the IAF calls its backseaters) to do his job and keep quiet.

Within a year or two of the Phantom's arrival in Israel in 1969, and certainly by the end of the 1973 Yom Kippur War, pilot and navigator had forged an iron team, perhaps even stronger than American Phantom crews.

For all their successes, most Israeli pilots eschew identification beyond being part of the overall team. Indeed, some of the interviews I conducted for this book met with initial resistance. A few pilots asked why write such a book and made sure that I knew that they were only doing their jobs at the time. However, there were also several pilots who were anxious to tell their stories.

Some men were animated, enthusiastic as they retold their dogfights above the marshes of Egypt or the mountains of the Golan. They sought out maps to accurately describe the setting of these engagements. Although more than 20 years had passed for some, they were still firebrands, eager young lieutenants and captains in flashing Mirage or Nesher delta-winged fighters, seeking out the enemies of Israel with 30mm cannonfire and Shafrir missiles.

Then there were the more subdued pilots, some of whom it was hard to imagine flying at or near supersonic speeds, lower than 50 feet above the desert pursuing a MiG-21. Yet, they had done so and lived to tell about it.

And, finally, why write a book about *Israeli* aces? These pilots are, by definition, the most tangible symbols of IAF success. Although the lack of flashy medals and publicity tends to put individual Israeli pilots in softer focus than their counterparts in other countries, they are arguably the most effective of all the IDF component organizations.*

At the beginning of his interview, one fighter ace guardedly asked me, "So, is this going to be another book about *all* the aces, all over the world?"

"No," I said, "I want to write only about Israeli aces." He settled back into his chair, a satisfied smile softening his face.

"OK, it is a good story."

Peter B. Mersky
Norfolk, Virginia

*Author's Note: The IDF award system consists of three main medals, austere even by other simple systems, like that of Great Britain. Little more than 1,000 individual medals have been awarded since 1948, and only 37 awards of the highest medal have been given.

The first level is the E-tour HaMofet (Medal of Bravery), a blue ribbon, given for exemplary conduct. The second medal is the E-tour HaOz (Medal of Courage), a red ribbon given for bravery. The E-tour HaGevora (Medal of Valor) is the IDF's highest award, whose yellow ribbon commemorates the yellow Star of David that Jews in Nazi Germany were forced to wear.

Besides these personal awards, the IDF issues campaign ribbons to commemorate the wars of 1948, 1956, 1967, 1973, and the war in Lebanon in 1982. There are unit awards and individual certificates of commendation as well.

Only one IAF member has received the Medal of Valor, E-tour HaGevora, the pilot of an Auster liaison aircraft during the War of Independence in 1948. Although flight crewmen *have* received the first two medals on occasion, there are so many candidates for the E-tour HaGevora in the IAF that it is thought better to not award any, thereby promoting the feeling of teamwork in a common cause.

To the memory of Brigadier General Asher Snir, respected pilot, officer, and warrior.

TABLE OF CONTENTS

Chapter 1	In the Beginning	9
Chapter 2	Building the Force	17
Chapter 3	Experience in Combat After Suez	21
Chapter 4	Ace-Maker: The Mirage	27
Chapter 5	Making an Israeli Ace	35
Chapter 6	1967: IAF Triumphant	41
Chapter 7	The War of Attrition: The Happy Time	53
Chapter 8	The Russians Up the Ante	63
Chapter 9	Buildup to Catastrophe	85
Chapter 10	War on the Holiest Day	91
Chapter 11	Recovering From the Wakeup Call	103
Chapter 12	New Aircraft, Same Mission	113
	Appendices	124
	Bibliographic Essay	126
	Index	127
	Area Map	8
	Sinai – Suez Map	66
	Syria – Lebanon Map	67

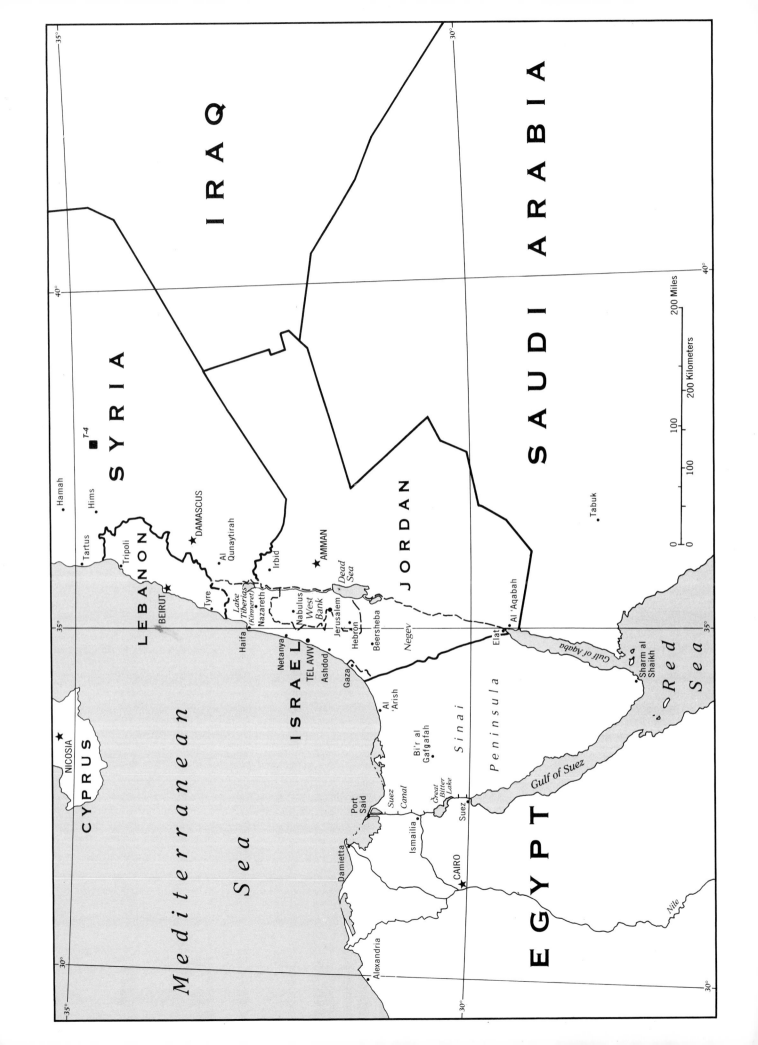

1

IN THE BEGINNING

*The Israeli air force was created by men and weapons – in that order; men
are the most important, and their weapons help them to express themselves.*
– Ezer Weizman, *On Eagles' Wings* (Macmillan, New York, 1976)

Most people will be surprised to learn that the first Israeli ace did not appear until the 1967 Six Day War. One would think that since Israel has had to defend itself constantly since its formation in May 1948, that there would have been ample opportunities for some enterprising Jewish pilot to gain the requisite five kills. Such was not the case.

There are several good books about the history of the Israel Air Force (note that it is the *Israel* Air Force, not Israeli Air Force), and this book is not intended to recount the story well told elsewhere. It is about the careers of a specific group of Israeli pilots whose accomplishments have gone largely unreported outside their own country. But some occasional background to the main story is necessary.

It is helpful to understand to some extent the Jewish mentality that persisted in forming a country from a combination of those people who had lived in what was then Palestine – some of whose parents had come to the Holy Land as long ago as the mid-19th century and before – and the huge influx of refugees from wartime Europe, survivors of the horrors of the Nazi Holocaust's concentration camps, former members of allied services, especially the British Royal Air Force (RAF) and army, and dreamers from other lands who saw in Israel a chance to find a new life, to establish themselves and their families in a new country that shared deep religious and cultural ties with their own heritage.

It wasn't easy. The British took over from the former Turkish rulers after World War I, and although they cultivated Jewish good will and participation in the Second World War against the Nazis and their Arab sympathizers, the British tried to rule post-1945 Palestine with an iron hand. They restricted the immigration of European Jews to their cultural homeland, sometimes with bloody results. The first two years after World War II became an undeclared terrorist war against the British that included some pretty unsavory, nationalistic factions that even the most ardent Jewish Zionists had trouble supporting.

Finally, the British realized that they could not keep on administering the troublesome Jews in Palestine. The only answer was to let them govern themselves,

to let them have their country back. The Arabs were horrified, then angry, and vowed to annihilate any Jewish state that appeared. Equipped with some of the best wartime British hardware, including aircraft like the Spitfire and Fury, as well as a small number of equally aesthetic and capable Italian Macchi and Fiat fighters, the Egyptians and Syrians, in particular, seemed able to carry out the threat.

To counter this threat, the Israelis had only a few ancient trainers and a small number of volunteer pilots. However, plans were afoot throughout the world to bring more and better planes to Israel, along with a large cadre of pilots, most of whom had flown with the American and British Commonwealth air forces.

The operation was tricky, and had to be carried out under the strictest security and operational conditions. The British had sold 21 Auster AOP.5s to the Israelis, and for a time, these high-wing, three-place observation aircraft were the best in the lineup.

The Austers, as well as the rest of the incredible collection of aerial cast-offs, were part of the Sherut Avir, literally "Air Service," a somewhat clandestine organization formed to supply Jewish settlements on the frontier. Most of the aircraft were based in and around Tel Aviv, on the Mediterranean coast, particularly on several ex-RAF fields.

The Israeli aircraft were prey to bombing attacks by Egyptian aircraft, especially the nimble Spitfires, which raided Ramat David airfield twice on May 22, 1948. Unfortunately for the Egyptians, the field was actually occupied by Spitfires of RAF Squadrons 32 and 38, which were protecting the final evacuation of British troops after the announcement of a Jewish state a week before. The second Egyptian raid found the British ready, and in the ensuing dogfight, the British Spitfires shot down three Egyptian Spitfires.

The Israelis organized three squadrons, based at Yavne'el (less than six miles from the Sea of Galilee), Tel Aviv (at Sde Dov, near the Yarkon River, which flows through the northern portion of the city), and at a few bases in the Negev. The aircraft of Sherut Avir did their best to counter the Arab attacks. By the end of May, the Sherut Avir had been reorganized and renamed; it was

A pilot gets into his Avia S-199 at Herzliya. The Czech Messerschmitt (which the Israelis named the "Sakin" ["Knife"], but which the hard-pressed pilots derisively called the "Mezec" ["Mule"]) used a Junkers Jumo engine, originally meant for Heinkel bombers, and a huge, three-bladed propeller. The big paddle-shaped blades show up well here. Generally, the spinners were red, but some debate remains whether the overall color of the aircraft was gray or more like khaki.

now the Chel Ha'Avir, the air arm of the Israel Defence Force (IDF).

As the War of Independence continued, many volunteers came to Israel to offer their services to the new nation. Not all of these volunteers were Jewish, and several were probably just looking for a war in which they could fly. Many, however, did believe in the cause of a Jewish state, and they also tried to round up more aircraft. When a truce went into effect on June 11, several types of aircraft had already arrived. When a second truce was arranged on July 18, the relative peace lasted until mid-October, allowing Israeli pilots to learn how to fly their new planes, sort of.

Nothing was more bizarre in these months of strange situations as the arrival of several crates in various American-built transports during May 1948. By the time other aircraft had been flown to Israel by Israeli and foreign volunteer pilots, the Chel Ha'Avir was the proud owner of 25 Messerschmitt 109s, the very symbol of Nazi Germany's infamous Luftwaffe.

Actually, the 109s were Czechoslovakian versions of the famous German fighter, and possessed only an external similarity to their Augsberg counterparts.

After the German surrender in May 1945, several Bf.109G-14 airframes had been sequestered near Prague with the idea of providing them with their normal Daimler-Benz engines. However, sabotage at the sugar factory used to store ammunition and the valuable powerplants destroyed most of the German engines and the Czechs had to find a substitute. (Twenty Daimler-Benz engines survived and were placed in the 109 fuselages. These fighters were designated S-99s and flew with the Czechoslovak National Air Guard.)

The only relatively suitable engines available were some examples of the 12-cylinder Junkers Jumo 211F, originally intended for Heinkel He.111H bombers, and which offered 100 less horsepower than the Daimler-Benz. Driving a big paddle-bladed propeller, the new engines were mated to the waiting airframes and the new fighters became S-199s.

The Messerschmitt was never an easy aircraft to fly, even when built to specifications. Its narrow-tracked landing gear made it prone to groundlooping, and its cockpit was only a narrow hole in the fuselage. The Czech version was even worse, acquiring the nickname of "Mezec" or "Mule," in service. Tricky to handle on the ground, the S-199 was also slow to accelerate, and its controls were touchy, overly sensitive. It was not for a ham-fisted pilot. In his autobiography, one of the young pilots, Ezer Weizman described the S-199 as "unfriendly, 'poker-faced,' ungracious and hateful."[1]

Six Israeli pilots traveled to Czechoslovakia to train in the S-199s under Czech instructors. One of the students couldn't handle the touchy Czech fighter and soon washed out. The transition period was fraught with peril, and more than one young Israeli had problems in merely taking off in the demanding fighter.

Eventually, the first four of the small planes were stuffed into transports and flown surreptitiously to Israel. The Chel Ha'Avir now had a small number of fighters and pilots to begin operational flights. Flying as loosely administered components of No. 101 Squadron, the S-199s were an immediate surprise to the Egyptian pilots who raided Israeli air bases at will or attacked Israeli ground troops with bombs and bullets.

On Saturday, May 29, 1948, the four S-199s scrambled from their base at Ekron (also known as Tel Nof)[2] to attack Egyptian units threatening the vital Gaza-Tel Aviv road, near the town of Ashdod. Flying as No. 2 was the young squadron commander, Mordechai "Modi" Alon. He and the other three pilots – Lou Lenart, Eddie Cohen and Ezer Weizman – headed for their target only 10 miles away.

Lenart was an American, while Cohen came from South Africa. Weizman, a native Israeli, proved to be the most enduring of the entire group of first-generation pilots; in fact, the nephew of Chaim Weizmann (note the second "n" that Ezer dropped as an indication of independence), the *first* president of Israel, has stepped into his uncle's place 45 years later as his country's president.

Swinging out over the Mediterranean, the Messerschmitts then turned back toward land. From their vantage point of 7,000 feet, they could see an entire enemy army strung out along the dusty road. Alon led his small formation down to strafe the Egyptians, who, after recovering from their surprise, began firing at Cohen and Weizman as they followed Alon and Lenart.

Cohen's aircraft was hit; he crashed nearby and was killed. When they returned to Ekron, the surviving three pilots realized that Alon's fighter had also been hit and was out of commission. Thus, on the S-199's first sortie, the Israelis had lost 50 percent of their operational complement, as well as suffering their first combat fatality. It was only 15 months later that the Israelis were able to find Eddie Cohen's crashsite. He might have actually been trying to land at an Egyptian field, which he had mistaken for an Israeli strip, and was shot down.

The next loss came the next day when Weizman and the fifth Messerschmitt pilot, Milton Rubenfeld, another American volunteer, headed out to bomb Iraqi and Jordanian armored columns. After one attack, Weizman watched in horror as Rubenfeld's plane began smoking. The pilot quickly bailed out, descending into a hornet's nest of angry Israeli farmers, who thought he was an Egyptian pilot and moved in to attack him.

Rubenfeld was able to finally convince the farmers that he was on their side and that he had actually been flying an Israeli fighter plane.

Now, the force was down to half of its operational aircraft.

While the Czech Messerschmitts and their pilots had been involved largely in ground-to-air action, it was only a matter of time before the first aerial encounters occurred. And it was most appropriate that the squadron commander, Modi Alon, achieved the first aerial kills of the Israel Air Force.

Egyptian Dakotas – military transport versions of the DC-3 airliner – converted to bombers approached Tel Aviv on June 3. In full view of the joyous inhabitants

Modi Alon as a flight sergeant in the RAF around 1943.

Lou Lenart poses by a squadron Avia S-199. As a U.S. Marine aviator, Lenart had flown F4U Corsairs in the Pacific.

below, Alon attacked the two enemy raiders, shooting down the first Dakota, which crashed south of Bat Yam.

The second Dakota tried to evade the Israel fighter, but Alon caught up with the transport-turned-bomber and sent it down, too. Tel Aviv erupted as the city shared in the glory of the air force's first public triumph.

Quiet, reserved Modi Alon tried to keep a tight rein on his squadron of foreign adventurers and Sabra zealots. It wasn't easy, and many times, the 27-year-old CO of 101 Squadron pleaded and cajoled his men to be more careful during nightly forays into Tel Aviv, all to no avail.

Alon came from a kibbutz on the Lebanon border, enlisting in the RAF in 1940 and flying Mustangs in Italy for a short time before returning to Israel to take up the fight for his native land. His tough, no-nonsense manner earned him a split decision regarding his management abilities: some people supported him, while others disliked his relatively humorless approach to what they saw as a life-or-death struggle that demanded occasional relaxation. However, all agreed that Alon was the driving force within 101 Squadron; his achieving the first victories of the IAF and its new fighter force proved it.

Besides Modi Alon and Ezer Weizman, 101 Squadron included an admirable collection of wartime personalities, many of whom had previous combat experience during World War II. Perhaps the pilot with the most tangible record was Canadian John F. McElroy. He had seen heavy combat during the epic siege of Malta in 1942, and had shot down eight German and Italian planes, receiving the Distinguished Flying Cross in the process.

He claimed two more Germans in June 1944 over the beaches of Normandy, France, and one more a month later, and received a second DFC. Thus, when he arrived as part of the foreign volunteer contingent (Mahal), he already had eleven confirmed kills plus three shared victories.

Another Canadian combat veteran of Malta, a squadronmate of McElroy, and one of the RAF's top aces, and the top ace of the Malta siege was George "Screwball" Beurling. He gained 26 kills over Malta and added five more by the end of the war. Beurling was killed in a crash in Rome at the start of a ferry flight to Israel on May 20, 1948. He was one of 20 Mahal pilots and flight crewmen who were killed in combat and operational accidents in 1948.

"One-Oh-One are lazy coons. They won't work in the afternoons...Off into the woods they'd creep, There to have a big, fat sleep..." (song probably written after the 1948 war) Hkrav Ha'Rishone (First Fighter Squadron), August 1948. No. 101 has its picture taken at Herzilya. Among the luminaries are: Ezer Weizman (standing, 7th from left), Modi Alon to his left, Rudy Augarten (standing 5th from right), and Chris Magee (kneeling, second from left, wearing a bandanna). Magee's red bandanna was an affectation the former Marine aviator carried from his days in the Pacific. Another former Marine F4U pilot was Lou Lenart (standing, 4th from the left). (via Rudy Augarten)

One more experienced Canadian fighter pilot would also show his skill in Israel. Joseph John Doyle had one confirmed victory in World War II, flying with the RCAF's No. 417 Squadron in Italy in 1944.

While the Czech Messerschmitts had filled a vital need, the Chel Ha'Avir pilots never felt very comfortable in the skittish cross-breeds. By late July, only a few S-199s remained in service, engaging in air-to-ground sorties and the occasional fighter sweep. A replacement was required – and found. Fittingly, the newcomer was the Messerschmitt's old wartime nemesis, the legendary Supermarine Spitfire.

Scrounging around abandoned RAF bases, the Israelis realized that they could rebuild a few of the derelict Spitfires, some of which were actually Egyptian fighters downed by Israeli antiaircraft fire or RAF Spitfires. The field at Ein Shemer northeast of Natanya was especially rich in Spitfire parts, although the base was under the guns of the Syrians.

As luck would have it, an Egyptian pilot had crashlanded his Spitfire near Herzliya after he had been hit while attacking the field at Sde Dov north of Tel Aviv on May 15. His aircraft was a writeoff, and the Merlin engine had seized after its vital glycol coolant reservoir had been hit by a single bullet. Israeli mechanics took a few undamaged parts and added them to a waiting Spitfire airframe. The aircraft was a conglomeration of parts from several different marks of Spitfires, including a Mk.9, 5B and even a late-model Mk.21.

To everyone's delight, the combo-Spit flew perfectly on July 23, piloted by Boris Senior, CO at Sde Dov and was soon joined by another fighter. But the IAF required more than piecemeal additions, and fortunately, by October 1948, another deal with the Czechs

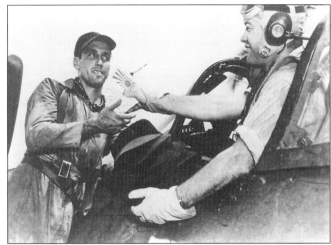

During World War II in the Pacific, Marine Capt. Chris Magee was VMF-214's second-leading ace, with only his CO, Major Greg "Pappy" Boyington (shown here in the cockpit of his F4U Corsair) ahead of him. Here, Magee poses with his famous skipper, displaying kill decals. Born in Omaha, Nebraska, Magee volunteered to fight for the new state of Israel, signing up in Chicago, then traveling to Czechoslovakia to train on the notorious Avia S-199. Although he had scored nine victories over the Japanese, Magee did not add to his total while in the Middle East. Most of his missions were close air support for the hard-pressed ground units of the Israel Army. Magee went back to Israel in July 1986 to receive his silver IAF wings. Magee died in December, 1995.

had been worked out, this time involving 50 Spitfires, most of which had been brought back by returning pilots who had served with the RAF. The new fighters began trickling into Israel.

The first Spitfires were used for photo-reconnaissance beginning in October, during what became the final phase of the War of Independence. Jack Doyle and Ezer Weizman flew recce missions over Jordan, the Negev, and Syria. On November 19, Weizman flew over

Rudy Augarten, one of the American volunteers, and an experienced P-47 pilot, stands by an Egyptian Spitfire he shot down, one of four kills he is *officially* credited with during the 1948 conflict. Combining these victories with his two kills over German Bf.109s in World War II, certifies Augarten as an ace, although not with the IAF. (via Rudy Augarten)

Ezer Weizman sits in his all-black Spitfire, one of the "perks" of being not only one of the founders of the IAF, but eventually, its commander. Weizman flew "his" Spitfire at air shows, and also as a transportation hack. One wonders how many times he wishes he were back in the cockpit as he serves as his country's president, following in the footsteps of his uncle Chaim Weizmann. (via Rudy Augarten)

the Damascus Airport at 14,000 feet, using a camera with a 14-inch lens.

Taking off from the former RAF field at Qastina (later Hatzor), with a P-51 escort, Weizman refueled at Ramat David and headed northeast. Arriving over his target, and using a relatively slow speed of 210 mph, he made three runs over the airport and eventually recovered at Ramat David, where the film was downloaded. It was the IAF's first photo-reconnaissance mission to an enemy capital.

A Mahal volunteer, Rudy Augarten, gained the first kill, an Egyptian Spitfire, for the IAF's new fighter on October 21, 1948. (He had shot down another Spitfire while flying an Avia on October 16.) On November 17, he claimed a third Egyptian Spitfire over the Faluja Pocket – a hotly contested area about 10 miles southeast of Ashqelon where the Israelis had a large number of Egyptian troops (one source lists 5,000 men) surrounded,

much to the particular discomfort of one participant, Major Gamal Abdul Nasser. The Egyptian Spitfire had been protecting a supply drop to the embattled Egyptians.

By the end of the year, Augarten had achieved two more official victories over Egyptian aircraft – a Dakota on November 4, which Augarten shot down while flying a newly arrived P-51 Mustang, and an Italian-made fighter variously identified as either a Fiat G.55 or, more likely, a Macchi C. 205V, destroyed on December 22 while flying a Spitfire. With four kills in the IAF, Rudy Augarten became the top-scoring Israeli pilot for the next 19 years. The IAF only recognizes four kills, and in 1986 sent him four citation certificates for the two Spitfire kills on October 16 and October 21, the Dakota and the Macchi, still misidentified as a Fiat.[3]

"After all these years," Augarten declared, "I would trust my logbook over the citations."[4]

Rudolph Augarten was a good warrior personality for the crusade of establishing the young state of Israel. He had flown P-47s with the USAAF's 403rd Fighter Group as part of the Ninth Air Force in Europe. He had to bail out on a patrol over the Normandy beachhead on June 10, 1944, after his Thunderbolt was hit by groundfire. He evaded the Germans for a short time, but was finally captured.

He succeeded in escaping on his second try, with five other POWs. He eventually found a group of U.S. infantrymen and returned to his squadron. He shot down two Bf 109s on October 3.

After the war, Augarten attended Harvard University in Massachusetts. However, the news from the Middle East in 1948 made him decide to offer his services to the infant Israel Air Force. After school finals, he left for Israel in June, going through Italy and Czechoslovakia, where he joined a group of Israeli fighter pilots as they trained on the Avia-Messerschmitts.

The young air force suffered a major blow, and lost one of its primary driving forces on October 16, when Modi Alon was killed in the crash of his Messerschmitt, No. 114 while returning from a mission. Besides getting the first two IAF kills on June 3, Alon had shot down an Egyptian Spitfire on July 18.

A Spitfire of 101 Squadron taxis at Ramat David. The year is 1950, and Rudy Augarten commands the base. Little more than a year after the War of Independence, it is unlikely that the fighter's markings and color scheme have changed. (via Rudy Augarten)

Two truces in June and July allowed the Arabs and Israelis breathing space and time to re-arm and strengthen themselves. Although the IAF acquired more Spitfires, as well as other British aircraft such as the twin-engined De Havilland Mosquito, and a few examples of America's premier wartime fighter, the North American P-51 Mustang, many were not ready for use when fighting resumed in October. The Israelis had 100 aircraft, but twenty percent was unusable. Five Spitfires and eight Messerschmitts were operational, but twelve S-199s and four Mustangs were not able to fly for various reasons. Thus, the Chel Ha'Avir was still fighting on the edge.

The two Canadians, McElroy and Doyle, began to get results by the end of the year. Doyle shot down three Egyptian Macchi fighters in December and January, while McElroy claimed two British Spitfires in a unique encounter in January 1949.

The RAF was not yet clear of the war zone by the new year. The British were pressuring both sides to stop fighting, even threatening to intervene militarily. The Egyptians finally agreed to a ceasefire on January 1, 1949; fighting would stop at noontime, January 7. A few hours before that time, the RAF's No.208 Squadron sent four FR Mk. 18s out from their base at Fayid near the Suez Canal to confirm word that Israeli forces had moved into the Sinai. Two of the RAF fighter pilots were credited with two victories over Egyptian Spitfires in May when the Egyptians attacked Ramat David.

Two Israeli Spitfires were up, flown by McElroy and an American, former USAF-test pilot Slick Goodlin, who had actually made the first flight of the Bell X-1, which later became the first plane to break the sound barrier (although with Chuck Yeager at the controls).

Amidst the confusion of action on the ground, dust storms and the excitement of an impending engagement, the IAF Spitfires dove on the British fighters. McElroy downed a Spitfire flown by Pilot Officer G.S. Cooper,

and went after another piloted by Sergeant Pilot Sayers. Goodlin engaged a third Spit, flown by Pilot Officer McElhaw, and shot it down. The fourth Spitfire with Sergeant Pilot Close at the controls was downed by Israeli groundfire at the opening of the fight. Perhaps the fire from the ground and the smoke from Close's aircraft was what the IAF pilots saw and mistook for an attack by the as-yet unidentified Spitfires.

By the time the IAF pilots realized the identity of their opponents it was too late. Three of the four RAF pilots were eventually returned to their unit, however, Sergeant Sayers was killed. The engagement provoked the already unsympathetic British foreign secretary Ernest Bevin to threaten direct intervention against Israel, which seemed to restrict the new Jewish state's bargaining position with its Arab neighbors for the time being.

The Israeli War of Independence had lasted barely seven months, and even with a ceasefire, the fighting would continue, with constant excursions by both sides into the other's territory. From Modi Alon's first kills on June 3, 1948, the Israel Air Force's fighter pilots of No.101 Squadron had achieved twenty victories over their Arab (and unfortunate British) opponents. The Chel Ha'Avir had, in turn, lost approximately fifteen aircraft, though most to operational causes and not in air combat.

Endnotes:

1. **Weizman, Ezer. *On Eagles' Wings.* New York: Macmillan Publishing Company, New York. 1977.**
2. **Ekron was the name of the biblical Philistine town near the base. The names are used interchangeably when referring to the IAF airfield, although Tel Nof is currently the most used.**
3. **Recent research has confirmed the fact that the Fiats had barely arrived by late December 1948, but had not yet attained operational service. Therefore, the kill is most certainly a Macchi.**
4. **Rudy Augarten, letter to the author, October 29, 1993.**

An Avia mounted on a column as a gate guardian at Hatzor. Its successors — Mirage IIIs of 101 squadron — stand alert on their covered pads in the background. This aircraft's original Israeli serial is unknown, and after its condition deteriorated, it was moved in 1988 to the IAF Museum at Hatzerim and restored as D.112.

Augarten returned after the War of Independence to help train a new generation of IAF pilots. Here, he is flanked by instructors for Class "0." From left to right, Yeshayahu Gazit, Danny Shapira, Dan Dangutt (an American volunteer and former naval aviator), Augarten, Moti Fein (later Moti Hod), and Tibi Ben-Shahar. Gazit helped reform IAF flight training in the late 1950s, Shapira became an early test pilot, making the first flight in the French Mirage by an Israeli, while Moti Hod commanded the IAF during the 1967 Six Day War. (via Rudy Augarten)

A Mark IX Spitfire of 105 Squadron, Herzliya, 1953. The tail stripes are yellow-and-black.

2

BUILDING THE FORCE

As a tense peace settled over the Middle East, many of the foreign pilots left Israel, feeling that their job was done. A few returned to oversee the establishment of a training program, among them Rudy Augarten. Although he wanted to return to his college studies, he devised an initial schedule for the first classes of cadets for the IAF.

When the war ended on January 7, 1949, No.101 Squadron actually had only two Israeli pilots, Ezer Weizman and Sandy Jacobs. Sid Cohen, from South Africa, commanded both the squadron and the base, while Rudy Augarten ran operations.

In April, Augarten started a flying course at the fighter base at Qastina with four advanced students, who had gained preliminary training in Italy. Dan Dangutt, a former U.S. naval aviator, served as another instructor. The students trained on the AT-6, then soloed in a Spitfire.

By the time these first students graduated, the IAF had asked Augarten to run another group of 11 students, this time with three more American instructors. Augarten had been a USAAF instructor in 1943 at the big training base in Texas, Randolph Field.

"The Israelis I instructed were on a par with my American students. Later, the IAF made pilot qualification very selective, and as a result, they turned out superior pilots."[1] By 1950 Augarten commanded Ramat David Air Base.

His plans were flexible at best, however, as the air force found itself fighting logistical and political battles and beset by strong personality conflicts.

Besides organizational refinement, the IAF also desperately needed new, more modern aircraft, but had to be content, for the moment, with more castoff British planes – Spitfires and Mosquitos. While the Supermarine fighters retained some measure of capability – and who didn't admire the Spitfire's timeless looks and flying ability? – the De Havilland Mosquitos had special problems in the hot weather. Made of wood that was held together by glue, much like a child's model airplane, the ageing Mossies were literally coming apart in the air and could not be counted on.

Like servicemen throughout the world, IAF crews have composed many songs to commemorate or more often desecrate their equipment, leaders, or situations. One such lyric[2] concerns the "Mossie," or "Mozi," and its tendency to self-destruct.

Mozi is a mighty fine aircraft
Constructed of plywood and shit.
It never reaches the target,
And when it does, it gets hit!
Oh, why did I join the air force?
Oh, mother, dear mother knew best.
Here I lay on the runway,
With Mozi all over my chest.

By the mid-1950s, the IAF's fleet of Mosquitos was in disarray, and morale in Mozi squadrons was not high, especially when they were the objects of ridicule by other squadrons. But then, No. 101 took occasional shots at everyone.

We don't want to fly with One-Oh-Nine
Bomb with Sixty-Nine,
Train with Halperstein.
We just want to fly with Moti Fine.
We are One-Oh-One!

No. 109 Squadron was down to its last Mosquitos by 1955, while No. 69 struggled to keep its decrepid B-17s in the air. The place to be was definitely 101, which had begun taking deliveries of sleek, new Mystere IVs. (Moti Fine was Moti Hod's original name. He would rise to fame as head of the IAF in 1967.)

The Mosquitos and Spitfires came from France in early 1951. Italy sold the Israelis more Spitfires in 1952, while Sweden offered more Mustangs. While these additions were some comfort, the Israelis could only look longingly across their borders as the Egyptians re-equipped with British Meteor and Vampire jets. Soon, their new leader – one-time army major, now-Colonel Abdul Nasser – began flirting with the Soviet Union, which responded with massive shipments of arms, including MiG-15s, one of the top jet fighters in the world, and Il-28s, twin-jet bombers. The Soviets also began supplying arms to Syria, while the British supported the Jordanians.

Israel did acquire more Meteors, including NF.13s, a night-fighting, two-seat version, which gave the IAF its only night and all-weather capability for more than a decade.

Israel had wanted to buy twenty-four Canadair Sabres, which were North American F-86s built under license. The Sabre had forged a glorious record in Korea against the vaunted MiG-15, and for the moment, seemed to be the only western aircraft capable of dealing with the speedy little high-tailed Russian fighter. It

Meteor F.8s, probably of No. 117 Squadron, at Ramat David. The squadron also operated FR.9s, some of which can just be seen beginning with the fifth aircraft. (Note the camera windows in the nose.) An FR.9 of 117 Squadron scored the IAF's first jet kills when Capt. Aharon Yoeli shot down two Egyptian Vampires on September 1, 1955.

was a frustrating situation for the Israelis that would be repeated in the mid-60s when no less a luminary than Ezer Weizman traveled to Washington to plead for F-4 Phantoms, only to be refused.

The U.S. embargo against sending arms to the Middle East made the Canadian Sabre deal stillborn, and Israel turned to France, which was only too happy to sell off some of its first-generation jet fighters.

The first French fighter to join the IAF was an uninspired straight-winged design, which looked very much like its classmates of the first group of operational jets. The Dassault Ouragan had entered service with the French Armee de l'Air in 1952, but had been quickly outclassed by newer designs. However, the IAF was glad to take delivery of 70 Ouragans beginning in 1955. The planes would serve the Israelis well for 18 years, ending their careers in 1973 as OTU trainers. For all the third-generation aviators, the Ouragan became their first high-performance jet aircraft, one they would return to as instructors, and for some, even fly many combat sorties in.

Soon after the first Ouragans entered IAF service with No. 113 Squadron[3] at Hatzor, they were joined by a development of the basic design, the Mystere IVA, which featured swept wings and improved performance. Like the Ouragans, the Mysteres also served as operational conversion aircraft as well as first-line combat planes, providing many pilots with a comparison mount against the earlier Ouragan.

Two other French types arrived in Israel in the late 50s, the Sud-Oest Vautour and the Dassault Super Mystere. The Vautour entered French service in 1955. A large, twin-jet, single-seat attack bomber that could carry ordnance in an internal bomb-bay as well as on wing stations, it seemed to offer the flexibility and hitting power that the Israelis were looking for to replace their self-destructing Mosquitos and worn-out B-17s.

The first Vautours IIAs arrived at Ramat David in 1957 to serve with newly created No. 110 Squadron.[4] Further deliveries included two-seat IIBs, and like all of the aircraft in this large influx of French equipment, the

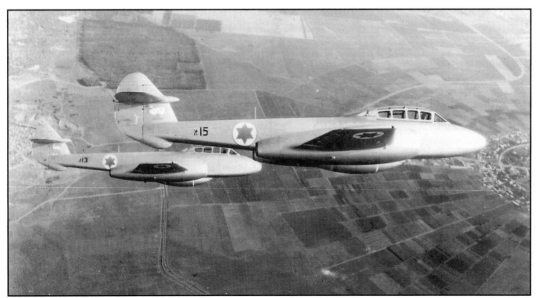

Two Meteor T.7s over Nahalal, near their base at Ramat David. The two-seat trainers were unarmed versions of the RAF's highly successful jet fighter. Six T.7s served with the IAF, the first arriving in June 1953.

Two Dassault Ouragans reside at the IAF Museum. Though sparsely marked, aircraft 113's number can hardly be coincidental since the type flew a major portion of its IAF service with the Wasps of No. 113 Squadron. (Author)

IAF eventually wrung every precious flight hour and operational sortie from the big bombers.

A few future aces flew the Vautour as their first operational aircraft. Colonel (Res) Oded Marom remembered the plane.

We started flying the French Ouragan; everything in French. Everything was different. The OTU course on the Ouragan was 60 hours. Then we went to the Mystere, which was very close to the Ouragan. I was 21 when they sent me to fly the Vautour. It was like the American B-66 or A-3. A giant aircraft, a miserable airplane, very heavy. I felt like a mosquito in the cockpit. When I saw what a monster I would fly, I was shocked.[5]

Lieutenant Colonel Ariel Cohen actually flew many combat sorties in the Vautour before transitioning to the Mirage.

I got my wings in 1969 as a fighter pilot. I flew Ouragans, then the Mystere IV, and just before I became an operational pilot in Mysteres, they moved me to Vautours, bombers! French bombers! I flew Vautours for eight months. Half of this period was during the War of Attrition. So, I had about 31 missions over Egypt, Syria and Jordan in the Vautour, bombing mostly bridges.

We could carry six 400-kg bombs in the Vautour's belly, as well as bombs on the wings, or fuel tanks. We flew all the types of Vautour – single-seater, two seaters with a navigator behind the pilot, and a clear-nosed version where the navigator sat in the nose. That version was used for surface bombing with a bombsight.[6]

When the Egyptians got their first supersonic fighter – the twin-engined MiG-19 – the Israelis began looking for a supersonic fighter to redress the imbalance. Although they approached Britain and America, they were rebuffed and again turned to France. The French had just placed its Super Mystere in service. The Israelis ordered twenty-four of the marginally-supersonic fighter in 1958, and had taken delivery of the entire order by early the next year.

Although it had a limited ground-attack capability, and was roughly comparable in performance and appearance to the American North American F-100 Super Sabre, the Super Mystere became the IAF's primary interceptor against the periodic probes by Egyptian fight-

A Vautour IIA attack bomber. Until the A-4 and F-4 arrived in the late 1960s, the big French bomber was the only dedicated attack plane that the IAF flew. Heavy and ponderous, the Vautour nevertheless scored an aerial kill during the June 1967 war. This Vautour IIA now greets visitors to the IAF Museum at Hatzerim Air Base in the Negev. (Author)

A P-51D Mustang of No. 101 Squadron, Hatzor, circa 1951-52. While two P-51s arrived shortly after the 1948 conflict from the U.S., most of the IAF's Mustangs initially came from Sweden in 1951. Once one of the world's most successful fighters, the Mustang served the IAF well for nearly a decade, and participated in what might have been the Mustang's last major conflict, the 1956 Suez Campaign. By that time, however, 101 had transitioned to French Mystere IVs. On December 1, 1948, American volunteer Wayne Pick got the first of the few aerial kills by IAF Mustangs when he downed an RAF Mosquito that was engaged in clandestine reconnaissance over Israel. Flying one of only two newly arrived American P-51s, Pick had been waiting in ambush at 30,000 feet to spot the intruder, which had been making itself troublesome during the past weeks. Finally, the spy plane appeared at 28,000 feet, and Pick managed to down the Mosquito, which fell into the sea off Ashdod. IAF Mustangs also claimed three Egyptian "Fiats," probably Macchis.

Rudy Augarten stands in the doorway of the squadron operations building. Note the roundel from an Egyptian victim. (via Rudy Augarten)

ers that scooted across the Negev, daring the Israelis to come after them.

Assignment to the Super Mystere squadron quickly became the most sought-after position for newly-winged pilots, and many aces spent most of their initial operational time in the cockpit of the sweptwing fighter. The Super Mystere also served a long time in the Chel Ha'Avir, flying through three major wars and numerous skirmishes. Thus, by the early 1960s, the IAF had quite a collection of tactical aircraft, most of them French.

Endnotes:

1. Rudy Augarten, letter to the author, October 29, 1993.
2. These and other songs quoted in this book come via Mirage ace and author Colonel (Res) Oden Marom.
3. *Air Enthusiast/ Thirty-Seven (September - December 1988.*
4. *Air Enthusiast Forty-Two*
5. Oden Marom, interview, Tel Aviv, November 19, 1992.
6. Ariel Cohen, interview, Tel Aviv, May 6, 1993.

3

ENTERING THE JET AGE

Although Israel had held onto her independence and had begun building a strong defense force, this decade saw the Arabs constantly probe the Jewish neighbor's resolve and abilities. Besides encounters on the ground, there were sporadic engagements in the sky. The Israeli pilots usually emerged victorious in these limited dogfights, absorbing the experience for future use.

One of the earliest engagements, and the first all-jet encounter in the Middle East came on August 29, 1955, when two IAF Meteors of No.117 Squadron,[1] the first Israeli jet squadron, intercepted two Egyptian Vampires. One of the Egyptian jets was hit and turned for home, preventing anything but a claim for a damaged aircraft by the IAF pilot. However, three days later, on September 1, Major Aharon Yoeli scrambled from Hatzor with another Meteor pilot to intercept two intruders near the town of Ashqelon.

The bogeys turned out to be another pair of Vampires, and Major Yoeli and his wingman, Yoash Sidon, caught up with the Egyptian pilots at 6,000 feet. Major Yoeli opened fire on one of the Vampires from 150 feet behind quickly tearing off the Egyptian fighter's left wing.

He then turned for the second Vampire which had by now turned south, trying to escape. Yoeli now found himself over his own kibbutz.

I wanted to bring the Vampire down in the kibbutz itself. It was doing various spins and turns, and I was waiting for it to finish its acrobatics. At 200 meters, I opened fire and hit the cockpit. The plane crashed into the ground just west of the kibbutz.[2]

Yoeli's twin victories were the first confirmed IAF kills since the War of Independence, and served notice to the Arabs that Israel could deal with any intrusions. No.101 Squadron would soon give up its ancient prop-driven Mustangs for new Mystere IVAs, while No. 113 Squadron at Hatzor acquired Ouragans. The IAF was rapidly modernizing its equipment, and training an entire generation of pilots to fly the jets. The new planes and crews would come not a moment too soon. The second Arab-Israeli War was on the horizon.

In a strong sense, the complicated 1956 Suez War was not just another Arab-Israeli confrontation,

Four of the first Israeli jet pilots pose in front of a Meteor at Ramat David. Standing are Aharon Yoeli (l.) and Danny Shapira. Sitting are Yak Nevo (l.) and Joe Alon. Yoeli scored the Meteor's first two kills in September 1955.

certainly not like the later wars in 1967 and 1973. Prompted more by Egyptian President Nasser's early pan-Arabism, and his desire to get the British and French out of the Middle East once and for all, the war quickly sucked in all the traditional players.

Angered by what he considered continued British interference, and American reneging of money to finance a pet project, the Aswan Dam, Nasser nationalized the Suez Canal in July 1956, a daring ploy, which he knew the Europeans could not abide.

Nasser had been nagging the Israelis for months, taunting them with cross-border incursions, on the ground and in the air. The Israelis were fed up and were planning several methods of attacking their neighbor in the west. At first, they thought they would have to fight the Egyptians, as usual, on their own, but the Israelis soon found themselves with two powerful allies, who promised the Tel Aviv government that if the Israelis would simply start the fight, the French and British would be right behind them.

The Israelis had been working on a paratroop assault against Egyptian bases in the northern Sinai, but the British and French weren't satisfied. They demanded a more direct threat against the Suez Canal. The Israelis then offered a second plan that would bring the assault much closer to the canal.

The IAF would provide its own air transport as well as initial combat air patrols. The French committed several squadrons of aircraft, including Mysteres and American-made Republic F-84F Thunderstreaks, as well as aircraft carriers with several squadrons of the Aeronavale. The British would field several RAF squadrons as well as four aircraft carriers with light attack bombers and fighters.

Besides Dakotas to drop the paratroops, the IAF committed most of its thin complement of aircraft – the last P-51s, a few Mosquitos, two ancient B-17s and a variety of jet fighters, including Meteors and recently obtained Ouragans and Mysteres.

The Egyptians had a much larger contingent with which to oppose the sparse Israeli force, including MiG-15s and MiG-17s, Vampires and even a few Meteors, as well as a fairly large number of Il-28 jet bombers.

Last-minute negotiations yielded nothing and the Dakotas of No. 103 Squadron made their drop on October 29. Meteors and Ouragans provided escorts, and French Noratlas transports, also from No. 103 Squadron, dropped jeeps and field weapons as the paratroops dug in. While the campaign in the Sinai opened, British and French aircraft bombarded Cairo and Egyptian positions along the canal in preparation for a vertical assault on Port Said on November 5. A ceasefire on November 7 finally ended hostilities.

Most of the air-to-air action during this 10-day war occurred over the Sinai. While Egyptian aircraft occasionally challenged the various British and French bombers that flew from Cyprus or the assembled carriers, they reserved their main force to confront the Israelis over the desert of Sinai.

Earlier in the year, on April 12, Lieutenant David Kishon of No. 113 (Wasps) Squadron had tangled with two Egyptian Vampires and shot one down. The young Ouragan pilot was sitting early evening alert at Hatzor when he got the call to scramble. The intruders were on a reconnaissance patrol over the Negev. In his first combat mission, Lieutenant Kishon fired a long burst at the first Egyptian jet, setting a wing aflame. The Egyptian pilot made an emergency landing and was captured. This was the first kill for the French Ouragan.

A ground crewman checks his Ouragan. Probably an aircraft of No. 113 Squadron, this fighter also displays the yellow-and-black fuselage stripe (rear tail fin) carried by many IAF planes during, and immediately after, the 1956 Suez campaign. Ouragans shot down at least five Egyptian aircraft in 1956 (one in August and four during the October Suez operation), as well as participating in the successful attack and capture of the Egyptian destroyer *Ibrahim-el-Awal*.

This Meteor NF.13 of No. 119 Squadron (note the insignia on the tail) shot down an Egyptian Il-14 transport carrying 16 high-ranking army officers on October 28, 1956. The kill was unique because it was the first night score for the IAF, the first victory by a "Bat" Squadron crew, and the last of three aerial victories scored by IAF Meteors.

Six months later, Wasp Ouragans met Egyptian fighters several times over the Sinai, although the Ouragans were primarily used for ground attack missions. On October 30, two Ouragans shot down four Vampires. On another occasion, while going after Egyptian armor, two Ouragans were jumped by four MiG-15s. In the dogfight, the Israelis dispatched one MiG; the three survivors fled.

The Mystere IV proved to be the top Israeli fighter in the Sinai. Both French fighters proved to be sturdy and stable, although the Mystere had a higher performance that let it meet the MiG-15 and MiG-17 on a more equal level.

At first, Egyptian air activity following the Israeli paratroop drop was sporadic, amounting only to occasional strafing attacks on IDF troops. In mid-afternoon on October 30, a patrol of 101 Squadron Mysteres headed for the large Egyptian base at Kabrit at the southernmost point of the Great Bitter Lake. In the lead was a man who would become one of the guiding lights of the second generation of IAF combat pilots, Captain Yakov Nevo, almost always known as "Yak." The three Mysteres – Yak Nevo, Yeshayahu Egozi and Yosef Tsuk – approached the busy enemy airbase as four MiG-15s took off.

All the Israeli pilots were concerned about firing on their own aircraft because of the general similarity from certain angles between the Mystere and the MiG-15 and MiG-17. Only the MiG's high-mounted horizontal stabilizers offered quick identification.

The Mystere pilots had very low flight time in their new planes; Tsuk had only 12 hours. Ezer Weizman later wrote that many young IAF pilots in 101 Squadron even registered their fear that the MiG-15 which, after all, had already demonstrated its lethal capabilities in Korea, would do the same to their new Mysteres. Weizman stifled his annoyance at such concerns and decided that it was only natural to be afraid of the unknown.

Now, one of these junior pilots watched the other two Mysteres in his formation open fire on the oncoming MiGs without success. Tsuk got off two long bursts with his plane's cannons and saw his MiG burst into flame. A general melee ensued and Tsuk found himself surrounded by a bunch of angry MiG-15 pilots. His Mystere took a hit in the starboard wing, but he kept maneuvering, trying to disengage.

Finally, as the Israeli formation began turning into the MiGs, the Egyptian pilots had had enough and ran, leaving Tsuk to rejoin his squadronmates with the first Mystere kill.

Yak Nevo had turned for home because his jet had begun oscillating as he dove on the MiG-15. He regained control and disengaged, but didn't tell anyone.

While he was to play an important part in future IAF successes, on October 31, 1956, Captain Yak Nevo was primarily concerned with bagging a MiG or two. He told his wingman to hold at 20,000 feet over the Egyptian-held town of El Arish, while he (Nevo) engaged a flight of *seven* MiG-15s. After making sure that the on-

A Mystere IV, perhaps of No. 101 Squadron in the late 1950s.

coming formation was a flight of MiGs and not Israeli Mysteres, Nevo closed the group of Egyptian fighters. Four MiGs disappeared into a cloud, but the solo Israeli fighter aimed at the remaining three MiGs. The fight quickly turned into a tail-chase, with the MiGs in line behind – or ahead – of Nevo's fighter.

He tried for a deflection shot on the MiG leader but missed. To add to his problems, one of his two 30mm cannon had seized, leaving him with half his armament. The fight had dropped dangerously low to the rocky terrain and Nevo decided to get out while he could.

As he climbed to rejoin his small group, Nevo got a call from the other Mystere pilots orbiting high above that two MiGs were hot on his trail, coming at him out of the sun, at almost a beam position.

Nevo maneuvered onto the tail of one MiG-15, whose pilot started twisting and turning, trying to brush off the Israeli fighter.

"The Egyptian piloting this MiG-15 certainly could fly!" Nevo reported later in one of the few expressions of admiration by IAF pilots for their Arab adversaries, many of whom the Israelis felt could just adequately fly their aircraft straight and level.

Yak finally fired his one cannon from 600 yards. He missed, and closed to 400 yards, missing again. The frustrated Mystere pilot finally got to 200 yards and fired off his remaining ammunition. This time he saw his shells tear a large hole in the MiG's right wing, black smoke trailing behind the damaged Egyptian fighter.

Out of ammunition, Nevo watched the MiG stagger toward El Arish. The Israeli pilot, already low on fuel, sped toward the enemy jet and pulled in front of him, forcing the MiG pilot to turn away, back toward Israel. However, Yak watched his fuel meter's needles drop unsteadily. There was nothing he could do if he wanted to fly home. He broke away, leaving the MiG to its fate.

Later, an Israeli scout pilot spotted a barely damaged MiG-15 in the shallows of the Mediterranean coast just off El Arish. The prize was retrieved by the Israelis and happily evaluated by IDF intelligence.

Yakov Nevo (his original name was Milner) had been born in Afula in 1932. Enlisting in the IDF in 1950, he got his pilot's wings a year later and became a Spitfire pilot. In September 1953, he was one of four cadets chosen to transition to the newly arrived Meteors. Quiet and introverted on the ground, Nevo soon acquired a mixed reputation as both a loner and an inspired pilot. Everyone had an opinion of the young captain.

As Nevo's standing grew, he attracted attention from superiors and junior pilots. While his seniors became somewhat leary of him, the younger pilots clambored to learn from Nevo, the acknowledged master of tactics and getting the most from an aircraft. He was at his best surrounded by his men, quietly smoking a pipe and listening to the conversation. When he finally commented, everyone listened.

Nevo had been part of a group of six Israeli pilots that had gone to France to train on the new Mystere, which Israel had bought to modernize the IAF. Originally, it was the Mystere II that the Israelis flew, and they were unanimous in their lack of enthusiasm for the new fighter. It was unstable at high speeds, had a short range and couldn't carry much ammunition or bombs. They recommended waiting for the improved Mystere IV, which the French had not offered for sale to the Israelis. Instead, they suggested the Ouragan. The six pilots went to another base in France and checked out in the straight-winged jet.

Yak Nevo's MiG-15 in the water off the Sinai coast. A major salvage effort is underway to retrieve the valuable war prize.

After a thorough testing program, Nevo's MiG became a gate guardian in a very undignified, but historically accurate position at Hatzor Air Base.

The first Ouragans arrived in Israel in October 1955, complemented the following March by the first Mystere IVs. In April 1956, 101 Squadron was reestablished at Hatzor with new Mysteres. Benny Peled, the squadron commander appointed Yak Nevo as his deputy. With even the most senior pilots – Nevo included – having limited time in the new Mystere IV, every flight was an instructional one. Typically, Yak Nevo pushed the new plane to its limits, trying to learn how it would react at high speed. In September, there were only 12 Mysteres in service.

The Sinai portion of the 1956 Arab-Israeli War saw no IAF losses in aerial combat; the Egyptians suffered the loss of three MiG-15s, and four Vampires, as well as several hundred on the ground from bombing attacks by Israeli, British and French planes. The IAF, in turn, had lost 15-18 aircraft, including 9-10 Mustangs; the survivors were quickly withdrawn from service. One Mystere was lost to ground fire.

The war had been a fairly quick victory for the Israelis, backed up by the British and French. However, it was the IAF and army paratroops that opened the conflict with only a promise of help from the two large European powers. The war also graphically demonstrated to the Egyptians that superiority in numbers was no replacement for quality in operators. It was a lesson they would have to be retaught several times in the next 20 years.

Although the Sinai remained fairly quiet for the next few years, and while Egypt rearmed from the seemingly bottomless well of equipment that was the Soviet Union, the IDF tried to facilitate its training operations and modernization, especially the air force. The Israelis were pleased with the Mystere and the Ouragan. The two French fighters had proven themselves quite capable against the relatively limited Egyptian opposition. And even with very low time in their aircraft, the Chel Ha'Avir pilots had done well.

However, it was not time to rest on laurels and the IAF quickly placed another new plane, the Super Mystere, into service with the Scorpions of No. 105 Squadron,[3] patrolling the tenuous borders of the Sinai, always on alert for intruders.

Super Mysteres first engaged the Arabs in November 1959, but the Egyptian MiG made it back home. Again, on May 25, 1960, two Super Mysteres scrambled toward four MiG-17s headed into the Negev. Two MiGs broke off, leaving the second pair to engage the IAF fighters. But, although one MiG was hit, it was only damaged and managed to make an emergency landing back at its base. Another encounter with MiG-17s two months later yielded the same results with no confirmed kills.

On April 28, 1961, two Super Mysteres met two more MiG-17s. In the twisting dogfight that ensued, one of the MiG pilots lost control of his aircraft and entered

25

Yak Nevo boards a Super Mystere, probably of No. 105 Squadron. The Scorpions are among the most identifiable IAF squadrons. If the aircraft does not carry the more traditional squadron badge of a scorpion on the vertical tail, the prominent red arrow, running the entire length of the fuselage, is another indicator. Several of the squadron's F-4s displayed the arrow marking. This view shows how surprisingly large an aircraft the Super Mystere was. Note the raised clamshell canopy, a rare method of design also used by the American Republic F-84F Thunderstreak.

a spin. He ejected, leaving his plane to crash onto the desert floor below near El Arish.

After the Suez Campaign, the IAF settled into building itself from within, continuing its modernization, and refining its tactics. Yak Nevo also continued to refine his own philosophies, not without an occasional problem or brush with controversy. Although he wanted to eventually lead the IAF, Nevo's loner personality and his "deep-thinker" reputation put many people off, including those superiors who might have helped him.

Nevertheless, Nevo wrote what many consider the first tactics manual for the IAF. He arranged exercises and developed many theories involving multi-plane operations during engagements. His manual established the aggressive tone for the IAF that carried it through the next 35 years.

In the air, Nevo was a virtuoso. He taught his younger pilots in the three dimensions of flying. He was hard to fly with, so great was his ability, offset by his competitive individuality. Benny Peled considered Nevo

the quintissential hunter, who thrilled at stalking and engaging his prey, using every drop of fuel.

As a young pilot, high-scoring ace Brigadier General Iftach Spector learned a lot from Yak Nevo, as did other pilots of later generations.

"Yak Nevo was a *pilot*," General Spector recalled, "a name to be remembered. He pioneered many things in tactics and taught us to analyze things."[4]

Endnotes:

1. *Air Enthusiast/Fifty May-July 1993.*
2. *Israel Air Force Magazine 1989 Annual*, p. 57.
3. *The Small Air Forces Observer, January 1993.*
4. Iftach Spector, interview, Tel Aviv, November 20, 1992.

4

ACE-MAKER: THE MIRAGE

Aircraft often become symbols to the countries whose pilots fly them or to the adversaries who fought against them. "Fokker" came to mean any German World War I fighter. The Spitfire became the ultimate symbol of British defiance against the Nazi assault of 1940, while the Mitsubishi Zero epitomized Japanese ascendancy in the Pacific for the first six months of World War II. F-86 Sabre meant Korean War air action, and "MiG" *still* means *any* Russian jet fighter to many people.

In the first fifteen years of its existence, the Israel Air Force used so many types of aircraft that no one plane captured the public imagination like the Spitfire, Zero or MiG-15. It was not until the early 1960s that the IAF had a plane with the svelte good looks and capabilities that the man on Tel Aviv's streets could easily identify. It became the symbol of Israeli audacity and ability, and the ace-maker for two generations of pilots: the Dassault Mirage IIIC.

While the Super Mystere brought the IAF to the next generation of jet aircraft, and countered the arrival of supersonic MiG-19s in Egypt, the Soviet Union raised the ante with the MiG-21, a clear-weather interceptor, small and rakish with a silhouette easily lost in the wide reaches of the sky. If the Soviets supplied these hot new fighters to their clients in Egypt and Syria, the IAF could be in trouble. An antidote had to be found.

There was also considerable – and justified – concern over the new MiG in the inner military circles of the

U.S. Air Force and Navy. Current fighters – even the exotic-looking F-104 Starfighter – were thought to be only marginally equal to the MiG, which as if in some curiously retributive prank, was given the decidedly unglamorous NATO codename "Fishbed."

As he had so many times before, and would again in another few years, Ezer Weizman, now commander of the IAF, searched for the newest and best equipment for *his* air force. He knew that the French were working on a delta fighter that could fly twice the speed of sound. He had seen a prototype as early as 1957, and again in 1959. He had gone to France to take a good, first-hand look at the small silver jet.

After some typically coy wrangling, the French agreed to let Colonel Danny Shapira, a highly regarded Israeli pilot, test-fly their new plane. In 1959, Shapira took the plane, with the evocative name of Mirage, up to 38,000 feet and went Mach 2, the 12th pilot to reach that speed in France. After other demonstrations, Weizman was desperately convinced: the IAF *had* to have the Mirage. One hundred would do very nicely. At $1.5 million apiece, the total came to $150 million (in 1959). Weizman had his work cut out for him trying to convince his own government to buy the new plane, and the French to sell it.

Finally, the French agreed to sell the Israelis 72 Mirage IIICs and three two-seat Mirage IIIB trainers. The Israelis quickly began modifying their new fighters, des-

Super Mystere 325 on the Scorpion flight line displays the squadron's distinctive red arrow marking the length of the fuselage.

Mirage 52 takes off past two Super Mysteres. Second-ranking IAF ace Iftach Spector began his list of 15 kills with a MiG-21 while flying this Mirage on April 7, 1967. He would score again in this plane, downing another MiG-21 on July 30, 1970. His total included 13 MiG-21s and two MiG-17s.

ignated Mirage IIICJs (the "J" indicating "Jeuf" or "Jewish"). In place of the small auxiliary rocket motor, the IAF requested two 30 mm DEFA (for Direction des Etudes et Fabrication d'Armament) cannon. The Mirage's original all-missile armament was in keeping with the then-current philosophy that also saw American designers deny the F4H Phantom internal guns in favor of air-to-air missiles.

The heavy-caliber guns would serve the Israelis much better than the rocket with its bulky fuel pack and cockpit controls, and the undependable air-to-air missiles of the period. Until the Yom Kippur War of 1973, most successful Israeli fighter pilots used their internal weapons with greater confidence than their air-to-air missiles. One of the reasons for this preference of the gun over the missiles was a lack of confidence in the early generation of missiles, which included early model American Sidewinders – usually AIM-9Bs that required the shooter aircraft to be almost directly behind the target – and the Shafrir I, which had a very short range and small warhead, and which performed dismally.[1] (The Shafrir did not achieve its first kill until after the 1967 war, on July 15; the victim was an Egyptian MiG-21.)

By 1973, however, the Shafrir II had gained the IAF's confidence to the extent that Mirage and Phantom pilots used the new Israeli-produced missile whenever possible. (The first Shafrir II kill was another Egyptian MiG-21 on July 22, 1969. By the 1973 war, the Shafrir II had thirteen kills to its credit, and during the Yom Kippur War the missile scored another 102 victories.) Guns were held in reserve and for when the IAF pilots were within 300-400 yards of their opponents.

During the period immediately after the June 1967 war, and through the War of Attrition (1969-70), Israeli aces used their cannons to get most of their kills. Major General Giora Rom described the intense training each Israeli pilot took to use his guns to their best advantage.

In 1967, we had first-generation air-to-air missiles; the enemy had the early Atoll, and we had the Shafrir I.

Both missiles were very limited. So, we tried to get cannon kills, as much as perhaps our adversaries tried.

It takes a lot of expertise, doing the same thing hundreds of times in training, a lot of training, where you really take your aircraft to the edge against extremely good pilots. In combat, there is a lot of tension; this is the real thing, after all. It's very simple: if you don't train to do it in combat, you can't just open your afterburner and shoot a plane down. It's a matter of how you fly your aircraft, the mental picture, not what we call a "dog chase."

When a dog chases another dog, he never comes forward; he always runs on the tail of the other. The whole idea in air-to-air tactics, when we're talking about gun kills, is to fly your aircraft not *after* your target, but to the *anticipated* point in space where your flight paths will cross.

When the kill is that easy, you don't develop a lot of respect for your opponents. It doesn't mean that next time you'll be "light headed" about him. Maybe the next pilot will be a top Syrian or Egyptian pilot.[2]

At the end of the day on June 5, 1967, Rom had three kills. He and his fellow pilots had trained long and hard for this moment.

It gives you a lot of confidence in your aircraft. When you put your viewfinder on another aircraft, find the aimpoint, pull the trigger, and the cannon shells hit where you aim, this is not a trivial thing. To reach a point where the aircraft is perfectly harmonized, when the guns are aimed properly, that takes a lot of work. You can't believe how much work we put in before the war to get to that point.[3]

The Israelis modified the radar in their Mirages, one of many changes that they typically made to whatever aircraft they bought – a practice that continues to the present day.

For instance, when we didn't have a radar lock, we incorporated something we called "constant range." We pressed a button, which gave us the aimpoint, the exact coefficient for 200 meters, 300, or 400 meters. We developed that before the Six Day War.

We got most of our kills in the war by using the constant-range capability. We learned how to make good range assessments. When you know you are 200 or 300 meters behind your opponent, you can save yourself all the agony of trying to gain a radar lock by just pressing the button. Even though the Mirage's radar was a very advanced radar, it wasn't as advanced as what we have now. If you knew how far behind your target you were, it was simple.[4]

Besides the training in air-combat maneuvering, the Mirages pilots paid close attention to other missions they would fly.

We spent our lives training and talking about training; for years, it was our job...

When the mission was ground attack, we carried bombs. The bombs and Shafrirs could not go on the same hardpoint. Sometimes we carried a Shafrir, but we always used our guns. I had one Shafrir during my earlier engagements. I launched it but it didn't work. I don't know why. It might have been my fault, instead of a problem with the missile. We didn't know how to sufficiently train to use the missile, not like today.

Perhaps the area in which the IAF trained its fighter pilots most intensely was that of air-to-air gunnery. A pilot had to be more than simply a good flier; he had to be a marksman.

We only had a couple of hundred rounds per gun, and so our bursts had to be very short. In fact, we felt very unprofessional if we didn't get the kill with the first burst. If we didn't, and we used a second or a third burst, in no time, we lost confidence. The pilot doesn't know if it's him or the aircraft; he begins shooting wildly.

Before the war, when we saw that a pilot had fired his guns, and the aimpoint wasn't steady on the fuselage of his target, we criticized him a lot.

Looking at gun camera films during the war, you might see that an Israeli pilot will take an extra 15-16 seconds to make sure he's aimed properly before firing. That's a long time to take without protecting your own tail.

The Mirage cockpit was a close fit for larger pilots and made use of every horizontal space for various devices, switches, and indicators. For aces like Giora Rom, however, the design fit like a glove. (via Giora Rom)

How did we determine if a pilot received a credit for a kill on a training flight? If the pipper wasn't steady on the target for a full second (16 frames on the film) – if it was only 15 frames when the pilot fired – there was no kill. Gunnery training was demanding, but the rules were so simple; there was no room for argument. It became almost a cultural component. We couldn't do it any other way in actual combat.[5]

By April 1962, the first two Mirages were in Israel. A new era was dawning for the Israel Air Force. When the two of the newest IAF fighters landed at Hatzor, all the IAF pilots came to see them. Young Lieutenant Eitan Karmi, at his first operational duty station, wandered around one silver Mirage.

"Mirage, Mirage," he mumbled to himself. Ezer Weizman watched the junior pilot.

"Do you want to fly this airplane?" the IAF commander asked.

"Yes!"

"OK," Weizman laughed, but quickly added, "but you are too young."[6]

It was true. Only second-tour, experienced pilots could apply – at first – to fly the Mirage. Captains and majors were recruited, but as these senior pilots' ranks were eventually exhausted, even lieutenants, like Karmi, got a chance.

All Israeli fighter pilots fell in love with the Mirage, dismissing its relatively few shortcomings, much as one would dismiss a lover's minor faults. And, in truth, many pilots looked on the Mirage as their first love. In describing their experiences in the Mirage, and perhaps later, the Phantom, their comparison between the IAF's two primary fighters was that of night and day. The Mirage was a lady, sophisticated and bright; the Phantom was a huge, powerful brute, without a trace of outer beauty. But, the F-4's inner beauty was appreciated just as furiously.

Brigadier General Amos Amir flew both aircraft, gaining seven kills in the Mirage.

Although I didn't have any combat experience in the Phantom, I think it was a great machine. But if you're talking about how a pilot loves his airplane, I loved the Mirage over the F-4. The Phantom was a big fighting machine; the Mirage was much more elegant, extremely maneuverable, very nice to handle. We all loved it.[7]

Major General Avihu Ben-Nun, who commanded the IAF in the late 1980s, flew combat in several aircraft, including the Mystere, Mirage, and Phantom.

Recalling the different types he has flown, including the new F-16, he said, "I liked the F-16 very much, but the Mirage was very *elegant*."[8]

The IAF's premier fighter squadron, No. 101 at Hatzor, was the first unit to receive Mirages. However, the 72 Mirage IIICs permitted the formation of another squadron, No. 117 (which had disbanded only a few months before), and the re-equipping of a Vautour squadron, No. 119, both at Ramat David. (Exchanging its Vautour IIAs for Mirage IIICJs in March 1963, No. 119 moved to Tel Nof.) Word of the Israeli's new fighter quickly spread, and the jittery Egyptians took delivery of their first MiG-21s in mid-1962.[9]

Captain Oded Marom had been flying the Vautour as well as instructing. He was one of the first group of six pilots chosen to transition to the Mirage. "We didn't have trainers," he recalls. "It was hard. During landing, the nose cocked up, the stick was very mushy, wobbly, and it was very difficult for us in the beginning to get used to the new airplane. My French instructor used a yellow grease pencil to mark on the windscreen where the horizon should be when we landed."[10]

After a year, the first crop of Mirage pilots was well trained. "We flew dogfights that nobody saw," Marom said. "The Mirage had many 'childhood' diseases," he remembered. Its Atar 3C engine rumbled every few minutes, which was very disconcerting. The Cyrano radar was not very good: "On radar we could only see aircraft at six or seven miles ahead of us, which was less than what I could see with my own eyes!"[11]

Public disclosure of the Mirage in IAF service was slow to come. However, when a U.S. Air Force RB-57A Canberra on a high-altitude reconnaissance mission entered Israeli airspace on July 19, 1963, it was intercepted by two Mirages with the blue Star of David on their wings and fuselages. After firing their cannon ahead of the big-winged American aircraft as an inducement, the two IAF deltas shepherded the intruder to a landing at a nearby base.

The relatively quiet period following the 1956 Suez War was beginning to deteriorate by 1962. The Israelis had begun irrigating the desert of the Negev with water from the Dan River in the north. Using a network of pipes that took water from the river through the Sea of Galilee, Israel had literally performed magic and turned a lifeless expanse into a lush, green farmland that grew practically anything. Furious, and probably not a little embarrassed, Egyptian President Nasser threatened to poison the water in the pipes. He was supported by the Syrians, looking down from the Golan Heights across the Sea of Galilee into Israel's breadbasket.

Between 1962 and 1967, there were constant incursions and artillery barrages against the kibbutzim and their farmers, who took to working their fields in armored tractors. Besides the big guns, the Syrians ran daily MiG patrols along the border with northern Israel, partly to harass the Jewish farmers, but also to take advantage of targets of opportunity. These tactics required standing air patrols by the IAF, and it was only a matter of time before the Mirage met its nemesis, the MiG-21, in combat.

Encounters in August 1963 and March 1965 between Mirages and Syrian and Egyptian MiG-21s had yielded only inconclusive dogfights. Captain Amos Amir found a pair of Syrian MiGs over the Golan Heights in April 1965 during a combat air patrol. The situation was tense at the time and there were ground operations going on. Amir and his wingman chased the MiGs almost to Damascus.

Each Mirage carried one Shafrir I missile. The new air-to-air missile had never been fired in action. Amir was in a good position behind one MiG and shot, but the missile failed to fly properly and fell away. The frustrated young pilot then fired his cannon, hitting the MiG in its underwing fuel tanks. There was a lot of smoke and the tanks fell away from the damaged Syrian fighter.

At first Amir thought he had shot the enemy plane down. But his ground (radar) controller shouted for him to return, and reluctantly he complied. Intelligence confirmed that the MiG had been only slightly damaged and the disappointed Mirage pilot had to wait for another chance.

Captain Yoram Agmon, a Mirage pilot from 101 Squadron finally made the first kill by a Mirage, and the first MiG-21 kill by the IAF, on July 14, 1966. Agmon had spent two-and-a-half years with the Nahal border guards before going to flight school in 1960. After the normal training sequence on Stearmans, Harvards, and Meteors, he moved on to the Ouragan and Super Mystere.

"I was lucky," he remembered. "I was one of the first to go to Mirages before being an instructor. I was one of the first four young pilots to go this route. I spent two years at 101 Squadron, and then became an instructor."

It was fitting that Agmon's opportunity came on July 14, Bastille Day in France which, after all, produced his Mirage. At this time, the Arabs were maintaining the pressure on the Israeli farmers and the Israeli water system in the northeast area around the Sea of Galilee, which the Israelis also call "the Kinneret," a Hebrew name for an ancient lyre, because the shape of the lake resembled that musical instrument.

To young Capt. Yoram Agmon fell the honor of scoring the first MiG-21 kill for the Mirage. Here, Agmon prepares for a mission. The symbol below his cockpit indicates the shatter pattern for his Mirage's cockpit canopy during ejection. Note the large single-looped ejection-seat ring behind his head. (via Yoram Agmon)

July 14 was what the IAF called "a war day." Periodically, the flight school closed, and the instructors flew on alert with their operational squadrons. From early in the morning, there were battles as the local farmers came under Syrian fire. Only the Mirage squadrons stood patrols, much to the disappointment of the Super Mystere pilots.

Captain Agmon checked 101's schedule at four in the afternoon, but he wasn't scheduled to fly. He asked the major in charge of operations why. The answer came that some other pilot was on the list. However, this pilot decided that nothing was going to happen so late in the day; he wanted to go home and allowed Agmon to switch with him.

We took off and began patrolling along the Syrian border, north of the Sea of Galilee. North-south, north-south. Then, the controller asked us to head west at full power. We had full tanks, and I used full military, which was enough. The other three used their burners, but I was able to keep them in sight. I wanted to save my fuel. Since I was the navigation officer in the squadron, I knew exactly where we were and that at that speed, with those external fuel tanks, my power setting would give the same performance as with afterburner – actually same speed, but double the fuel conservation.

The controller told the Mirage pilots, "Full power, *east*." Because of his conservation, Agmon had more fuel than the others. As the flight came to the border, he spotted two MiG-21s, very low, heading southwest, to the southern point of the Kinneret.

After getting permission from my lead, I dove toward the MiGs, but I lost them against the ground. I knew they were there, however, and I dove below the horizon, hoping to catch sight of the MiGs again above the horizon. Sure enough, I saw them about a mile-and-a-half away from me. They hadn't seen us.

I couldn't close them until they began to turn at the border. As they turned, I fired a burst with my cannon at one Syrian, but missed. I wanted the MiG to turn more so that I could get closer. I maneuvered toward him and fired again. This time, I hit him at the right wing root, severing the wing from the fuselage. He fell into the Yarmuk Valley. The pilot ejected. I saw the seat come out.

As the four Mirages joined up, the Israeli pilots could see the second MiG, but didn't have enough fuel to engage it. In fact, the other three Mirages did not have enough fuel to get home and recovered at Ramat David in the north. Agmon did have enough gas to make it home to Hatzor.

I tried to keep my emotions in check, but allowed myself a victory roll over the base. We held a small celebration with the pilots and mechanics. It had been a long time since the IAF had shot down an airplane, perhaps 10 years. When the armorers checked my guns, they discovered that I had used the same number of rounds as the number of our squadron.[12]

Agmon's Mirage (aircraft No. 59) had started a long, eventful career that would eventually see it become the champion MiG-killer of all Mirages, with 13 kills (including victories by two other prominent aces) before it left service in 1982.

A month later, a second Syrian MiG-21 was brought down by an IAF Mirage and to add further insult to injury, an Iraqi pilot defected to Israel in a brand-new MiG-21F on August 16. The defection had been elaborately planned by Israeli intelligence, who painted the silver MiG with red trim and gave it an "007" side number on the nose, an allusion to the fictional James Bond spy character then enjoying a world-wide popularity.

Other engagements between Mirages and Arab aircraft continued through mid 1967. In a long, drawn-out encounter, squadron commander Major Ran Ronen, one of the rising stars of Ezer Weizman's air force, took on four Jordanian Hawker Hunters on November 13.

Jordanian pilots were acknowledged to be a cut above Egyptian and Syrian aviators, having been trained by the Royal Air Force. (Britain was still a patron of its former Middle East colony.) However, their capability was mitigated by their older aircraft. Nonetheless, the Hunter was a fine design, which had enjoyed a long and satisfying career with the RAF as well as with client states of the British; in the right hands, the Hunter could be a dangerous weapon.

However, Ran Ronen was one of the IAF's most capable pilots. In a characteristic burst of enthusiasm, IAF commander Weizman had penned a poem to Ronen after the young pilot ejected from a Mirage on October 11, 1963, while returning from a mission over Egypt. His engine had died but Ronen stayed with the plane guiding it away from a populated area before bailing out at only 800 feet. The Mirage glided to a relatively soft landing allowing Israeli mechanics to retrieve it and solve the problem with engine failures that had plagued the Mirages since their service introduction.

Now flying Mirages in November 1966, Ronen and his wingman jockeyed with the Jordanian fighters, eventually chasing one Hunter across hills near the town of Hebron. After eight minutes, Ronen put a short cannon burst into the Arab fighter, causing the Hunter to roll. Its pilot ejected, but hit the side of the canyon he was flying through and was killed.

The MiG-21 provided the IAF with its most worthy adversary for nearly three decades. A flyable example of the Soviet Union's most modern fighter would be an invaluable acquisition. On August 16, 1966, an Iraqi pilot flew his brand-new MiG-21F to Hatzor. This intelligence coup had taken three years of hard work to bring to fruition. Danny Shapira wrung the MiG out, and within a year, every IAF tactical squadron knew the MiG's good and bad points. Later, the Israelis painted their prize with bright red markings and a "007" serial, which was a broad-humored link to British author Ian Fleming's super spy "James Bond," whose adventures were enjoying a world-wide audience at that time.

Two Egyptian MiG-19s were dispatched on November 28 by Mirages that had responded to calls for help from the pilot of an IAF Piper Cub over the Negev. The twin-engined MiGs had attacked the tiny spotter plane whose pilot did his best to stay low and maneuver against the Egyptian pilots. Concentrating on their prey, the MiG pilots did not see the Mirages approach until one fired a huge Matra 530 missile. The Matra took out one MiG and the second went down before the withering cannon fire from the second Mirage. The encounter marked the first time that an air-to-air missile had been used in combat in the Middle East, and was a definite portent of things to come, even though the IAF quickly found other, more capable missiles to replace the troublesome French-developed Matra.

On April 7, 1967, over the Golan, after a morning of intense action, the IAF attacked Syrian positions that had been firing into the Jewish settlements. Mirages were on CAP and two of the IAF fighters engaged four Syrian MiG-21s, shooting down two near Damascus. Lieutenant Iftach Spector got his first kill – one of three Israeli kills in the fight – over the Syrian capital. He and his wingman split a second kill.

Captain Avi Lanir found a third MiG-21. He closed to 600 feet and ended up chasing the Syrian almost to Damascus. Lanir waited patiently until he was in range and lined up on the enemy jet, and then fired his can-

non. Almost instantly the MiG exploded, leaving the Israeli pilot no choice but to fly through the debris of his victim. He brought his once-silver Mirage, No. 60, back to his base, covered with soot, to the delight of his squadron.

A half hour later, another dogfight developed near Israeli positions on the Golan Heights. Three more MiGs were shot down by Mirages – a total of six MiGs for the day – again with no IAF losses. (By April 1967, the Israelis had shot down 13 Arab aircraft since the 1956 war, 10 of which had gone to Mirage pilots.)

As heady a day as April 7 was for the Chel Ha'Avir, the eventual outcome was to simply exacerbate the already tense situation between the Arabs and Jews. The Soviets did not help matters by feeding false information to the angry Egyptians, claiming that an American pilot had been shot down and captured while flying for the Israelis.

President Nasser of Egypt was bent on forcing a war on the Middle East and intensified his inflammatory rhetoric. The whole region was about to explode.

Endnotes:

1. *Air International,* March 1986, Israeli reader's letter.
2. Giora Rom, interview, Washington, D.C., March 6, 1992.
3. Ibid.
4. Ibid.
5. Ibid.
6. Eitan Karmi, interview, Tel Aviv, May 3, 1993.
7. Amos Amir, interview, Tel Aviv, May 5, 1993.
8. Avihu Ben-Nun, interview, Tel Aviv, November 20, 1993.
9. *The Small Air Forces Observer,* September 1993.
10. Oded Marom, interview, Tel Aviv, November 19, 1992.
11. Ibid.
12. Yoram Agmon, interview, Tel Aviv, May 6, 1993.

While serving as the IAF's primary interceptor in the early 1960s, before the arrival of the Mirage, the Super Mystere also flew a ground-attack mission. This aircraft sits on the alert pad, ready to answer a call for close air support with additional fuel tanks and bombs.

Squadron commander Ran Ronen (second from left) walks with three of his pilots from their Mirages after a mission. Ronen was a rising star in the pre-1967 IAF. He retired as a brigadier general.

5

MAKING AN ISRAELI ACE

Every air force has an established program by which it trains pilots. Training organizations in the U.S. Navy and the U.S. Air Force are probably the best known because of the openness of American society: many books and magazine articles as well as scores of movies have been produced detailing every phase of a neophyte pilot's training.

For the Israel Air Force, however, the training period is so interwoven with the operational forces that revelation of many details, other than a general discussion, is frowned upon, if not completely discouraged. The most obvious link between the training units and the operational squadrons is the fact that flight instructors fly with their regular squadrons at least once a week, often on actual missions – in peacetime on patrol, reconnaissance, or low-level training flights close to Arab borders. This is in stark contrast to the practices of U.S. and other Western air forces.

The typical Israeli flight instructor, a 25-year-old IAF captain, is at least two to three years younger than his counterpart in the American Navy, Marine Corps or Air Force. It would be hard to imagine an American instructor leaving his students for a day or two to "strap on" an F-14, F/A-18, or F-16 to fly a reconnaissance mission over Iraq. Distance from U.S. training bases would have something to do with such a procedure, but not with the overall Western training culture.

When the cease-fire brought the War of Independence to a halt in January 1949, and Israel's existence was secure – for the moment – the survivors of those previous frantic months began thinking of how to continue training pilots.

While searching for newer, more sophisticated aircraft the IAF designed a training doctrine that was impressive in its uncompromising demand for perfection. Ezer Weizman's motto, "The best to the air force!" was a rallying cry that became more than a recruiting slogan; it was a way of life.

By 1956 the IAF training sequence was fairly well established. It required nothing less than strict obedience to the production of only the best, most qualified young pilots, even if that meant that barely ten percent of each incoming class received wings, which was more than often the case. It was a harsh regimen, one that was not easy to adhere to, particularly in times of reduced numbers of pilots in squadrons and low pilot-production rates.

Major General Giora Rom, Israeli defense attaché in Washington, gave a succinct insight into the IAF's training philosophy:

We need quite a few fighter pilots, but we still put a strong emphasis on selection and making sure that only the best will graduate. Our "ancestors" understood that flying fighters is a very demanding profession, and we can't compromise. Just because you need 30 fighter pilots, you don't just take the first 30 pilots you have. You take only the fittest people. If you need 30, but only have 15, so... We may be short of pilots, but we want to make sure that only the best will graduate.[1]

Little has changed since the first formal training schedules in the late 1940s. Certainly aircraft have come and gone, but the tenet of only the best graduate from IAF flight training remains as strong as ever. And the pressure doesn't stop after the emotional winging ceremony. General Rom continued:

It's a little different today. We have built our force and now only have to produce enough pilots to compensate for those who leave or for attrition. Originally, we had to produce a large number of fighter pilots, because even after we get our wings, there is a constant process by which you can be washed out at any time, even in your operational squadron. Our philosophy is that if

A closeup of Lt. Rom peering purposefully from the cockpit of his Mirage, His large, rounded helmet is typical of the period. The knurled knob and slot in the helmet's center worked a smoked visor that the pilot could bring down to shield his eyes from the sun and glare. (via Giora Rom)

you're not good enough in the squadron, you don't fly any more.

You can't fly an F-15 or F-16 just because you got your wings a few years ago. If you're not good enough, you won't fly. We grade ourselves all the time. We can't give a $30 million aircraft to someone who can't fly it properly. I got my wings in 1964, at 19. Even then, we kept to this philosophy about flying complicated jet aircraft.[2]

Most Israeli pilots begin their flight training perhaps three years earlier than their American counterparts. When an IAF fighter pilot is 25 he is probably a captain and already a designated flight leader, with perhaps several operational missions to his credit. He has not gone to college.

In contrast, U.S. Air Force and Navy pilots and officer crewmen *must* have college degrees and commit to a lengthy period of "payback" service after graduating from flight training. Thus, by the time the American aviator finishes the two-year training syllabus and joins his first operational or fleet squadron, he is at least 24, a Navy lieutenant (junior grade) or Air Force first lieutenant, and has five to eight years of obligatory service ahead of him. At the end of that time he will be approaching 30. At that age, most Israeli pilots and crewmen will have already been out of active service for four or five years, and will have settled into the routine of reserve flying, keeping their skills sharp, ready for mobilization within 48 hours.

The IAF acquired its first jet aircraft in June 1953 – two Gloster T.7 Meteor trainers from the British. Pilot training was already well underway in Israel, and producing exquisitely capable fighter and attack pilots whose only purpose in life was to fly and fight. Only those relatively few ambitious souls who wanted to make the Air Force their life's work and attain higher responsibility and rank sought the collateral administrative duties that squadron command brought.

Before the training, there should be the strong motivation to fly. Most successful pilots will say that their first and strongest dream was to fly and that the dream never left them. Mirage ace Lieutenant Colonel Eitan Karmi expressed the feeling poetically:

I knew when I was young that I would like to be a pilot. I came from a city, Petah Tikva, not far from Tel Aviv. It had a small airfield, which still exists today, though not for flying. In those days – in the 1950s – it was the flight school for the IAF.

I would stand for hours by the fence, watching the Stearmans and Harvards. My dream was not to fly, but just to *touch*, to touch the airplanes. Then the dream came true and I got my wings.[3]

While a few pilots – Israelis included – decide relatively late (in their 20s) to enter flight training, most have strong motivations from their earliest years. Just to be accepted for flight training sometimes requires that strong dedication. As in most national flight-training programs, the IAF wanted nearly perfect physical specimens – with excellent eyesight, coordination, and emotional stability, as well as a demonstrated ability to work well with others as part of the team.

The majority of physically qualified and motivated youngsters who stayed the course could at least find an initial "seat" in some class of future aviators – particularly in the 1955-1965 decade when the IAF was building itself up. But there were those who ran into unanticipated problems, and only their special brand of dedication and chutzpah eventually got them to this important, though by no means final, goal. A unique, even bizarre, example of a pilot who nearly never was is Colonel G.

[Author's note: Security concerns for pilots who still fly operational missions as this book is written require the use of initials.]

Coming from Kibbutz Negba some 30 miles from Tel Aviv, G. was brought up in the traditional frontier-farmer life style, a background that the IAF prizes above others because it gives recruits an appreciation for hard work and for machinery as well as the important understanding of working within a team.

G. lived through the War of Independence as a ten-year-old. He devoured books about flying, read all the biographies of Britain's wartime aces, and joined the Gadna Forces, a youth corps, which gave high-school students an obligatory introduction to Army life and security concerns along the frontier. In Gadna, G. was exposed to many phases of Israel Defence Force life, including naval and undersea operations, paratroops, and aviation.

By the 1956 Suez War, there was a new generation of air-minded young hopefuls including G., who could not wait for their 18th birthday and induction into the IDF, which would lead to acceptance into flight training. The 1956 war shelved such thoughts, however. Recently inducted trainees filled in where they were needed. G. assembled rockets for Israeli attack bombers at Hatzor in October 1956. When the war ended in November, he seemed a shoe-in for flight training and went for a final battery of tests.

He was surprised to find himself now confronting the formidable bureaucracy of the IDF whose doctors had decided that this promising young candidate had an undefinable medical problem that would prohibit him – for the time being – from becoming a pilot. G. fumed, stuck with kitchen or cleaning duty on the base.

Like many young Israelis, he would not sit still; he wanted to give things a shove and went to his commanding officer, a Mystere pilot from 101 Squadron, who was actually in charge of the pool of trainees under medical hold.

"Look," G. Said, "if I'm not fit now, I don't want to spend my time doing nothing. I want to do something."

"What do you want to do?" his CO asked.

G. drew himself erect. "I want to join the paratroops."

The Air Force officer refused, saying, "We want you here. Perhaps we can train you as a tower controller or radar operator, maybe a mechanic."

"No," he replied firmly, "I don't want to be a 'jobnik'!" He used a derogatory term for people who spent their careers behind desks. "I want to be a fighter pilot!"

His commander arranged a meeting with the base CO, Moti Hod, who would rise to command the IAF, during the 1967 war. Hod liked the young trainee's attitude and approved his transfer to the paratroops.

However, when G. went through the medical exam for his new career, he ran into the same doctor who had marked him unfit for flight training. The doctor did not remember his earlier judgment and certified G. acceptable. Then the doctor checked his files and realized his error. He demanded his letter of approval back.

"No!" G. replied. He was not about to let control slip through his fingers this time and stood his ground. Qualifying as a paratrooper, G. eventually made 495 jumps and was a member of the IDF's parachute demonstration team. He left active duty in 1959 and returned to his kibbutz, where he spent the next three years trying to satisfy himself at home and participating as a reservist. But he never forgot his dream to fly and re-applied for training.

The early 1950s were difficult years for the Israeli armed forces. The battle-hardened veterans of 1948 were now reservists and the IDF's regulars were low on morale and training. It took a massive rebuilding of the force, driven by the IAF and the paratroop battalions, to initiate a new era for the IDF. They needed experienced veterans, and G. had what they needed.

In turn, he was concerned that he would soon be too old – he was approaching 24 – to begin flight training. He was running out of time. With six years of military experience, he was more mature and had gained several useful contacts in the IDF that could help him. IDF medicine had also grown a little and after some investigation, it was decided that because of his athletic endeavors, G. had a "sportsman's heart," which gave somewhat different, but unacceptable, indications during testing. He finally won his case and in 1963, after seven years of frustration, he began flight training. But his troubles were not over.

Because of his experience and paratroop record, G. skipped the military phase of the training syllabus and was well on his way to becoming a pilot as one of the top students of his class. However, four months before graduation, he learned to his consternation that he would be going to helicopters.

"Why?" he asked the commander of the flight school.

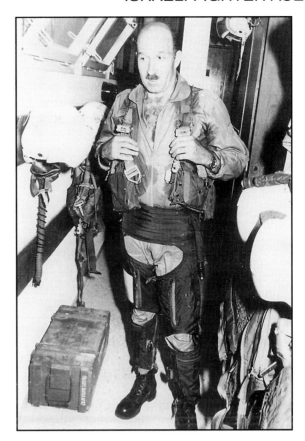

Moti Hod returns from a flight. Credited as the man who steered the IAF through the tumultuous and heady days of the Six Day War, Hod was a tough kibbutznik who was one of Israel's first jet aviators.

The colonel told him that the doctor who had signed off on G.'s medical qualifications had done so saying he could only fly helicopters. Fortunately, G.'s file was sent to a U.S. Air Force cardiologist in America who straightened things out with the IDF bureaucracy by explaining that there was nothing that would keep him from flying fighters. But it took time, and he reported to the helicopter training squadron. He told his instructors it was a waste of time.

"No," they said, "if everything comes back OK, then you'll change, but if not..."

Two months later, he ran into Moti Hod, who by now was the deputy commander of the Air Force. Hod asked him how he was doing. G. related what was happening and was sent to see the legendary Ezer Weizman who now commanded the IAF.

"I don't care what you do," G. played his last card. "I'll sit in your reception hall until you send me to fighter training."

"OK," Weizman said after a while, "go home and let me think about it."

The next day G.'s helicopter training squadron held a major exercise, but he did not fly. His CO honored his request not to fly while he waited for Weizman's decision. Finally, the phone rang.

"I didn't sleep all night thinking about you," the caller complained without identifying himself, but G.

knew who it was. "You SOB, get your things and go to the fighter OTU. I don't want to hear another word!" The phone went dead.

Thus, after eight years and obstacles that would have deterred many other young men, G. reported to a jet training unit to fly Super Mysteres, second only to the newly introduced Mirage as the top assignment for new pilots.

Although he was a top student, he couldn't go directly to Mirages, which were considered much too valuable at this early stage [1964] to give to newly graduated pilots. Only after a year's tour with the Super Mysteres, could a pilot actually fly the Mirage.

G.'s drive and determination were unique, even in a society of uniquely motivated young men. His ultimate success, however, was fortunate not only for him, but for the Israel Air Force: by 1973 he would become the IAF's top ace.

The road to wings is generally the same for any nation's military pilot program; only the training required to fly a specific aircraft varies. Normally, the candidate or cadet will undergo some form of harsh indoctrination to military life, something akin to jumping into 30-degree water wearing only a pair of bathing trunks. The initial shock – usually "lovingly" administered by non-commissioned officers – is intended to quickly weed out those people who immediately show they cannot tolerate even this level of pressure.

Further military training follows – in some cases with commissioning as an officer before flight training – and eventually is combined with the candidate's first flights. These initial flights usually determine if the student is prone to air sickness or is otherwise uncomfortable in the air.

As the syllabus continues, and students become more involved with controlling the aircraft, their instructors quickly give them increased levels of responsibility for the aircraft and mission – including flight planning, mission briefing and aircraft preflight inspection. In the air, everything is graded – control technique, response to in-flight problems (usually "faked" by the instructor...but not always), navigation, fuel management and conduct of the mission.

The categories are generally similar in every phase of flight training, whether primary or advanced, only the expected level of competency changes.

In the United States, particularly in the post-Vietnam period, although a hopeful pilot commits to anywhere from five to eight years *after* getting his wings, if he washes out, he's likely to simply be discharged from the service. However, Israel can find a use for practically everyone somewhere in its defense forces, and is not likely to discharge an otherwise physically qualified youngster from military service.

Located west of the desert town of Beersheva in the Negev, Hatzerim Air Base reminds one of Navy and Marine Corps bases in the American southwest, especially Texas and Arizona. The flat desert terrain lies under a deep blue sky, with only a few stratus clouds for variation. Several aircraft are usually in the local pattern including Tzukits and Piper Cubs, or a visiting F-4E Phantom. Even for an F-4, the Phantom looks immense beside the base's trainers.

Following the shock treatment of entry into the IAF at Hatzerim, candidates discover whether they will, after all, truly enter flight training, or will simply be dropped without having had even one flight. It's a tough time, this initial "socialization and screening phase." For those who remain in the program after a gut-searing roll call in the base auditorium, the work has just begun.

Selection phase includes classroom work and the first flights in the Piper Cub, of which Hatzerim surely the largest single gathering of these little World War II-era "grasshoppers" in the world today. Immaculate in gray-and-orange livery, the Pipers line the ramp alongside Hatzerim's shortest runway.

"The aircraft doesn't matter that much," observed Lieutenant Colonel O., the chief flying instructor of the IAF's Flying Academy.

The IAF is not looking to train pilots at this early stage. Rather they want to see how the recruit reacts to flying in general, and various situations, and how he absorbs and learns from his early experiences. During this portion, the candidate also learns a little about chart reading and radio communication. A little less than half of the initial group survives this prep stage, during which time the recruits live in a "tent city" near the flight line.

In one unusual aspect of this initial phase older pilots introduce the candidates to their first military aircraft. The IAF cannot afford the luxury of retiring a man just because he has reached an arbitrary age. These veterans – usually reservists – still serve as IAF flight instructors in the Piper Cubs or Tzukits, even though they may be in their late 40s or even early 50s.

"We're a small country," O. explained, "and we have to take advantage of every resource."

The recruit now enters the preparatory phase, going through more training in soldiering, including field trips, day and night marches and living in tents. The washout rate here is ten percent.

After the preparatory phase, and eight months into the course, the recruit becomes a "flight cadet" and moves to the primary stage, and the principal 'ab initio' trainer, the Tzukit, an updated version of the veteran Fouga Magister jet trainer originally purchased from France, but later manufactured in Israel. The Fouga – as the type is universally known in the IAF – has had a long, distinguished career in the IAF, and even saw extensive combat during the Six Day War as a ground-attack aircraft.

The Fouga, with its distinctive butterfly- or V-tail, is a very simple machine, and indeed, does not have ejection seats (which made its low-level combat missions in 1967 among the most dangerous in the IAF). In

Probably one of the longest-lived jet trainers, the Fouga Magister served until December 1994 as a carrier-training aircraft for the French Navy. Like many trainers, the type has also seen combat, most notably with the IAF during the Six Day War. Small, and simply equipped, the two-seaters were camouflaged (oddly, they also carried day-glo pink nose and tip-tank strips) and thrown into battle as anti-armor attack bombers.

the event of a bailout, each one of the crew must blow off his canopy, roll the aircraft inverted, unbuckle their seat harnesses and drop from their cockpits. Fortunately, the highly reliable Fougas have a good safety record.

After nearly 100 dual and solo flights and 20 months of hard work, those primary flight cadets with top grades move to advanced jet instruction. Students with lower grades go on to helicopter, transport or navigator training. Advanced fighter cadets fly A-4 Skyhawks, on night, navigational, and formation hops. They also fly basic air combat maneuvering (ACM) missions. The advanced phase also has a heavy syllabus of classroom work. The washout rate at this advanced stage is low.

Navigators come from the same ranks as the initial pilot trainees, and, unlike U.S. military services, are required to have a pilot's 20-20 vision and other physical attributes. Navigator students in advanced training fly the Fougas or helicopters, depending on their pipeline. They then move on to the TA-4 Skyhawk for advanced training, or the Bell 206. Fixed-wing navigators also fly the twin-engined Beechcraft, similar to the Navy's T-44.

The advanced helicopter-navigator course involves training in low-altitude flight and the use of night-vision goggles. Transport navigators train in C-130 Hercules and twin-engined Aravas.

Near the end of the course, all the flight students – pilot and navigator – reunite for the Officer Training Phase. This includes training in leadership as well as "jump" school, and occasional short tours with other IDF units. The washout rate is low here, but those that do leave still receive their commissions as officers.

The successful cadets finally receive their wings and officer commissions at an impressive ceremony, which is held usually at the Flying Academy, or atop the ancient mountain fortress of Masada. A nighttime winging ceremony in this vastly symbolic venue bestows a lifetime memory for the happy cadets.

Instructor pilots (IPs) come from operational squadrons. The IAF does not believe in using newly graduated aviators as instructors as does the U.S. Navy. The IAF wants students to know that their IPs are fully operational pilots and can be recalled to squadrons to fly combat missions.

Every week the instructors visit their operational squadrons to fly missions in an F-4, F-15 or F-16. The skill they have gained before their instructor tour is too valuable, too precious to lose for a two-year stint as instructors.

After many years of producing top-rated pilots, the IAF looked into the psychological aspects of their program. A major negative aspect of the IAF's highly successful program was discovered in regard to the inordinately high stress level during training. While high stress is a common, and universally accepted aspect of any military flight training, the IAF studies found that the stress was even higher because there was no feedback for the student, who seldom knew on a daily basis how he was doing. IPs seldom responded to this basic need of any student.

Now, the IAF uses "all-aspect" instruction, addressing individual problems, including extra instruction, but maintaining the high standards that were set long ago for flight cadets.

"People are getting better and better," Lieutenant Colonel O. declared. He was referring to the generation of cadets who have grown up with video games, which require rapid assessment of information on a screen and quick reaction.

He learned to fly before he entered the service and belongs to the older generation of aviators that flew the aircraft without a lot of displays or high-tech avionics. However, he is not unappreciative of the technical advances represented by such newer IAF aircraft as the F-15 and F-16, which he has flown on operationally; he commanded an F-16 squadron.

O. said, "As an instructor, you have to divide how much training the student receives in each phase. Today's advanced aircraft require more linkage to the battlefield. And, you will always need a gun."[4]

This training scheme, far different than that of other major air forces, and to a degree suited to the unique environment of Israel and the temperament of the Israelis, has proved highly successful.

Endnotes:
1. Giora Rom, interview, Washington, D.C., March 6, 1992.
2. Ibid.
3. Eitan Karmi, interview, Tel Aviv, May 3, 1993.
4. Lt. Col. O., interview, Hatzerim, November 11, 1992.

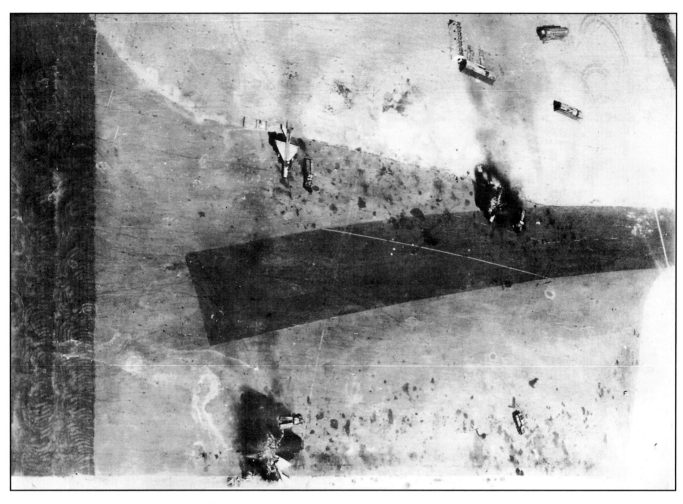

Above: The Egyptian air field at Abu Suweir after initial IAF strikes on June 5, 1967

Below: This Egyptian MiG-21C has been riddled by Israeli attackers. Note the MiG's canopy tilted open, indicating that its pilot might have been in the aircraft when the IAF struck and made a hasty exit from his fighter. Early-model MiG-21s employed an ejection system that involved the canopy tilting forward and leaving the aircraft with the pilot and his seat, thereby providing wind-blast protection.

6

1967: IAF TRIUMPHANT

Much to his chagrin, 22-year-old 1st Lieutenant Giora Rom fidgeted in his Mirage, envying his friends who were nearing targets in Egypt while he stood on ground alert at the IAF base at Ekron (Tel Nof). Still, he knew there was a reason for his remaining behind, and he also knew that there was a very good chance that he would be in combat before the day – June 5, 1967 – was over. He later described his feelings, "...when I leaned forward to fasten my shoulder harness, I literally felt that I put the quarter-million people in Tel Aviv on my back." He and only three other Mirage pilots were the sole defense of the vital Israeli city. It was an awesome responsibility for one so young.

Rom was not a kibbutznik. He was one of the city-born generation of new pilots. Although he was a "sabra," his parents had emigrated from Poland in the 1920s when teenagers. They had been in Palestine during World War II and Giora had been born in 1945. (The Hebrew word "sabra" is how the native-born Israelis refer to themselves. It is the word for the fruit of the prickly pear: tough and thorny on the outside, but sweet and tender on the inside.)

Raised in the bustling city of Tel Aviv, Giora had attended a military boarding school because he wanted a challenge. The school prepared students for careers in the IDF, mainly as ground officers; however, Giora dreamed of flying in the IAF.

After going through the barrage of tests and interviews, he entered flight training. It would be a tough road to the wings of an Israeli pilot. The washout rate was proudly acknowledged to be a constant 90 percent. Indeed, in his class of 130 cadets, only 14 graduated: four went to transport-pilot training; only 10 moved on to fighter training. Two months later, one fighter trainee was reassigned to fly helicopters.

When I got my wings, the Mirage was a new aircraft and we sent only the best to those squadrons. We didn't select these pilots by computers, or randomly. We considered every pilot's performance in all areas – flight school, personality, safety, everything.

At that time, only I and another pilot were selected for Mirages, 18 months after I graduated from flight training. We also had four pilots in the class, who had just finished their period of instructor duty. In fact, they were *my* instructors.[1]

There was no designated Mirage training squadron, no FRS (fleet replacement squadron) or OCU (operational conversion unit). Every four months a conversion course to the Mirage began. Every four months, one of three squadrons – at first, there were two Mirage squadrons (No. 101 and No. 117), then a third (No. 119)[2] – received the new pilots for Mirage training. After conversion, they could be sent to one of the other two Mirage squadrons to fill vacancies.

Then, to increase the level of operational ability, the air force decided that pilots would become operationally qualified only in the middle of their *second* squadron tour, which made the entire conversion to Mirages a six month requirement.

Lieutenant Rom and his squadronmates made up a very competitive group. "We competed with the aircraft; we competed with our friends. It was a demanding time, but that's the way we did it."

They flew an average of two sorties each day, although the time was only about 30 minutes per flight. Missions in Israel are much shorter than other countries. The time for an average air-to-air sortie could be as little as 25 minutes. The young Mirage pilots normally didn't take any reserve fuel tanks for air-to-air training missions.

Besides air-to-air, they also trained in air-to-ground missions, which prepared them for the Six Day War. "We did a lot of ground-attack missions in the Mirage III," General Rom recalled. "The Mirage with its external fuel had the longest range next to the Vautour. But the Vautour was quite heavy and had a limited self-defense capability. The Mirage could do anything, once you dropped the reserve tanks."[3]

The Mirage carried two 250-kilogram (550-pound) or 500-kilogram (1,100-pound) general-purpose bombs, mainly the 500-kg bombs, under the belly.

A few months before the Six-Day War, Rom began his flight-instructor tour. He had three years of experience as a pilot, flying the Ouragan, then the Super Mystere. The Ouragan was his squadron's OCU aircraft; all ten pilots in the training squadron were also considered operational. The Ouragan would also be used for ground attack in 1967. General Rom notes, "It's too expensive to keep a separate training squadron, and even today, we do not have dedicated training squadrons."

Rom flew Ouragans for four months. Out of nine pilots, five were sent to fly the Mystere IVA, while the last four – including Rom – were sent to Super Mysteres in an operational squadron for a year. After that, he and another pilot went to No. 119 Squadron to fly Mirages.

When the 1967 war started, the IAF had about 200 fighters, including Fouga Magister trainers. We sent all of them out to attack Egyptian air bases, but we kept 12 Mirages for air-base defense alert. Two pairs in each of the three squadrons.

I was on alert while all the others were taking off with bombs, I sat there with one air-to-air missile and my cannons. I finally got into the war about an hour after the first strikes.

H-Hour was 0745. My section was scrambled at 0845. I was No. 2. I flew across the canal to Ismailia to a base called Abu Suweir.[4]

As Rom and his leader, Captain Eitan Karmi, neared Abu Suweir, they could see columns of smoke from burning aircraft, hit on the Egyptian runways during the first strikes. Gutted Il-28 bombers stood by the bombed-out runways. Suddenly, Rom spotted a MiG-21 trying to take off.

"Number 1," the young pilot called his leader, "can you see them?" Karmi had seen the MiG and warned his wingman away, quickly destroying the MiG with a burst of cannon fire.

"It was beautiful," Karmi said. "Cannons from 750 feet. Then I got another. Giora also got two, but we got separated. It was a big 'balagan' – a big mess."

Looking around, Rom saw a Mirage being chased by two MiG-21s. He lit his afterburner and sped to help his comrade. At 600 feet, he fired his Mirage's 30mm cannon, but did not hit the MiG. He closed to 450 feet and fired again. This time his aim was good and the MiG exploded.

He returned to Abu Suweir and took on another airborne MiG-21, which also went down. Although he saw yet another MiG, Rom knew he was short of fuel and reluctantly let this third target escape. Eventually the excited young Mirage pilot landed back at Ekron. It had been an eventful morning. He had shot down two MiGs on his first combat mission. But the day was not over.

The third Arab-Israeli war in 19 years resulted from constant Arab – mainly Egyptian and Syrian – political rhetoric and military pressure. President Nasser's calls for a united front against the Jewish state, as well as removal of UN peace observers raised Israeli hackles, but Tel Aviv lived with the largely mental harassment. (Ezer Weizman called Nasser "this new Saladin" in a sarcastic comparison to a respected Arab leader of the late 12th century.) There were other more direct assaults, however, including incursions by Palestinian raiders, and constant attacks on Israeli kibbutzim and farms by Syrian artillery. These actions had focused Israeli attention more to the north than westward toward Egypt as the probable flash point for war.

However, what finally made the Israelis decide on military action was Nasser's movement of entire divisions into strategic positions in the Sinai along the border with Israel, a formal alliance between Egypt, Syria, and Jordan, and Nasser's closing the Straits of

Eitan Karmi in Mirage 732. The kill roundels below the cockpit show one Egyptian and two Syrian aircraft destroyed, although the practice was to mark the victories scored by that aircraft and not by a specific pilot. (via Eitan Karmi)

Tiran to Israeli shipping. The straits were Israel's only link to shipping lanes. Nasser must have known – just as he did when he nationalized the Suez Canal in 1956 – that his move was unacceptable, and that war was inevitable.

The French government had become afraid of upsetting the delicate balance of power in the region. In a surprise move, on June 3, the French embargoed all arms shipments to the Israelis, including delivery of 50 new Mirage V ground-attack aircraft, *already bought and paid for.*

To an extent, the French killed a golden goose. The large Israeli purchase and initial success with the Mirage had given the delta-winged fighter high-level publicity and had re-established the French aircraft industry as a world leader. However, the embargo pushed the IAF toward eventually reequipping almost entirely with American aircraft within the next two years.[5] Major General Moti Hod, who commanded the IAF during the 1967 war, is generally credited with getting the air force ready to fight and win the war, as well as saving and eventually implementing the 'Moked' plan of first strikes. He said later that one of the achievements of his tenure as IAF commander was the doubling of the size of the IAF *and* turning "a force completely outfitted with French weapons into an American air force."[6]

It took nearly three weeks for Israel to respond to the Egyptian challenge. The government of Prime Minister Levi Eshkol struggled toward a decision to strike first – the element of surprise and a devastating first strike were at the heart of Israel's defense. The threat of the combined Arab forces arrayed against Israel was considerable, at least on paper. The alliance of Egypt, Syria, Jordan and Iraq, with other brother Arab states – such as Algeria, Libya and Morocco – ready to join at a moment's notice, gave the Eshkol government some pause. But in the end, there could be only one choice.

Fortunately, the senior pilots of the IAF had, for years, nurtured just such an offense plan – code named 'Moked' (Focus). Major Yak Nevo, now a Super Mystere pilot with his old squadron, No.105 (Scorpions), had been largely responsible for writing the plan, but it was Moti Hod, now the commander of the IAF, who had filed the plan away, waiting for the right moment. The first week in June 1967 was that time.

Nevo left 105 Squadron in 1961 to serve at the IAF Headquarters in the operations division, where he evolved what became the first-strike plan of the brilliant June 1967 war.

Since it had the largest Arab air force, Egypt was the primary target of an initial strike. The relatively small, but potentially potent, force of Egyptian Tu-16 Badger bombers had to be destroyed along with as many of the more threatening MiG and Sukhoi fighters and fighter-bombers as possible. Scattered around a dozen airfields, the MiG force would be hard to destroy all at once.

After what amounted to a security blackout for the night of June 4/5 – not even the pilots who would fly the mission knew about it until they were briefed in the early hours of June 5 – flights of Israeli aircraft – nearly 200 in all – launched from the various bases scattered around the tiny country. Most headed northwest, out over the Mediterranean. Mysteres, Super Mysteres, Mirages and Vautours – each toting a few bombs – then arced back toward Egypt. To help ensure maximum surprise by lulling the Egyptians into thinking everything was normal, flights of Fouga trainers took off, climbed high above the desert, where their pilots broadcast the usual radio calls.

At 0845 (Cairo time) the first waves hit 11 Egyptian bases, including El Arish, Jebel Libni, Bir Thamada, and Bir Gafgafa in the Sinai, Kabrit, Inshas, Cairo West, Abu Suweir and Fayid along the Suez Canal. Ten minutes later a second wave struck 16 bases, followed by a third wave. The main targets were the air bases concentrated along the Nile River and its delta. El Arish was only 15 minutes flying time from Israel, but Beni Suef, the most distant base, took one hour to reach. Thus, the takeoffs had to be strictly orchestrated so that the first air strikes at 0745 would have achieved surprise before the long-range Vautour bombers of No. 110 Squadron from Ramat David hit Beni Suef at 0810. The Vautours carried special bombs developed in Israel that buried themselves vertically into runways before exploding, leaving potholes and rendering the runway useless. Some dibbers used timers that made them explode a long time after the raid, thereby keeping the runways in a state of disrepair. These concrete "dibber" bombs were responsible in large part for grounding much of the Egyptian aircraft that had not been destroyed by bombs or strafing attacks.

The plan was vaguely reminiscent of the Japanese surprise attack on Pearl Harbor on December 7, 1941. The enemy had been caught literally asleep, and with a one-two punch, the attackers had nearly destroyed and demoralized their victims in a stunning demonstration of airpower. Israel committed its entire air force in the opening rounds much like a desperate gambler on a winner-take-all last throw of his dice.

The Egyptians tried to respond, but the relatively few MiGs that rose to do battle that morning were pathetically ineffective.

The surprise factors which the Israelis had carefully considered included the particular hour, when the Egyptian morning alert would have stood down, watch shifts were changing, the swing over the Med to avoid any radar coverage, and strict radio silence in the attack force. The main objectives were obtained: surprise and destruction of the Egyptian air force, particularly its long-range bomber force, and making the airfield runways temporarily inoperative.

By the time the morning's attack force had returned to Israel, most of Egypt's aircraft lay in burnt-out

Capt. Asher Snir sits in a Bat Squadron Mirage. (via the Snir family)

ruins along the runways and in the revetments of decimated airfields. Returning pilots estimated more than 200 aircraft destroyed. It was a singular achievement for the Israelis and their small, but efficient air force. The world gaped in wonder – and admiration.

Within 10 minutes of landing, the returning strikers were refueled and rearmed by hard-working ground crews, beginning one of the miracles and reasons for the eventual success of the next five days. The mechanics and armorers provided a shuttle-like capability for the IAF. Most IAF pilots averaged three sorties on June 5. Many Arabs believed that the U.S. was supplementing Israeli missions with American planes and crews, flying in support of the small Jewish air force.

In the early afternoon the IAF turned its attention to Syria, hitting airfields near Damascus and the remote base known as T-4, 75 miles *northeast* of Damascus. (The original mission against the international airport at Cairo had been scrubbed while the Mirages were taxiing out. Instead, the attack would be against T-4, which was a dispersion base that had apparently received 15-20 MiG-21s and two Il-14 transports.)

Four Mirages from No. 119 Squadron participated in the long-range attack. Their pilots were Eitan Karmi, Asher Snir, Eliezer Prigat and Giora Rom. Asher Snir quickly engaged a flight of two MiG-21s patrolling over the base. Snir, who would become an ace, later a brigadier general, and one of the most respected officers in the air force, shot down one of the Syrian fighters while the other Mirages strafed the airfield. The MiG was one of three kills that Snir scored in the war.

As Giora Rom, on his third mission of the day, made his attack runs at more than 550 knots, he saw a MiG closing in on Prigat. Rom called for the Mirage to break, and punched off his own drop tanks to engage the enemy. The Syrian pilot fired two missiles, neither of which hit Prigat's airplane. Prigat screamed for help and Rom responded, lining up the MiG and firing his cannon. The silver MiG went down right over its home field, spinning and trailing a long plume of smoke before it hit the ground.

After the 90-minute mission, Rom was low on fuel. He barely had enough to land at Tel Nof. After a few hours sleep, Rom awoke at 0330 on June 6 to brief for another mission, a patrol over the northern Sinai, near the Egyptian base at El Arish. Although he and his flight saw two Su-7 Fitters, the Russian-built fighters were shot down by Mirages from another patrol.

On his third strafing pass, a 37 mm anti-aircraft shell struck Rom's Mirage right under his ejection seat, sending shrapnel into his leg. The shell knocked out his plane's electrical system and damaged the control system; he could barely fly the crippled French fighter. He headed for the IAF base at Ramat David, fighting the stiff control column with two hands. He managed to land and was taken immediately to the hospital at Afula.

"I spent one day in the hospital, but I found out that my wound was not that serious. So, I ran away to get back to my squadron."

In typical fashion, Rom had prevailed on some of his friends to smuggle in a new flight suit. He got to the hospital's gate in his wheelchair and boarded a shuttle bus, making it back to Ekron by 1400. At first, his CO, Ran Ronen, forbade him to fly without a doctor's okay, but the energetic lieutenant finally prevailed over all obstacles.

At 5 PM, I launched on a ground attack mission with two other Mirages against an Egyptian armored column on the road between Ras Sudr and

Sharm el-Sheikh in southern Sinai. As we headed for the tip of the peninsula, we were vectored to intercept Egyptian MiGs.[7]

The Israeli controller told the Mirages to punch off their drop tanks and head north at 20,000 feet. Looking far below, Rom spotted the sun flickering off two silver MiG-17s closing in on two Israeli Super Mysteres.

A dogfight quickly developed, the Mirages and MiGs mixing it up until the MiGs had had enough and tried to escape. Scraping the desert floor at 30 feet, the MiGs headed for the safety of the Suez Canal. Rom pursued them and hit the second MiG from 600 feet.

He fired another burst, this time from 900 feet, still only 30 feet above the desert. Pieces began flying off the MiG and its canopy blew off. Rom approached the MiG and was surprised to see that the cockpit was empty, the warning lights flickering. The Egyptian pilot had, in fact, ejected without Rom seeing him go. The MiG soon stalled and crashed.

He pulled up to search for the second MiG. Rom looked at his airspeed indicator; he was doing 710 knots (more than 800 mph) in full afterburner.

"This was the fastest I had ever flown at low altitude," he remarked.

In the blinding light of a setting sun, he spotted the second MiG over the canal, near Ismailia. The MiG pilot saw the Israeli plane as well. Alone over the canal, the two fighter pilots, one Egyptian, one Israeli Sabra, dueled in a close-turning dogfight. The voice of his flight leader intruded on the radio, calling for Rom to return.

"You don't fight alone," his leader warned. Rom knew the wisdom of that warning but kept turning with the MiG. Finally, after another minute, he fired at the MiG-17, sending it into the ground. He returned to his base where he found the atmosphere subdued, somber. Three days of war had begun to have their effect on the normally exuberant young Mirage pilots. To make matters worse, because of his late return, Giora Rom could not even get a meal from the base's cook.

The base's atmosphere could not take away what Giora Rom knew was a milestone, not only for himself, but for the air force: he had become Israel's first ace, and in only three days. No one had previously achieved the magic five kills in the Israel Air Force, not even the early legendary eagles of 1948, Augarten and Alon. Four was the highest number until June 7, 1967, and Lieutenant Giora Rom's engagements with two MiG-17s.

"I was lucky enough to find them and get them both," he said.

The Israeli air tactics were those of Germany nearly 30 years before – blitzkrieg, a lightning war, involving quick, devastating strikes in slashing air attacks. In little more than six hours most of the aircraft of Egypt and Syria had been reduced to burnt-out shells, resulting in only a relatively few aerial encounters between the opposing sides. Only a few Israeli pilots saw MiGs in the air, and fewer still got kills. Rom was the only one to get five during the war. It was a mixed blessing.

The next day, I was put on the slow road in the squadron because everyone wanted a chance to shoot down MiGs. I had already five kills, and most of my friends had no kills. Some had one. It was very competitive. They were flying two or three sorties a day; I got to fly maybe one. A few days later, the war was over.[8]

The second MiG-17 downed over the canal was Giora Rom's last kill. He remained in Mirages for the

First Lieutenant Giora Rom stands beside Mirage 755, probably at Tel Nof. Shooting down five Egyptian and Syrian MiGs in three days (two on his first combat mission), Rom became the IAF's first ace, beginning a brilliant career that saw him rise to the rank of major general. His Mirage's natural-metal finish shines, indicating the loving care that IAF groundcrews lavished on their charges. (via Giora Rom)

Asher Snir shot down three MiGs in June 1967, and eventually scored 13.5 kills, while rising to one-star rank. This photo shows the intense young Mirage pilot in 1967 some time during the Six Day War. (via the Snir family)

sults of his efforts. Later that night, he proudly displayed prints of four MiGs burning in the sand that he had destroyed.

With all his success, Snir was happy and in control. He was not prepared for personal losses. Thus, when Giora Rom approached him with news of squadron casualties, Snir listened quietly. Then, after a long pause, Rom told him that one of the lost pilots was a particularly close friend. Snir took the news hard and retreated into a private corner to cry.

At that moment, the CO walked in. Ronen took his young pilot into his office and told him that he couldn't afford the luxury of such a public display of emotion.

"You're not the only one that lost a friend here. We're all in the same boat, and that's war. Concentrate on winning. After the war there will be plenty of time to mourn."

Ronen's tough words left Snir confused. However, Ronen was widely respected and his comments carried weight. Eventually, like everyone around him, Snir steeled himself to the horrors and the personal losses of war.

Ran Ronen and his method for dealing with personal tragedy was typical of IAF pilots, who even today try to mask their true feelings, allowing few but close friends – friends who have experienced the same type of loss – to know their thoughts. But this way of absorbing adversity seems to have worked for those men who have survived two and three intense wars.

next six years, but did not score again. However, his adventures were not over.

Although the overall Israeli victory was stunning, it was not achieved without cost. One IAF pilot in ten was either killed or captured. Some men ejected safely only to be killed on the ground by angry Arab farmers and peasants. The shock of losing close friends so quickly dampened the enthusiasm of many Israeli pilots.

Immediately after the war, during a television interview, thin, intense Captain Asher Snir had declared that as long as he was alive, no one would bomb Tel Aviv. He had struggled to complete jet training and join Ran Ronen's No. 119 Squadron at Tel Nof. After the first few missions of the war, he had downed MiGs and attacked ground targets. He had shot down his first MiG on the raid to T-4, on the afternoon of June 5, the long, first day of the war.

Snir lined himself up behind the silver Syrian MiG-21 and fired – he missed. Doggedly hanging onto the tail of the twisting MiG, Snir stomped on a rudder pedal, swerving his plane's nose as he fired again. This time, he was on target, and the enemy plane went down.

On the second day of the war, Asher Snir was part of an attack against the Egyptian base at Inshas. Instead of kibbitzing with the rest of the pilots after they returned home, Snir developed the film from his gun camera himself. He didn't want to wait to see the re-

That most determined of determined aviators, G. was one of the Mirage pilots in 101 Squadron. Although he had flown a few combat sorties in Super Mysteres before the June war, and three missions in Mirages during the opening day of the 1967 war, he had yet to see any real action.

At 0430 on June 7, he was standing alert with his squadron commander, Major Amos Lapidot. The two pilots were scrambled toward the Egyptian airfield at El Arish; there was heavy tank action in the area – there had been a big fight the previous night – and the controllers said there were enemy aircraft nearby.

G. and his CO went down to 5,000 feet where they encountered heavy flak but no MiGs. They pulled up to 20,000 feet to avoid the flak. G. looked down and saw three Su-7s coming from Bir Lachfan, where the big fights were. He saw another section of two Mirages, perhaps from his squadron.

Then another Mirage also approached. These Mirages went after the Su-7s, which had shot down a Super Mystere with rockets over Bir Lachfan. The Super Mystere pilot had flown Mirages with 101 but when the war started, he returned to his previous squadron because he didn't have enough experience in the Mirage.[9]

The Su-7s – Russian-built ground-attack planes with the reputation for being built like the proverbial tank – made a chain with the Mirages: Su-7, Mirage, Su-7,

Mirage, Su-7, Mirage. Only the lead Sukhoi had nothing to shoot at. The Sukhoi in the middle was in the best position, but he missed. As G. looked on from above, the first two Mirage pilots hit their targets, and the two Egyptians went down. G. told his leader that he was going to join the third Mirage in pursuit of the third Sukhoi.

> I gained a lot of speed coming down from such a height and by the time I joined on the other Mirage, he had launched his Shafrir I aerial missile. At the time, we said that the Shafrirs went like "autotanks," our drop tanks, like a brick headed straight for the ground. The other pilot couldn't close the Su's, and he had used up all his ammunition.

> "I'm sorry," he called me, "I've nothing left."

> "OK, I'll take him," I replied. I was in full burner and closed the Su-7. Now, the Sukhoi was not maneuverable but it had a *huge* engine — it was a big airplane — and it was very fast.

He had chased Su-7s three times for very long periods at 50-100 feet, at 750-800 knots, straight-and-level over the dunes. It was impossible to shoot them down. G. was 50-60 miles south of El Arish, very low, and at 750-800 knots. At last, he got to about 1,000 feet behind the Sukhoi. He put his sight's dot on the enemy plane and squeezed the trigger...nothing!

> I checked inside the cockpit and found that the circuit breaker for the cannons had popped out! It was one of the few circuit breakers that is left out before takeoff. I was so excited that I had forgotten to push it back in.

> I did so and was still about 250 meters behind the Egyptian jet. I fired a short burst, and the Sukhoi exploded in the last third of its length. Only the portion forward of the wing came out of the blast. It pitched up, then down, and hit the ground. The pilot had no chance to eject. I was so close, so fast that I had to pull something like 9 G's to avoid the explosion.

> My lead had been wondering what had happened to me, but I found him and we flew back to Hatzor.[10]

As a point of interest, Captain Yitzhak Barzilay, another Mirage pilot from 101, had scored the first Su-7 kill of the war, and probably in history, during a mid-day attack on Abu Suweir on June 5.

As a junior pilot one future ace was involved in one of the most controversial events of the short conflict. (His identity must be protected because of the lingering sensitivity of the incident) On Thursday, June 8, with almost everything in the war going Israel's way, the Egyptians were nearly out of it, and Israel was marshaling its forces for a thrust into Syria. Naturally, security about what would be the invasion to the north was tight, and the last thing Tel Aviv wanted was a third party spying on their preparations.

Returning from a mid-morning attack on an Egyptian convoy, the ace and his flight leader were sent to check out an unknown ship off the northern Sinai coast. They had been looking for Egyptian tanks along the road between Bir Gafgafa and the canal, about 80 km or 50 miles, but didn't find many because the Egyptians had retreated west. They found four batteries of ZSU-57 AAA mobile guns. They attacked, and one of the wingman's bombs went directly *inside* the hatch. "After a war, everyone runs to see the damage to see how he did. Several weeks later, I found the ZSU I had attacked. There were only small pieces of metal left."

The Mirage's DEFA 30mm cannon was the best weapon for attacking convoys, everything. The trucks would spread out. We'd hit the head and the tail of the convoy. The drivers would run away, and leave the trucks for us to strafe on the road. We used very short bursts — we only had about seven seconds of fire, 135 rounds per gun.

On the way back from the June 8 mission against the ZSUs, the controller told the flight that there was something in the sea, 10-15 miles north of the Bardawil, off the northern coast of the Sinai, in the Mediterranean. It was an unknown ship, and the controllers asked the Mirage pilots to find it.

"The Cyrano radar in our Mirages was good for spotting big ships on the water," the ace commented. "It was very hard for it to find airplanes in the skies, but ships on the water it could do. My flight leader's radar wasn't working and I took the lead. I saw the ship, a very big, gray ship. It had three or four cranes, plus all kinds of antennas."

As far as the Israeli pilots could see, the ship was unmarked, no signs, no flags, nothing. It looked like a freighter, and they flew around it a few times, very low, trying to determine its identity and nationality.

After the Mirage pilot reported to the controllers, they said, "Go away, immediately! It may be a *third* force!" It wasn't Egyptian, nor Syrian, and not Israeli. Could it be American or even Soviet? The Mirages left and landed at Hatzor. The pilots debriefed and looked at the pictures they had taken of the ship. Soon after they had recovered, several IAF aircraft attacked the mystery ship with rockets and strafing runs. Israeli small craft also launched torpedoes.

Eventually, the story came out. The ship was the USS *Liberty* [AGTR-5], an intelligence-collection ship, festooned with antennas. Of the 286 officers and sailors in the ship's complement, 34 men were killed and 171 were wounded in the Israeli attack. The ship's commanding officer, Commander William L. McGonagle, had been badly wounded, but refused to leave the bridge during the attack.

Some time during the Six Day War, now-Lt. Col. Yak Nevo (l.) is involved in an animated discussion with Capt. Yosef Tzuk (r.) while then-Lt. Eitan Peled (c.) looks on. Eleven years earlier, Tzuk had claimed the first kill for the Mystere IV at Suez. Eitan Peled eventually became an ace in the F-4, but only after flying 16 missions in the 1967 war, five in one day. Note the prominent Scorpion squadron shield beside Yak Nevo.

The pilots involved personally regretted the attack and the thought that they had killed Americans. By the same token, they questioned the intelligence of sending the ship so close to a combat zone. In fact, American authorities had signaled the *Liberty* to move further away from the coast. However, the ship did not receive this vital direction because the message had been routed through the Philippines!

Although Israel apologized and made financial reparations, the story of the *Liberty* is still a sore point for both sides. For their part, the Israelis steadfastly claim that the ship made no attempt to identify itself, by flag or by answering radio calls from Israeli boats. Also two Israeli inquiries to the U.S. naval attache in Tel Aviv regarding any American ships in the area resulted in negative replies.

Whatever the reason, from the *Liberty*'s and Israeli viewpoint, the ship was in the wrong place at the wrong time, and many Americans died. Relations between Israel and the U.S. were greatly strained.

Several future aces flew missions during the 1967 conflict, which soon became known as the Six Day War because of the short duration of hostilities. The name connoted the amazingly swift and total victory of the Israel Defense Force over the combined might of several Arab states that were, on paper, much more powerful than their small neighbor.

Many pilots like Avihu Ben-Nun, and Eitan Peled spent the war flying ground attack missions, averaging three missions each day, and sometimes more.

Ben-Nun flew the Mystere, while Peled flew the Super Mystere. "The Super Mystere," now-Colonel Peled says, "was a simple airplane – two bombs, some fuel. I flew 16 missions in five days."

Avihu Ben-Nun had been in the first strikes against the airfield at Fayid. He had started the mission with four Mysteres, two of which were flown by very junior pilots. As they flew low over the Mediterranean, Ben-Nun saw his No.4 aircraft rising and falling above the water. The pilot was obviously having trouble, but because of the ultra-strict radio silence, Ben-Nun could not call him. The fourth Mystere suddenly plowed into the water, leaving the three surviving aircraft to fly on.

As they approached their target, they saw a large four-engined An-12 transport that had lumbered into the first wave of attackers. Ben-Nun excitedly lined up the Cub (the NATO name for the big Soviet-built transport), but the young Israeli pilot's guns didn't fire and the Cub flew on to a safe landing.

A few years after the war Ben-Nun learned that the Cub had been carrying several high-level Egyptian officers, who were returning from an inspection of their forces in the Sinai.

Yak Nevo had gone to the U.S. to gain a master's degree in 1966, then rejoined his old squadron in time to fly Super Mysteres in the June war. He flew a strike on June 5 against the big Egyptian base at Kabrit, where his group destroyed most of the base's MiG-17s on the ground.

Returning from the strike, the Israelis encountered Egyptian MiG-21s. All his planes were low on fuel, and the flight leader would not allow his men to turn to fight the enemy planes. However, the MiG pilots had other ideas and a battle quickly developed. The leader and his wingman broke at low speed, stalled and crashed. After the war, Nevo, Peled and other pilots took a helicopter out to where their leader had crashed. They found the body of the wingman on the ground by his aircraft.

He was barefoot and his throat had been cut, the work of Bedouin nomads.

Major Oded Marom, the ex-Vautour pilot, was in a 101 Squadron Mirage on a strike mission on June 5. He was now the squadron's deputy commander. His cockpit was far removed from Rishon Le Zion, the settlement he had grown up in six miles from Tel Aviv. He had learned farming and had originally decided that it would be his life's work. He had even gone to an agricultural school near Herzliya.

He detoured to volunteer for flight school and flew the usual types of trainers. The IAF flew two models of the British Gloster Meteor in training: the two-seat T.7 and the Mk 8 single-seater. "The Meteor had toe brakes for taxiing," Marom recalled, "and they sounded like a big diesel truck – shoosh, shoosh." He got his wings after Meteors and was sent to fly the Vautour. Then on to instructing, and finally, Mirages.

Our mission was to attack airfields and destroy their runways. It was a joke, because the Mirage could only carry two 500-kg bombs. We used to fly 250 miles to drop two bombs without any modern compass. All we had was a magnetic compass. We had directional gyros, but they tumbled whenever we bent the aircraft around. There were no beacons, no TACANs, nothing. Just a map and a compass.[11]

When the Six Day War started, Marom led four Mirages from Hatzor on the 0745 strike to Cairo West, back in the Egyptian desert, a flight of more than 250 miles. They strafed a number of Tu-16 bombers.

We went twice to Cairo West, then to Bilbeis, near the Nile. The IAF was fighting in three areas simultaneously – Egypt, Syria and Jordan.

A pilot could brief in the morning for a strike into Jordan, and the targets could be changed to Syria in a minute. We could launch from Hatzor, and within a few minutes, headquarters would turn us 90 degrees to the left, toward Jordan.

"Many MiGs over Haifa, over the Kinneret," the controller might say. We'd light our afterburners and head north. In 10 minutes we'd be in a dogfight over Syria, when our initial target was in Egypt. This was war in the Middle East.[12]

On June 8, Marom was part of an attack against Egyptian tanks near El Arish. On the way to the target, the radar controller told the Mirage pilots about two MiGs over Jebel Ma'ara, south of El Arish. The Israeli pilots changed direction and eventually saw MiG-19s.

"You never saw such a miserable aircraft as a MiG-19," Marom declared, "like a big cigar. Fat fuse-

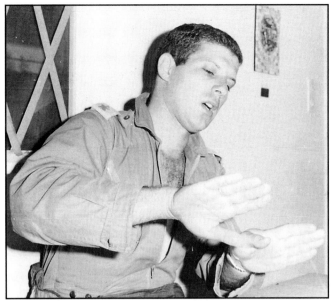

Maj. Oded Marom could be from any fighter squadron as he uses the universal hand movements of pilots everywhere to describe a mission during the June 1967 war. Originally a Vautour pilot, Marom was a member of the first group of IAF Mirage pilots. He gained victories in three wars, eventually accumulating 11 kills.

Iftach Spector (c.) and Danny Shapira (r.) on a post-mission debrief presumably with their wingmen at 101 Squadron's operations building during the Six Day War. Note their heavily loaded G-suits, which typically carry everything a pilot might need in the cockpit, such as additional charts, and personal items.

49

lage, short wings like a bug, and it flew the same – like a bug."

The MiGs started to turn lazily to the left. They were the first enemy aircraft Marom had ever seen in the air. Suddenly his wingman started to shout in a high voice, "MiGs! MiGs!"

"Get to the back," Marom told him, "45 degrees!"

With no radar, and from 600 meters, I put the pipper on the No.2 MiG. After a short burst, he exploded. His left wing departed and he rolled inverted. He crashed in the middle of a big crater.

I was 300 meters behind the second MiG. I put my airbrakes out and tried to slow down. Then, I pressed the trigger, but nothing happened. The mechanics told me later they had found a loose connection. But, when you're sitting behind a MiG at 300 meters, with no guns, you're pretty frustrated. I told

Mirage ace Amos Amir strafed Egyptian Tu-16 bombers on the opening day of the war, June 5, 1967. This frame from his gun camera shows the effects of his plane's cannon on a Badger. (via Amos Amir)

my wingman to take my place and he shot the second MiG down. We both made victory rolls over our base.[13]

Amos Amir, who had been frustrated during an encounter with a Syrian MiG over the Golan in 1965, got his first kill during the June war. Watching his friends score, he had come up dry until the fifth day of the war, June 9. He led four Mirages toward an Egyptian target near the Dead Sea, near the Gulf of Suez.

The controller called to tell them about a flight of four MiG-19s. Amir quickly engaged and destroyed one with his cannon, while his wingman took care of a second MiG. After their comrades went down before the guns of the Israeli Mirages, the two surviving MiGs ran.

On the afternoon of June 6, four Vautours of No. 110 Squadron launched with an escort of Mirages to bomb the Iraqi airfield H-3. The mission was required because an initial strike the day before had not done enough damage. This time the IAF meant to take out the Iraqi base. After a flight of 45 minutes – long by Middle East standards – the Vautours climbed to bombing altitude but ran into Hawker Hunters, which were apparently finishing their patrol over the base; their landing gear was down.

Yehuda Koren, another Mirage pilot, quickly closed on the second Iraqi fighter, which was turning on final. Matching his speed to that of the Hunter, Koren maneuvered to about 750 feet behind the British-built jet. The Israeli pilot checked his tail; it was clear. But he could also see the four Vautours dropping their bombs; he knew he had to break away.

The Iraqi pilots were now aware of the IAF's presence. They tucked up their landing gear and turned to meet the threat to their base. An alert Vautour pilot called that an Iraqi was lining up on a Mirage. Koren thought it meant him and broke hard, punching in his afterburner. However, he soon realized that the bomber pilot's warning was for another Mirage element, and he looked for another Hunter.

He found one at 6,000 feet, about half a mile in front of him.

Koren closed to 1,500 feet and began shooting, hitting the Iraqi plane, chopping off pieces, and even activating the Hunter's drag chute. The Hunter went down, but Koren's engine had ingested the gases from his long burst of cannon fire – a common problem – and it stalled. The Mirage pilot got a relight at only 2,000 feet and at 325 knots airspeed.

Looking around, he saw a MiG-21 heading for one of the Vautours. Calling a warning, Koren made for the MiG, which overshot the Vautour and went into a vertical climb, aiming for another Vautour. The Iraqi pilot was oblivious to Koren's approach, and was a fairly easy shot as he crossed in front of the Mirage. Nine hundred feet from the MiG, Koren fired a short burst and the MiG's right wing burst into flames. The MiG rolled over and crashed into the ground.

Even a Vautour pilot scored a kill – the first and only aerial victory for the bomber. Captain Ben-Zion Zohar had chased a Hunter that was after another Vautour. Coming off his bomb run, Zohar had to change his gunsight from bombing to guns, and as he did so the Hunter crossed in front of him. Zohar fired at close range, and the Hunter went in from an altitude of 200 feet.

It was only now that the young bomber pilot could concentrate on delivering his bombs. As he finished his run, a MiG-21 approached. Zohar called for help and a Mirage pilot told him to get away; he would engage the MiG. It was probably Yehuda Koren seeking his second kill of the day.[14]

During the war Major Ran Ronen was the CO of No. 119 Squadron, based at Tel Nof. In company with the other two Mirage squadrons, No. 101 and No. 117, 119 had seen much action, providing escort for strike missions as well as ground attack sorties, especially against Egyptian armored columns in the Sinai.

As men like Iftach Spector and G. were discovering, the pilots of 119 Squadron learned that their Mirages' 30 mm cannon were very effective anti-tank weapons. The Israelis found that if they could maneuver so that they attacked a tank from behind, the tank's radiator, fuel and ammunition stock, located in that vulnerable area, would reduce the target to a charred hulk.

Ronen had nearly missed his place in line during the hectic launch for the initial strike on June 5, shortly after 0700. He was to lead four Mirages as escort for the strike force against the Egyptian MiG base at Inshas, near Cairo. As in all military operations where radio communications are restricted – or in this case, forbidden – mistakes and misunderstandings occurred, and Ronen found himself behind a section of Vautours instead of with his own flight. Cursing to himself, he quickly rolled to an available spot on the runway and took off, pouring the coal to his fighter to catch up.

Ronen and his pilots arrived as scheduled over Inchas, and proceeded to drop their 500-kg (1,100-pound) bombs on the base's runways. Although they had planned to make two runs over the field, and with intense antiaircraft fire from the ground emplacements bracketing their Mirages, Ronen's flight made three more passes, this time using their cannon to strafe the MiG-21s in their revetments. As he took his flight home, Ronen counted 15 MiGs afire.

The morning strikes were a complete success, and Ronen led his fighters down to strafe what remained of the Egyptian air force. During the day Ronen and his squadron hit one Egyptian airfield after another. In the afternoon they launched toward Al Ghurdaqa, near the Red Sea, nearly 600 miles from home. (Twenty-four years later, American Navy helicopter and transport crews would come to know the desolate airfield at Al Ghurdaqah (although they misspelled, or mispronounced, the name as Hurghada) as they staged from the Egyptian base to fly out the busy aircraft carriers and ships of the U.S. fleet in the Red Sea during Desert Storm.)

Dropping down to attack altitude, the Israeli attackers began seeing heavy anti-aircraft fire as they approached Al Ghurdaqa. Undeterred, the Mirages bombed and strafed, until they were engaged by MiG defenders. The MiG-19s swarmed around the Israeli fighters, but eventually lost four of their number, two to Ronen, himself.

The Six Day War was definitely one-sided in favor of the Israelis. The Israel Air Force came of age, spearheading the IDF attack, and gained worldwide attention and recognition. Depending on sources and the time of publication, actual figures vary, but the number of Arab aircraft destroyed is 450 to 469, including 60 to 79 downed in aerial combat. The vast majority was destroyed on the ground during those devastating attacks in the early hours of the war on June 5. The three Mirage squadrons' scores were relatively low for the six days, most of their kills coming in the first two or three days. No. 119 was the high scorer with 19 kills, while 101 and 117 tallied 17 and 12 Arab planes downed, respectively.[15] (Other IAF planes gained several aerial kills, but the Mirage squadrons, whose main mission was, after all, air superiority, scored the most victories.)

By far, June 5 had been the busiest day, both in the air and on the ground. Twenty-seven Arab aircraft had been shot down by IAF fighters, followed by 14 more one June 6.

Egypt was by far the greatest loser. Its large air force was decimated, and many of its Soviet-trained pilots were killed. Egypt admitted to losing 34 pilots in aerial combat, in air-to-air engagements and from groundfire.

For its part, Israel admitted to losing only 46 to 50 aircraft, and 20 to 24 pilots killed. Although these numbers represented more than eight percent of the IAF, they were still acceptable in view of the total victory accomplished in so short a time against such apparently overwhelming odds.

Egypt was eventually able to organize some retaliatory sorties, flying more than 150 missions against Israeli positions in the Sinai and along the canal. The IAF racked up 3,279 sorties with its fighters and fighter-bombers.

Although less experienced by a wide margin than their Israeli counterparts, Egyptian pilots accounted for several IAF planes. These successes, however, were occasional and did little more than rouse a disconsolate fighter corps. The Egyptians found that while their MiG-21s could keep up with the delta-wing Mirages, the Russian fighter's limited armament – the early models only had two Atoll air-to-air missiles – afforded little backup and limited dependability. Thus, when an Israeli plane presented a target to an Egyptian fighter, the frustrated Egyptian pilot was never sure of the kill.

The Israelis had little knowledge of the current capabilities of their opponents until they met them in combat over the Sinai. Because so many Egyptian fighters were destroyed on the ground, the IAF usually had superior numbers in aerial engagements, and it was not uncommon for a flight of two or three MiGs or Su-7s to find itself engaged by at least eight Mirages. Unless one was very courageous, and an outstanding pilot, there was little to do but break and run.

Apparently, Egyptian MiG pilots also had to consider their escape systems when engaging Israeli fighters. During a visit to a USAF base in California in 1992, three senior Egyptian pilots related what had to be more than a darkly amusing coincidence. In their younger days, the general and two colonels had flown MiG-21s. All three had been shot down by Israeli Mirages. When they ejected, they all had broken their left arms.

The Soviet seat was a rugged design that used a mine-type explosive charge instead of the rocket motor favored by western designers. The result was a very powerful ride up the rails. All three Egyptian pilots had kept their left hands on their throttles while using their right hands to pull the handle.

Arab losses were short-lived. Embarrassed by their Arab clients' poor showing, the Soviets quickly re-supplied Egypt and Syria with aircraft and other munitions.

The Jordanians, arguably the best among the Arab pilots, had also lost nearly all their tactical aircraft and ceased to be a functioning air force. (Jordan's King Hussein had received offers of immunity from Israeli attack if he stayed out of the war. But, after a meeting with his senior staff, who demanded their king either shoot them or fight Israel, he entered the battle. Hussein's Arab loyalties would also lead him into ill-advised support of the Iraqis during the 1991 Gulf War.)

The Syrians were probably better off, having received concentrated Israeli attention only during the final days of the war. But, like the conflict in the south and west, the outcome over the Golan Heights was seldom in doubt.

For the young pilots in the Mirages, Super Mysteres, Mysteres and Ouragans, the war validated their training and the teachings of their seniors. For men like G., Oded Marom, and Giora Rom, the June war was only the beginning of careers that would see them achieve greater accomplishments and face old enemies again.

Endnotes:

1. Giora Rom, interview, Washington, D.C., March 6, 1992.
2. *The Small Air Forces Observer*, September 1993
3. Giora Rom, interview, Washington D.C. March 6, 1992
4. Ibid.
5. In early January 1968, a French deputy, and a widely known World War II fighter ace, Pierre Clostermann, revealed that France had, in fact, sent 20 Mirages "on loan" to Israel to be used solely for defense of the nation. The Mirages arrived on June 4, the day before the war began, with the Israeli Star of David already on them. Some people thought that one of the reasons for President de Gaulle's anger over the initial Israeli assault may have stemmed from his sending these additional fighters before the IAF attack, for which he bent the rules of his own embargo.
6. *Israel Air Force Magazine 1989 Annual*.
7. Giora Rom, interview, Washington, D.C., March 6, 1992.
8. Ibid.
9. G., interview, Tel Aviv, November 19, 1992.
10. Ibid.
11. Oded Marom, interview, Tel Aviv, November 19, 1992.
12. Ibid.
13. Ibid.
14. Capt. Ben-Zion was one of only 51 members of the IDF to receive a citation from Chief of Staff Yitzhak Rabin during the war. Since the IDF did not have a traditional awards system at the time, these certificates – without an accompanying medal – were among the highest awards for valor an Israeli service member could receive.
15. *The Small Air Forces Observer*, October 1992, June 1993.

Aharon "Yalo" Shavit in a Super Mystere. A Mystere IV pilot with 101 in 1956, he commanded the Scorpions of 105 Squadron during the June 1967 conflict. He rose to the rank of brigadier general.

7

THE WAR OF ATTRITION: THE HAPPY TIME

While most readers recall the 1967 and 1973 Arab-Israeli conflicts, they only remember in general terms the period between these major wars. Yet, all Israelis know that from the summer of 1967 to the summer of 1970, an intense, but undeclared war played itself out over the Sinai, the Suez Canal and the Golan Heights.

By the end of June 1967, Israel found that it had nearly tripled its size, having conquered two important geographic areas, as well as perhaps the most important city in the world from a religious standpoint. The huge, largely desert expanse of the Sinai still hosted tribes of Arab nomads, as well as cities and towns, particularly in the northern tier.

The strategic Golan Heights secured Israel's vital growing areas in the Galilee from Syrian harassment, and for the most part, ensured the supply of water so vital to Israel's agricultural industries.

Then there was Jerusalem, "Yerushalayim Shel Zahav" ("Jerusalem of Gold") as Naomi Shemer, one of the most popular song-writers in Israeli titled a beautiful lyric that became something of a second anthem during and immediately after the Six Day War. Books and poems, songs and essays have been written about this ancient enclave that has seen more than its share of rulers. Yet, it was not until Israeli paratroopers finally stormed through the gates of the walled city that Jerusalem was liberated to become the property of the entire world, and especially of its three greatest religions.

In less than a week, the Arab coalition had lost major territorial and emotional possessions that its individual members had held for many years. It was a change not to be taken lightly, by either the victor or vanquished. Certainly, President Nasser in Egypt did not laugh off the losses, and he vowed to continue the fight against Israel, if not in another major war, than a "war of attrition," a conflict that would eat away at the enemy's defenses and will by its shear duration.

With a massive transfusion of equipment from his Soviet sponsors, Nasser felt sure he could eventually wear the Israelis down to the point where he could mount another major attack, and this time win.

Flushed with the scope of their triumph in the Six Day War, the Israelis rejoiced in their new-found world status. No more the defenseless Jews of the village, or the pitiful victims of the Nazi Terror, but a nation of Davids who had beaten the Arab Goliath. While deserved, this enhanced view of themselves probably harmed the Israeli military stance, and additional successes only made the surprise Arab advances of October 1973 that much greater and unexpected. In July 1967, however, the IDF, and in particular, the IAF, could be excused if they indulged in a little breast-beating.

Unlike the period following the 1956 Suez War, the months after the 1967 war were anything but peaceful. Beaten but not extinct, the Egyptian air force roused itself quickly, spurred on by Nasser's rhetoric and Soviet aid.

By Thursday, June 8, 1967, the fourth day of the blinding Israeli drive against its Arab tormentors, there seemed little the Egyptians could do to stem the tide from the east. At the end of the day, even with victory close at hand, the IAF stood watchful alerts at its widely dispersed airfields. Captain Yoram Agmon, the young pilot who had gained the first kill of a MiG-21 barely less than a year before over the Kinneret, sat in his Mirage. He had been on alert for two hours and he waited impatiently for his relief.

He became aware of animated activity below him. He looked down to see his mechanics jumping wildly for joy. He couldn't determine the reason. He signalled one of them up his fighter's ladder.

"Nasser's resigned!" the technician shouted happily.

Agmon could scarcely believe the news. He didn't dare. And yet, here it was, something tangible besides burnt-out tanks and dead bodies in the desert. The dangerous, hated leader of the Egyptians was in disgrace. It was too good to be true. And it was.

Knowing the inevitability of the defeat only a few days away, Gamal Nasser took the diplomatic offensive, and offered himself up to his countrymen as the reason and scapegoat for the humiliating Israeli victory. It was a shrewd gamble that paid off. The Egyptian populace would have none of it and, in crowds that swarmed onto the streets of Cairo and other cities, demanded that their leader remain at the head of the foundering Egyptian state.

Thus, though he had lost the war, and had badly embarrassed his Soviet patrons, Nasser was in firm control even as Israeli troops smashed into central Jerusalem, recaptured the ancient city, and turned their attention to Syria and Jordan.

After the ceasefire, fighting continued to erupt along the Suez Canal. The Israelis were stretched too thin to adequately monitor all their newly won territory. Two weeks after the war, Captain Agmon scrambled for a patrol near El Arish, the Egyptian airfield that had been spared by the Israelis, who wanted it for their own use in the northern Sinai. As Agmon and his wingman climbed out, he knew from his controller's voice that something was up.

"Your ear becomes attuned to their voices," he said. "A few times, I had made decisions based on this understanding. Sometimes a pilot has to be a 'musician'."[1]

An Egyptian ground attack was in progress, and Agmon brought his flight down from 25,000 feet to 6,000 feet. It was nearly sunset and the lower altitude would let the Mirage pilots see better any aircraft silhouettes coming from the west. As they went to a combat spread formation, Agmon told his wingman to look for exhaust trails.

Suddenly, he spotted two outlines going straight up. Maybe they would break toward the ground, but the ground was nearly invisible in the growing darkness.

The bogeys were Egyptian strafers lining up on the Israeli troops below. Agmon made a tough decision to wait until the enemy planes finished their first runs; he did not want to risk shooting friendly troops.

As the first Egyptian attacker – it turned out to be an Su-7 – pulled up from its pass, Agmon fired, hitting the big fighter-bomber, sending it down near the Israeli positions. The Arab pilot survived and was captured. Although Agmon later saw some of his enemy's affects, he had his eye on the control stick from the Sukhoi.

"A very ugly stick," Agmon declared, "very cluttered." He wanted the memento but had to surrender it to IDF intelligence, who promised eventually to return it to the victorious Mirage pilot, who is "still waiting."

Recovering at their base, Agmon met one of the ground commanders who had seen the engagement. He learned that before the flight of Sukhois had appeared, perhaps 10 minutes before, another strafing attack had been made, and the Israeli troops were furious; where was their air force to protect them? Thus, when Agmon and his flight appeared just before the second attack, the army troops cheered as they watched the Mirage dispatch the Egyptian jet.

Avihu Ben-Nun, who had flown Mysteres during the Six Day War, returned to his Mirage squadron in July as a major and deputy commander. Like many of his contemporaries, Ben-Nun had actually seen limited combat operations before the war. Indeed, on July 19, 1964, in company with his CO, he had flown an important reconnaissance mission over Egypt.

The two specially-equipped Mirages carried five cameras – one forward-looking, two vertical and two obliquely-sighted – to photograph ground-to-ground missile sites west of Cairo West Airfield. The sites had been built with the help of German scientists and the date was only four days before the observance of the Egyptian Revolution.

The two Mirages climbed to 36,000 feet over the Mediterranean, where relatively safe from Egyptian defenses, they could use their big 36-inch telephoto lenses. Mission complete, they climbed to 50,000 feet and went supersonic, Mach 1.6, back to Israel.

However, the CO's camera had been having problems, and Ben-Nun, the squadron photo officer, also found that his camera's IMC – image motion control – was not working. Thus, the camera couldn't compensate for the Mirage's speed over the ground, thereby promising blurred images of the targets.

The young pilot began taking notes on his kneeboard pad, even as his controller warned of approaching MiGs. But the Israelis were too high and too fast. Nonetheless, the Egyptians reported having shot down the intruders.

"Six MiGs chased us, firing missiles. It was the first of 10 times that I was reported to have been shot down," he commented dryly.[2]

Fortunately, between Ben-Nun's notes and the film, the pilots got the required information.

Now, three years later, Avihu Ben-Nun was standing Saturday alert. He had volunteered, even though post-war festivities in Jerusalem were in full swing. He was anxious to get back into the cockpit because it had always seemed that he was away when Mirages found MiGs.

After flying several patrols over the canal, Ben-Nun was preparing to finish his tour and return home. It was nearly dark, and normally, patrols didn't fly at night. However, he and his flight were scrambled once more. The controller called MiGs over Port Said, which was too far away. The Israelis didn't have very modern radar in the Sinai so soon after the June war.

With the sun already below the horizon, Ben-Nun strained to see toward the west. Perhaps eight miles distant, he spotted two dots. He racked his Mirage into a turn and punched off his fuel tanks, accelerating toward the bogeys.

His wingman was looking somewhere else when Ben-Nun turned, and lost sight of his leader. To make matters worse, Ben-Nun had dropped his tanks at too high a speed, and when the tanks left the underwing pylons, they also took his missiles with them! In the dark, he couldn't know that he now had only his cannons.

He finally made out the enemy: four brand-new MiG-21s. But as he looked around, Ben-Nun realized he was alone. He called for his No.2, saying he was over the water off Port Said, but the wingman couldn't see him.

As the Egyptian and Israeli fighters passed each other, the MiG pilots started climbing in circles, struggling to get up to the Mirage's altitude. They were sitting ducks and Ben-Nun began lining up a target when his controller warned of four more MiGs. The first four turned toward the south as Ben-Nun tried to launch a missile. Only then, did he realize he had none. He had to get closer to use his cannons.

He approached the trailing MiG as the first and second Egyptian fighters turned back to help their comrade. The high-altitude engagement was already at 37,000 feet.

The Mirage's cannons fired, and the 30mm shells hit the MiG. There was little time to observe its demise, however, and Ben-Nun racked his fighter into a turn to get away from the other two MiGs. Now he could see four more MiGs above him – maybe the first flight returned to the fight.

As he broke, Ben-Nun's engine had a compressor stall – a common situation for the French engine. He dove 90 degrees and got a relight. He headed back home at low altitude, with his first kill, but still thinking how many kills he could have achieved if he had his missiles.

These early skirmishes signalled that, although soundly defeated, the Arabs were not convinced to leave Israel alone. Indeed, the situation was the opposite. Incensed by the poor showing of his military, Egyptian President Nasser determined to rebuild his army from the ground up, dismissing senior officers and redefining the leadership process. He also went after new, more capable weapons from the Soviet Union, most of whose leaders considered the mercurial Egyptian president inept, or at best poorly supported by an equally inept military that didn't know how to properly use the high-quality weaponry that their Russian patrons gave them.

There was little thought actually that the Israelis had beaten the Arabs simply because the Israelis were better-trained, or more aggressive. To the Egyptians, it was simply a matter of finding better leadership, and acquiring state-of-the-art weapon systems.

Israel, too, needed more and better equipment, particularly in the air. The French embargo on the already-purchased Mirage 5 ground-attack fighter, as well as another embargo that the US placed on initial shipments of A-4 Skyhawk ground-attack planes, put the IAF in an even more desperate situation.

For the moment, however, while the Egyptians went shopping, and the Israelis considered their next moves, sporadic, occasionally heavy fighting continued along the Suez Canal through early 1969. Dogfights over the Sinai, artillery barrages, and sporadic naval engagements offshore, accompanied by commando raids were the order of the day. The Egyptians possessed superiority in artillery pieces, and used it. On September 8, 1968, they fired more than 10,000 shells against IDF positions along the canal, for which the Israelis bombarded Egyptian oil refineries and the cities of Suez and Ismailia. The war of the guns continued through May 1969.

To contend with Egyptian intrusions, and to provide a forward airfield, the Israelis repaired the former Egyptian base at Bir Gafgafa, 50 miles east of the Suez Canal, the same base from which Nasser had announced the closing of the Straits of Tiran that May, precipitating the June war.

The base was near the Biblical town of Refidim, and was an outpost with few amenities. Sand and dust were everywhere, and the hard-pressed maintenance troops struggled to keep aircraft cockpits, engines and control surfaces free of the grit.

The IAF faced another problem – manpower. With more than 20 pilots killed or imprisoned during the 1967 war, the small air force's manning levels were down con-

The forward base at Refidim in the desolate north-central Sinai became a major launch point for IAF Mirage pilots to intercept Egyptian MiGs and Sukhois. Also known as Bir Gafgafa, Refidim was captured from the Egyptians in the Six Day War. Here, Israeli ground troops inspect the control tower. They have already run up their national flag on the tower's roof.

siderably. Although the training sequences were stepped up, the IAF's belief in its quality-first doctrine prevented a reduction in standards. Thus, the buildup required time while the IDF met the ongoing threat across the canal.

The extra manpower would have to come from Israel's reserves. While regular air force fighter pilots served weekly tours in the Sinai, sitting alert in their Mirages at Refidim, they were supplemented by reserve pilots who scrounged time away from their jobs. Many of these reservists flew for Israel's two main airlines — El Al, the international carrier, and Arkia, the internal airline. If they couldn't schedule time off from their flights, the airline pilots would call in sick for a couple of days to spend time in the cockpits of their fighters in the Sinai.

"It was like the American Wild West," then-Major Oded Marom recalled. He had relieved Amos Lapidot as the CO of 101 Squadron. "The fields were very rough, and we had to treat our Mirages with care. There was a lot of dust and smoke." Indeed, the desert west of Bir Gafgafa quickly acquired the nickname "Texas," to indicate its bleakness and the free-wheeling "gunfights" that characterized the next year's action.

With a four-plane detachment temporarily stationed at Sharm el-Sheikh, Marom and his pilots patrolled day and night. Usually, two Mirages would sweep back and forth at 20,000 feet, their big underwing fuel tanks extending the missions as the pilots waited for their controller's call.

On July 7, 1967, Marom and his wingman heard, "Two MiGs near you, 10 miles, bearing 270."

The Israelis could soon make out two MiG-17s heading toward them. The MiGs were low, perhaps 500 feet above the desert floor as they headed toward the Israeli base at Sharm. Maybe they were on a training mission and had lost track of their position. No matter.

Marom and his No.2 punched off their fuel tanks and quickly passed Mach 1 in their dive toward the enemy fighters. The Egyptians' controllers must have finally alerted the MiG pilots because they suddenly reversed their direction back toward Egypt. The Mirages were on the MiGs, but it would not be an easy kill. The nimble, little MiG was more agile than the delta-winged Mirage, and Marom had trouble lining up his target. In the meantime, his wingman became concerned about their fuel.

"Shut up!" Marom told his No.2, as he concentrated on getting the MiG in front of him. It had occurred to him that the Egyptians were trying to drag the two Israelis farther toward their base so that Egyptian flak could dispose of the IAF fighters.

At last, Marom had a shot. The MiG went down right at the shore. The second MiG broke sharply to the left and spun into the ground, its pilot probably unnerved by the fate of his leader.

When they returned to Refidim, Marom and his squadron were constantly engaged. In 10 months, they shot down 107 enemy aircraft. Several of the young Mirage pilots became aces during this period of intense activity.

By mid-1969, the undeclared fighting had been given a name, fittingly by its Egyptian creators. Nasser broadcast that he would pursue a "war of attrition" against his Israeli foe, thereby finally wearing him down to the point where an Arab coalition would emerge victorious.

Throughout 1969 and 1970, the Arabs taunted and harassed the Israelis, drawing them in, testing them. Usually, the Arabs paid the price of the dance, but it did not seem to matter. Time was on their side, they thought. Indeed, although the IAF pilots knew they were at war — even if the government in Jerusalem and Tel Aviv wouldn't openly admit it — they also looked at the expansive dogfights above the Sinai as a "happy time," a period of unrestricted hunting that enabled them to sharpen their skills for the time when they would confront the Arabs again en masse.

One night, shortly after taking command of No. 119 Squadron, Major Amos Amir was patrolling over the Mediterranean. He knew that two Egyptian bombers had raided El Arish, and he thought he might catch them as they flew home. Disregarding the controller's chatter, he scanned the skies, finally catching a glint of moonlight on aluminum at perhaps 5,000 feet.

Typically, his Mirage's radar struggled to display the target. "Mainly 'green grass' on the scope," Amir remembered. "I turned it off and told everyone on the radio to keep quiet. I had to concentrate."

Descending to the bogey's altitude, he saw an Il-28 and got on its tail. He fired a Sidewinder, an early model AIM-9B that required such a dead-certain shot. It was his fifth kill.

Amir fought throughout the War of Attrition, eventually gaining six kills to add to the one he made during the June war. He says, "None of my kills were very tough." But twice he found himself in a difficult situation; both times he did not shoot anyone down and was lucky to survive the fight.

A Syrian MiG-17 saddled in on his Mirage, and began firing. A second time, Amir intercepted a MiG, slowed his fighter and got into position. He squeezed the trigger but the cannons didn't fire.

As he checked inside the cockpit, he didn't see another MiG coming behind him. Only his wingman's warning alerted the distracted pilot to the danger on his tail.

"When you're flying a Mirage, you don't maneuver away from a MiG-17 behind you," he said ruefully. "The only thing you can do is dive.

Returning home, he found that a problem in the electrical wiring prevented his guns from firing.

"It was a picture to remember with a MiG-17 filling my sights and I couldn't fire. Both MiGs got away. They were lucky; so was I."

With Nasser's calling it a war of attrition in March 1969 – the Hebrew name was "Milchemet Hatasha" – the conflict seemed to intensify, with almost daily clashes in the air and on the ground, counterpointed by artillery duels across the Suez Canal. G., still with 101, got his second kill during the eventful day of July 20, 1969, which saw the IAF begin an intensive 10-day campaign against Egyptian artillery and missile sites on the west bank of the canal. In response, the Egyptian Air Force mounted its largest operation since the Six Day War. While flying Mirage No. 82, G. found a MiG-17 and shot it down with cannonfire.

A third kill came on September 11. This time, he was in Mirage No. 59, which would eventually become the highest-scoring veteran of the IAF with 13 kills by various pilots (including three aces – Agmon, Spector and G.). He saw Egyptian Su-7s and MiG-17s returning to Egypt after attacking targets in Israel. After disposing of one MiG, he saw his wingman shooting at a Sukhoi from a great distance, so far that his ammunition was exploding on the ground.

"I thought we were being fired on from the ground," G. said. When he called his No.2 to warn him, the wingman replied, "No, it's me."

By this time, G. was flying formation with the Sukhoi. The Israeli pilot looked across the 50 meters to his enemy as the pilot of the second Mirage called that he was out of ammunition. G. quickly pulled up and behind the Sukhoi to finish him off, but the Arab pilot had apparently had enough and punched out.

At this time, such kills where an IAF pilot did not actually shoot fatal bullets into the enemy plane were credited to his squadron rather than to his personal score. Several aces therefore have one or two more kills than their official tally.

G.'s second and third kills had been participants in large Egyptian attacks against IDF positions and facilities. The third kill on September 11 had been part of a 102-plane raid into central Sinai.

September 11, 1969, was a day to remember for Giora Rom, too. Scheduled to join the first conversion course for the newly arrived F-4 Phantom, Rom was recalled to 119 Squadron to fly a mission into Egypt.

He took off as No.4 in a four-plane flight headed for the Egyptian air base at Al Mansurah, 36 miles east of the canal. The Israelis found six MiG-21s over the field and Rom began chasing two of them.

He overtook his quarry and launched a Sidewinder, which struck one of the MiGs. Pieces flew off the Egyptian fighter, but it remained in the air. The MiG turned right with Captain Rom in hot pursuit, trying to get close enough to use his cannons. But Rom happened to turn in front of two other MiG-21s, one of whom launched two missiles at the Mirage, No. 718. The first Atoll missed, but the second struck Rom's Mirage below the tail and blew up.

On July 24, 1969, Amos Amir shot down a MiG-21. The Soviet-built fighter's delta wings show up well in this series of frames from the gun camera of Amir's Mirage. (via Amos Amir)

Rom knew he was in big trouble as he fought to keep his shuddering fighter in the air, but there was little he could do. He had to get out.

"In no time – seconds – I had lost three hydraulic systems; I had no control."

He tried to eject at 18,000 feet but the seat didn't fire. He pulled the face curtain twice, and finally went for the secondary handle between his legs. The seat went up the rails, thrusting him out of the cockpit at 15,000 feet and Mach 1.2. As he left the cockpit, Rom broke his left elbow and injured his right thigh. It was the beginning of a four-month ordeal for the young pilot.

At 14,000 feet, his seat fell away and the main chute deployed, leaving him to drift down for 20 minutes. A large group of Arab farmers gathered to watch the drama above them. They had seen the Israeli pilot eject and were preparing to give him a proper welcome. As he descended closer, Rom could see the farmers gesturing and screaming at him.

Like many military aviators, Israeli pilots tried to stay with their airplanes as long as they could to keep from bailing out over hostile territory. Stories from returning pilots who had survived internment, and rumors circulated about those who did not return, made escaping imprisonment a pilot's first priority after the mission, itself.

Israel had plenty of information on the treatment of its pilots during earlier conflicts, as well as on American flight crews struggling to survive in North Vietnamese prison camps.[3] US Air Force crewmen had also had horrible experiences at the hands of their North Korean captors in the early 1950s. Clearly, to descend into your enemy's hands was something to be avoided at all costs.

However, Giora Rom had little choice, and he wondered what would happen as he drifted down toward the group of highly agitated Egyptians.

Rom hit the ground hard and was immediately set upon by the crowd. The farmers finally hoisted the badly injured pilot onto their shoulders and carried him to a nearby village. Following established procedures, he said little to the men around him, not even giving them the satisfaction of asking for water even though he was very thirsty.

Just before dark, he was loaded onto a truck, which took him to a small military hospital in a small city, Simbal Win. An Egyptian doctor tended to his wounds, and by the next day, he was in a prison undergoing interrogation.

"We talked for 12 hours. I was in solitary confinement, but sometimes, they'd take me out on a stretcher to photograph me for the media or for interrogation.

"'I'm a pilot' I kept repeating, 'a captain in the Israel Air Force.' I must have said it 500 times."

In excruciating pain, he struggled to maintain his demeanor and strength in front of his captors. By that evening, the Egyptians had taken him to a hospital for more treatment.

Eventually, Israel arranged a POW swap, and Rom was repatriated in December. He spent the next four months in rehabilitation and slowly began to recover. By 1973 he was back flying.

"It's strange," he muses, "and for reasons I can't fully explain, I never felt afraid, or that I was losing control. I just kept repeating, 'I'm a pilot, an officer in the IAF.' I always made them treat me as an officer, always insisted they call me 'Captain.'"

Giora Rom in a Mirage. After several months of treatment and therapy, the young ace got back into the cockpit. (via Giora Rom)

American-built A-4H and A-4N Skyhawks have served the IAF well for more than 25 years. Simple, strong, and adaptable, the A-4 now serves as an advanced trainer as well as equipping a few remaining IAF attack squadrons.

At the end of the Six Day War, IAF senior officers knew that they had to find newer, more capable aircraft. While the Mirage, and older types such as the Ouragan, Mystere, and Super Mystere had done well in the crucible of that incredibly intense period of operations, they lacked overall mission capability. The Israelis had too many planes, each of which could only do one mission at the cost of others. The air force also required a dedicated ground-attack plane, something that could bring a heavy load of ordnance to the battlefield to protect the ground troops against the Egyptians' guns.

In the mid-1960s, before the war, the Mirage V promised to provide that important close air support capability, but the embargo immediately before the war scuttled those plans. As before, Israel sought help from its American sponsor. The A-4 and F-4 were the front runners, especially the huge Phantom. Ezer Weizman had gone to Washington in 1965 to ask for a shipment of McDonnell's powerful worldbeaters, but was rebuffed by the Johnson administration, which thought that equipping the IAF with the F-4 would affect the delicate balance in the Middle East. America did agree to send an initial shipment of 48 A-4s, however. It wasn't all the Israelis had wanted, but it was something.

Things weren't all they seemed. The Americans knew they needed their F-4s for the growing involvement in Vietnam, but the A-4 was nearing the end of its service life in frontline squadrons, and besides, Vought's stubby A-7 Corsair II was in full production and would replace the A-4 in Navy squadrons and join Air Force units by the end of the decade. If Israel could make use of the unsophisticated little attack-bombers, where was the harm?

The A-4s began arriving in late 1967, after overcoming a U.S. embargo after the June war. The A-4H and TA-4H models supplied to Israel were similar to the A-4F and TA-4F that the U.S. Navy and Marine Corps used. The Skyhawks joined operations almost immediately, and over the years, several shipments made the A-4 numerically the most important type in the IAF inventory by the early '70s.

Obtaining the Phantom proved more difficult, especially after the flashy victory of the Six Day War, and the quagmire of Vietnam that drained so much of the overall American military effort and budget for nearly a decade.

The Israelis persisted after the initial rebuff of Weizman's 1965 request. President Johnson met with Israeli Prime Minister Levi Eshkol in January 1968, and finally agreed to sell the precious aircraft to Israel. The ecstatic Israelis quickly planned two squadrons of Phantoms, delegating two young fighter pilots as the first commanding officers, Shmuel Hetz and Avihu Ben-Nun. Both men had seen combat before and during the June war, and both had proven to be not only fine aviators, but leaders, qualities that were needed to transition a new squadron to such a fantastically complex and sophisticated platform as the F-4. Hetz would command No. 201 Squadron, nicknamed "the Ahat," or "First," while Ben-Nun would lead No. 69 Squadron, "HaPatishim," or "the Hammers." No. 69 was one of the original squadrons of the War of Independence when it flew decaying B-17 Flying Fortresses secretly donated by sympathetic American Jews.

The new Nixon administration gave the final okay to the deal in December 1968 for 44 F-4Es and six RF-4Es, strictly USAF models, with a valuable internal 20 mm cannon mounted directly beneath the Phantom's imposing snout. The "R" models were fitted for photo-reconnaissance operations. Typically, the Israelis made hundreds of modifications to their Phantoms. The type represented a complete departure in crew concept for the IAF. Dedicated to the traditional single-seat mentality, the Chel Ha'Avir now had to train two men to fly its new aircraft.

The addition of a non-pilot officer to work the Phantom's radar and radios required lengthy indoctrination and training. (The backseater acquired different names depending on the service. The U.S. Navy and Marine Corps called them radar intercept officers (RIOs), while the US Air Force referred to them as weapons system officers (WSOs). Seemingly unimpressed with such descriptive nicknames, the IAF simply called their F-4 backseaters "navigators."

Having someone behind them was initially unnerving to many of the transitioning Mirage drivers. A veteran single-seat pilot is used to, indeed thrives on, being solely responsible for the flight and accomplishing the mission. Its success or failure is completely in his hands. It took some time to accept the presence and voice of another officer in the rear cockpit.

Iftach Spector become an ace during the War of Attrition, on March 6, 1970, flying a Mirage over the canal. In company with another Mirage and two Phantoms, he met a flight of MiG-21s, which had gone after the F-4s. It was a typical Israeli ploy to bait the Egyptians into combat. He got one MiG as its pilot lined up on an F-4.

The shot was somewhat harder than normal because one of Spector's fuel tanks had not come off, thereby leaving his fighter in an asymmetrical configuration.

"The Mirage was a very light aircraft, and it was really difficult...I could have entered a spin." He used only 15 rounds to get the MiG. It was the ninth kill for his Mirage, No. 59.

This new assignment was only the beginning of an association with the Phantom. In 1971, he was ordered to form and command a third F-4 squadron, No. 107. He tried out the new plane from the back seat, making two flights a day to learn the Phantom.

"We called it 'the Hammer'," he says, obviously impressed with the airplane's seemingly unlimited power and speed. "It took time to learn this new, more sophisticated aircraft. The Phantom should be flown by experts. It's not easy to fly, but it gives you a special feeling when you succeed."[4]

He also had to get used to having a navigator behind him. There were times when that task seemed most difficult of all.

"My ears throbbed from all the talk in the cockpit," he said. "You're not talking!" he told his navigators at first. "Don't tell me that you've locked on the enemy with your radar. I can see it on *my* scope."

Spector was not alone in his initial ambivalence toward his backseater. Eventually, the pilots accepted, and welcomed, their new team members.

Actually, the IAF navigator had to meet the same physical requirements as a pilot – reflexes, ability and 20-20 vision, unlike the US services who normally relaxed the vision requirements to a great extent. While many navigators were those trainees who just couldn't complete the pilot training course, many were simply ordered to become navigators because of the IAF's need to fill the cockpits.

Yoram Agmon was in the first group of Israeli crews that went to George AFB, California, for the USAF course on the F-4. After completing the course, these men would then be the nucleus instructor group who would begin training other Israeli crews in Israel. While it was an honor and an exciting opportunity to be at George, many of the IAF pilots were desperate to be back home, participating in the War of Attrition.

"Every day we'd listen to news reports about how many planes the IAF shot down," Agmon remembered. "'Today, five MiGs were killed over the canal...11 MiGs...' The Attrition War, from an air-to-air point of view was busy, happy. Whenever you wanted, you could get a MiG. But, here we were with our newest fighter that we couldn't bring home yet."[5]

Their American hosts understood the Israelis' anxiety. One day, after returning from a training sortie, the Israelis looked at their status board, and gaped. Someone had written, "It's almost 11 am, and no kills have been scored by the Israelis. What happened?" It was worth a good laugh that helped relieve the tension.

"The only trouble we had in transitioning from the French Mirage to the American F-4," Agmon reported, "was the change in size and...its *ugliness*. The Mirage, even the Mystere or Ouragan, were like ladies. Now here is a plane with a huge nose, a big tail that droops, and the whole aircraft looked so heavy. How could it fly, how could it dogfight? It took only one flight to change our minds."[6]

The first crews were eager to bring their new mounts home. The Phantoms were needed. The first A-4s had already seen considerable action and had proven their worth. Now, their new teammates could answer the call. The Israelis finished their training at George in late July 1969. The first four F-4s arrived at Hatzor on September 5 with all the pomp the Israelis could muster. Prime Minister Golda Meir and Defense Minister Moshe Dayan turned out for the welcoming ceremonies, much as David Ben-Gurion headed the list of dignitaries more than a decade earlier for the arrival of Israel's first Meteor jets. The Israeli press immediately dubbed the imposing warplane "the Hammer," and Moshe Dayan got an introductory ride and the traditional dousing afterward.

The time to celebrate was short, however, and the Phantoms were soon in action against the Arabs. The first of the Phantom's officially claimed 116 victories in Israeli service nearly went to Yoram Agmon, the man who had scored the Mirage's first kill of a MiG-21 in July 1966.

On November 11, 1969, Agmon led two "Ahat" Phantoms in a low patrol near the Suez Canal. The pilot of the second F-4 was another member of the first class of Phantom pilots, Captain Ehud Hankin. An excellent pilot, Hankin was a close friend of Agmon.

As they listened to their radios, the two Phantom crews learned of a big dogfight nearby. Agmon asked his controller about it.

"Yes, it's a big battle," the man on the ground admitted, "but it's not for you." Agmon couldn't resist.

He and his wingman crossed into Egypt and soon saw fuel tanks falling. With full afterburner, he climbed to 20,000 feet, followed by Hankin. The F-4s' powerful

This "clean" F-4E makes a low pass over a runway.

radar soon showed bogeys – two MiG-21s. Agmon locked the MiG up and fired a missile. Nothing.

"It's yours," he told Hankin. He watched as the second Phantom fired a missile, which obliterated its target. Undeterred, Agmon went after the second MiG. The two fighters wound up low over the desert. Agmon had punched off his two wing tanks, but his big centerline tank wouldn't budge.

"We were in a scissors, and we were getting deeper into Egypt. We had broken the limitation speed with a centerline tank." It wasn't his day, and Agmon broke off, rejoining Hankin, who, along with his navigator, Major Eyal Ahikar, had achieved the first kill by an Israeli Phantom.

"At least I was involved in the downing of the first MiG by an Israeli Phantom," Agmon said.

It was a tradeoff, however. A week later, Hankin and his navigator, Major Shaul Levi, were hit by groundfire during a raid and forced to eject over Israeli territory. (Fate would not be so kind four years later. Hankin and Levi were killed in action during the Yom Kippur War.)

While the Phantom quickly assumed a major role, the Mirage was still the primary air-to-air fighter, with 101 Squadron and 117 Squadron still flying the veteran delta. (No. 119 had been tapped to fly the F-4.) New pilots had joined 101, fresh from training after the June war.

At the age of three, Lieutenant Moshe Hertz had emigrated from Russia with his parents in 1949, and then attended all the regular schools before going through technical training to become an IAF mechanic. He entered flight training in 1963. After graduating in 1965, he was assigned to Ouragans, while serving as an instructor.

When Israel closed the first agreement with the U.S. for Phantoms, Hertz was given the choice of transitioning to either the F-4 or the Mirage. Anxious to get into fighters, and knowing that he would have to wait yet another four months for a class on the Phantom, he chose the older aircraft, which still held considerable appeal for young would-be fighter pilots.

By July 1970, he was still a senior pilot in the Ouragan OTU, but was assigned to 101 Squadron for operational missions. On July 10, he flew his first combat mission with Iftach Spector, by now an ace, as the flight leader. After a short briefing, four Mirages flew toward the Suez Canal. The Egyptians continued to attack Israeli positions with either artillery or aircraft.

Spector, Hertz and their flight arrived at their patrol point at 20,000 feet and orbited, waiting for MiGs. Soon four MiG-21s showed up. Spector got one almost immediately with a missile. Moshe Hertz selected a MiG and shot it down with guns.

"We maneuvered in and out of the clouds," he said. "The Egyptian tried to lose me but I was too close. I put the pipper on him and with a short squeeze of the trigger, I got him. Later, the ground crew told me I had used only 60 rounds."

The Israeli pilots were becoming, little by little, more confident in their air-to-air missiles. Up to this point, the balky first-generation Sidewinders and Shafrirs had been considered second choice, long-range weapons because of their undependable performance. The AIM-9B Sidewinder demanded nearly dead-on tail shots, and the Shafrir I was just not ready for combat. However, the appearance of the Shafrir II in the late 1960s gave the IAF a dependable, effective missile. The Shafrir II had a larger warhead than the Sidewinder, and it was more reliable than the AA-2 Atoll, which was a copy of early AIM-9s.

Shlomo Weintraub, a Mirage pilot with 117 Squadron, got the first kill with the Shafrir II on July 22, 1969, over an Egyptian MiG-21. After a slow start, Weintraub seemed to be one of the IAF's young rising stars.

Unfortunately, he was killed in action on February 2, 1970. After flying one patrol mission along the Syrian border, he had volunteered for another flight. The mission would use a favorite Israeli tactic – a trap to lure Syrian fighters into action. Taking off as the wingman for his squadron commander, Uri Even-Nir, who had shot down a Lebanese Hawker Hunter near Beirut during the Six Day War, along with two other Mirages, Weintraub began trolling back and forth along the Syrian border, low, below 100 feet. It was a dangerous altitude; the Syrian flak was heavy.

Yehuda Koren, now the deputy CO, was one of the other pilots and he saw Weintraub's Mirage pull up. Koren called to the junior pilot, as did Even-Nir, but there was no reply. Koren flew alongside the Mirage but the cockpit seemed empty. Weintraub must have bailed out, for whatever reason.

The Syrian flak was becoming more intense, but the other pilots lingered, watching the pilotless Mirage arc higher and higher, until at 12,000 feet, it stalled and dived, crashing into the ground in a large fireball.

Later, the squadron learned that Shlomo Weintraub was, in fact, still in his aircraft, having been probably knocked unconscious, by a lucky hit from the enemy flak. He was hanging so far forward in his straps that no one could see him in his seat, and it appeared that the Mirage was empty. At the time of his death, he had four kills.

In August 1970, G. took off with another Mirage in company with two Phantoms from Major Shmuel Hetz's No. 201 Squadron – with Hetz in the lead F-4. It was one of the Phantom's first missions in IAF service. G. began a short patrol, tempting the Egyptians to launch their own fighters. Actually, the trap was spring-loaded since the Israeli pilots were among the best in their respective squadrons – a device created by the IAF commander himself, Moti Hod, who selected 10 pilots to form an elite team of shooters to patrol every day from sunrise to sunset in flights of two Mirages over the Suez Canal.

Blessed with superb eyesight, G. spotted enemy planes at 12 miles, closing very fast, near Mach 2. Incredibly, Hetz took his two Phantoms into a zoom climb as the two Mirage pilots engaged the MiG-21s.

G. quickly launched a Sidewinder, an early model that required its Mirage to be within 600 meters of the target's dead six. With only two seconds of burn time, the missile guided right up the tail of the MiG and exploded, but the Egyptian fighter survived – apparently without its afterburner, however.

G. turned his attention to the MiG's wingman, pulling to 350 meters of the second Egyptian. The Israeli started firing his cannon just as he received a radio call to return home. Meanwhile the Phantoms were nowhere to be seen.

"Perhaps they were somewhere *near the moon*," recalled G., remembering the F-4s' powerful exit at the start of the engagement. Leaving the second MiG, G. asked his controller where Hetz was.

"They're still engaged," the man on the ground replied, indicating that Hetz had found some MiGs. G. decided to engage two new MiG-21s. He closed the wingman and shot at him from 150 meters, using the remainder of his ammunition. The MiG remained in the air, however, and G. changed places with his wingman, who would deliver the coup de grace. But in the time it took for the two Israelis to change their positions, the MiG disappeared among the trees near Ismailia. The only credit G. received on this mission was a damaged for the last MiG.

However, on March 27, 1970, he was patrolling with three other Mirage pilots. Again, he saw the MiGs first and went after two of them. His wingman, a junior pilot, was having difficulties and G. ended up protecting *him*, which was an immediate invitation for the Egyptian pilots to attack.

"Break, break!" G. called as he turned into the threat and shot down two MiG-21s in short order with cannon fire. He was now an ace.

Endnotes:

1. Yoram Agmon, interview, Tel Aviv, May 5, 1993.
2. Avihu Ben-Nun, interview, Tel Aviv, November 20, 1992.
3. In October 1970, Israel charged Egypt with "grave breaches of the Geneva convention," regarding treatment of Israeli POWs. The charges stemmed from knowledge that a captured IAF pilot had died after having been shot down that August. He had apparently been beaten by his captors.
4. Iftach Spector, interview, Tel Aviv, November 19, 1992.
5. Yoram Agmon, interview, Tel Aviv, May 5, 1993.
6 . Ibid.

8

THE SOVIETS UP THE ANTE

The Arab numerical superiority made it impossible for Israel to trade combat casualties with Egypt and Syria. Instead, Israel adopted a policy of "asymmetrical response," which relied on a heavier retaliation than the original attack.

As the attrition war ground on, several attempts at a ceasefire failed. Israel rejected a American-brokered arrangement in November 1969, and in January 1970, in an attempt to force Nasser to end the war, Israel attacked bases and facilities deep inside Egypt. (These strikes had the reverse effect, however, and forced Nasser to seek a way to retaliate through increased Soviet aid.)

It was clear that the IAF could roam at will over Egypt, and its planes occasionally "thumped" Cairo with sonic booms, much to the discomfort of the infuriated President Nasser. (Syrian pilots also indulged in these dramatic, though relatively harmless, visits to the enemy's home, sometimes treating coastal inhabitants to "MiG music.")

Jordan's moderate King Hussein began having problems with the Palestine Liberation Organization (PLO), which had set up its headquarters in his country after the Six Day War, after being pushed out of the West Bank. PLO teams continuously raided Israel, then retreated back across the border into Jordan.

Obviously, Israel would not endure such infractions and soon IAF jets were pounding PLO bases in Jordan, much to Hussein's embarrassment, and the growing anger of the Arabs.

Hussein finally began his own internal cleanup campaign, launching several intense military operations against PLO enclaves. Syria believed that this action came from direct Israeli involvement and tensions between Israel and Syria increased.

The brashly capable Israelis added further to Nasser's fury when a helicopter-borne commando team captured an entire Soviet-built air-defense radar station, 100 miles south of Suez on December 27, 1969.

Unable to retaliate against the Israelis, Nasser quickly found scapegoats in his own army, and executed 14 officers and enlisted men the following January, having charged them with gross negligence and cowardice.

Frustrated in preventing the Israelis from wandering in and out of their airspace with their own fighter aircraft, the Egyptians began developing a missile defense umbrella. President Nasser went to Moscow on January 22 to plead for more weapons, including surface-to-air missiles. After four days of cajoling and threatening, he got a Soviet pledge of support and a promise to provide a better air defense network. It was the start of a "peaceful" Soviet invasion of the land of the Pharaohs. Advisers, technicians, and flight crews flooded into Egypt, taking over entire sections of cities and land adjacent to the Suez Canal.

Late-model MiG-21Js arrived in March and April, followed by battalions of SA-3 Goas surface-to-air missiles. The SA-2 Guideline missile was well known to American fliers in the Vietnam War, but the more-potent SA-3 had yet to be encountered by Western fliers.

The June 1 edition of *Newsweek* reported that the Russians planned to have 480 missiles in place by September 1, along with some 15,000 Soviet personnel. Estimates of between 20,000 and 28,000 Soviet technicians and advisers were also to be in Egypt by that date. The August 1970 issue of *Air Force Magazine* estimated that 100-150 Soviet pilots had arrived, along with 75-100 MiG-21Js. Thus, the Israelis watched the Soviet buildup with considerable alarm.

The idea of engaging MiG-21Js flown by Soviet pilots was also discomforting. Not because the Mirage and Phantom pilots worried about superior skills of the Russian pilots, quite the contrary. But what would the USSR do after the IAF disposed of several of its vaunted MiG-21s? Even the ever-confident Israelis could not fight a major conflict against the overwhelming might of the Soviet Union.

For their part, the Americans also viewed the situation with growing concern. If the Russians continued to help their Egyptian and Syrian clients – particularly if they also manned the advanced missile systems and aircraft – what should the U.S. position be? Clearly, the Soviet-Egyptian-Syrian alliance could not be allowed to accelerate without stepped up reinforcement of Israel.

The Soviets argued that if the Americans could not keep the Israelis from attacking the Arabs, then the Soviets would simply have to keep supplying and aiding *their* "friends" in the area.

In the meantime, the IAF sent its planes against Egyptian guns and bases along the canal. The A-4 Skyhawk and F-4 Phantom were quickly proving their value – tough, able to tote large amounts of ordnance, and also deal with the Arab air threat.

The Soviets appeared to initially avoid direct combat with the Israelis. The Russian MiG-21s hung back, orbiting over the canal or to the west, farther inside Egypt. The Egyptians, however, particularly the "pupils" of the Russian advisors and technicians, were fast becoming disenchanted with their helpers. The Russians' brusque, aloof style, along with their unintelligible language, alienated their Egyptian hosts, many of whom had spent their adult lives fighting the Israelis and knew a thing or two about what they were doing.

Soviet crews also manned other types of Russian-built aircraft – bombers, maritime patrol and electronic intelligence gatherers – and operated from at least five major Egyptian bases, shadowing U.S. Sixth Fleet carriers in the Mediterranean, and orbiting off the coast of Israel to listen to Israeli and American transmissions.

By mid-April 1970, Israel was sure that Soviet pilots were flying the MiG-21 air patrols over Egypt, and decided to stop the deep-penetration strikes by the IAF, sticking to a self-imposed 25-mile-wide strip along the canal's west bank. For the moment, the Russians seemed to accept this arrangement.

The Israelis had known for some time that Russians were in the cockpits of the new MiG-21Js, menacing in their two-tone brown desert camouflage and red stars. (Although the Russians flew their larger aircraft – the Tu-16 Badger and Il-38 May "snoopers" – in Egyptian markings, they evidently made no such attempt to hide the true nationality of the MiG-21s. Several Israeli pilots reported engaging late-model MiGs with Soviet national markings.) Listening in on the radio chatter between the tower at Cairo West and the MiGs, the Israelis could hear the rapid, impatient Russian as the MiGs sortied from the big Egyptian base.

Flying as surrogate members of client state's air force was not new for Soviet pilots. In 1939, many of the I-15 and I-16 fighters that Russia made and supplied to China to fight the invading Japanese were flown by Soviet "volunteers." Soviet pilots also flew as clandestine members of the North Korean Air Force during the Korean War, 1950-1953. Recent declassification of documents have only now disclosed how deep the involvement was, and how successful Russian MiG-15 pilots had been against American F-86s.

Newspaper and magazine stories in the American and European press reported clashes – many listed diplomatically as "unconfirmed" – between Soviet-piloted MiGs and IAF fighters, particularly in late March 1970. One account in the April 2 edition of the *Washington Post* claimed that Israeli jets had downed nine MiGs in two engagements near the canal, four on March 25 and five on March 27. The report said that although most of the Soviet MiG pilots ejected safely, at least one crashed with his plane. The MiGs had been protecting the new SA-2 and SA-3 sites, which were also manned by Soviets.

Perhaps emboldened by a U.S. refusal in March 1970 to sell more A-4s and F-4s to Israel, the Soviets intensified their participation in operations. Nasser's ground forces also took heart from the Russian presence at the SAM sites and in the MiG cockpits.

Israel issued a short statement on April 29, 1970, outlining the Soviet Union's intervention in the Middle East, its installation of missile sites along the canal, and the presence of Russian MiG pilots.

"Israel will continue to defend itself against all aggression which violates the ceasefire arrangements and which aims at renewal of war in the area...Israel will continue in its firm stand and in its quest for true and lasting peace," the release concluded.

As they had been since the War of Independence in 1948-1949, the keys to the IAF's successes and its continued survival were its flexibility and high training standards. Air force commander Brigadier General Moti Hod said, "We strive for perfection, but the Arabs never admit their mistakes...The channels are short here. If a man comes up with a good idea, we can push it through very quickly."[1]

IAF training continued, as did sorties against the canal SAM sites. The IAF used several captured Russian jets to educate its pilots on the strengths and weaknesses of Egyptian and Syrian fighters. At least three MiG-17s, a MiG-21 and an Su-7 were flown regularly by Israeli pilots in this period.

The first two MiG-17s were delivered by Syrian pilots who had mistakenly landed at Betzet, a small airfield in northern Israel, on August 12, 1968. Syria claimed that the two young pilots had become disoriented in bad weather and had to land when their fuel ran out. An Israeli farmer working in a nearby field said that the Syrians told him they thought they were in Lebanon.

A defecting Iraqi pilot flew the MiG-21 to Israel in 1966 after a fiction-like series of meetings with Israeli agents and "handlers" in Iraq. The pilot of the Sukhoi Su-7 had bailed out over the Sinai, leaving his unmanned plane to make a smooth landing in the desert! The Israelis scooped the big jet up, repaired it, and soon had it flying again.

Moshe Dayan, now Israel's Defense Minister, referred to the growing number of advanced Russian radar and SAM thickets, countered by burgeoning Israeli ECM capability, when he promised that the summer of 1970 would be "electrifying...electronic." He was right. By mid-July, Israeli F-4 and A-4 pilots no longer looked upon MiGs and Sukhois as their main enemy. A man in another plane could be seen, fought, and beaten. But a missile, aimed and fired by a technician safe and secure in a bunker was terrifyingly impersonal; the enemy's face was gone. Combat-experienced Israeli pilots felt their mouths go dry and their throats tighten as they neared the canal and its briar-patch network of SAMs.

The high-flying, eager aces of the IAF are quick to point out how the fight had changed – for them and for their fellow pilots in the attack jets. Several aces direct attention to the bomber pilots in the Skyhawks and

The former gate guard at Hatzor now resides at the IAF Museum in the Negev at Hatzerim Air Base. Its new serial number D. 112 (the Hebrew letter "dah-led" is to the right of the decimal, Hebrew being read right to left) represents Modi Alon's aircraft on June 3, 1948, when he scored the IAF's first victories, shooting down two Egyptian Dakota bombers over Tel Aviv. (Author)

Right: A P-51D Mustang preserved at the IAF Museum. Painted in the unique colors of No. 116 Sq. It carries the symbol commemorating the squadron's daring wire-cutter missions during the Suez War. On Oct 29, 1956, four 116 Mustangs flew across the Sinai towing weighted cables to cut Egyptian phone lines. But the devices didn't work, and the intrepid Israeli pilots used their planes' propellers and wings to do the job. (Author)

Below: An F-4 struggles at slow speed to fly formation with Weizman's black Spitfire during an air show. The Spit wears 101 Sq. markings. (Gil Arbel)

Sinai-Suez

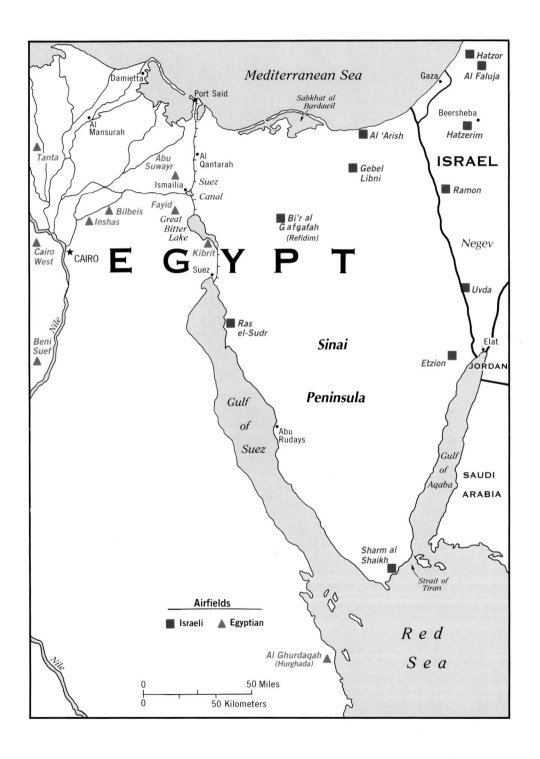

Syria-Lebanon

This Mirage III carries 11 kill markings — 10 Syrian and 1 Egyptian — indicating *its* record, and not that of a specific pilot.

Right: Wearing the same camouflage and markings, Mirage 158 (a coincidence) was the runner-up to No. 159, and the IAF's second highest-scorer with 11 kills.

Below: A rare, inflight view of Mirage 159, the champion MiG killer with 13 victory roundels below its cockpit. It started its career in the silver-and-red markings of No. 101 Sq, and now, at the end of its service life, some time in the early 1980s, it wears desert camouflage, and the rudder markings of what initially appear to be that of No. 117 Sq. However, they may indicate another "shadow" unit of 117, sometimes referred to as No. 190 Sq.

A lineup of Neshers and their crews emphasizes the type's long, black radome and desert camouflage. Note the four kill roundels below the cockpit of the second fighter.

Right: Now a lieutenant colonel, Oded Marom poses by a 101 Sq. Mirage with seven kill symbols, although the roundels usually referred to the plane's record rather than a specific pilot's score. Marom's flight jacket is of interest, showing his rank on epaulets, and the IAF shoulder badge. (via Oded Marom)

Below: A fine study of a late-model Egyptian MiG-21. Like many classic aircraft, the little Russian delta can still be found in many parts of the world, especially in third-world countries.

Probably taken in 1970, this photo shows Major Iftach Spector in a Mirage III. The aircraft sports three kill roundels, but they may not be Spector's, although by that time he was close to ace status. The Mirage's natural metal finish shows up well as does the small French fighter's rather cramped cockpit. (via Iftach Spector)

Below right: A lineup of Phantom tails on the Ahat flightline. (Gil Arbel)

Below: In 1980, this flight of camouflaged Mirage IIICs and IIIBs (two-seater trainers that retained most of their combat capability) lines up to take off from Eitam for the last time before the desert Sinai base was returned to its former Egyptian owners as part of the agreement between Israel and Egypt. By this time Mirages were grouped together in a unit either administered by or considered a shadow portion of No. 117 Sq. Thus the striped, blue rudders on these four aircraft are either the contemporary form of the first jet squadron's marking, or a derivation of the same.

A study of how war and operational losses thinned the ranks of the first IAF F-4 crews. The top photo shows the first group in the U.S., as they began their training. Standing in front of the first Phantom scheduled to leave for Israel in 1969 are (*r. to l.*): Eyal Ahikar, David Yair, Shaul Levi, Avihu Ben-Nun, Shmuel Hetz, Menahem Eini, Yoram Agmon, Rami Harpaz, Yitzhak Peer, and Ehud Hankin. Hankin and Levi were killed in action in 1973, and Hetz was killed in action in 1970.

In the lower photo, taken 20 years later, in front of the *same* F-4 in Bat Squadron markings (*r. to l.*): Eyal Ahikar, David Yair, Avihu Ben-Nun, Menahem Eini, Yoram Agmon, and Rami Harpaz. (Yitzhak Peer was not available for the photo.) Ahikar, Eini, Harpaz, and Peer spent several years as POWs in Egypt, while Ben-Nun rose to command the IAF.

71

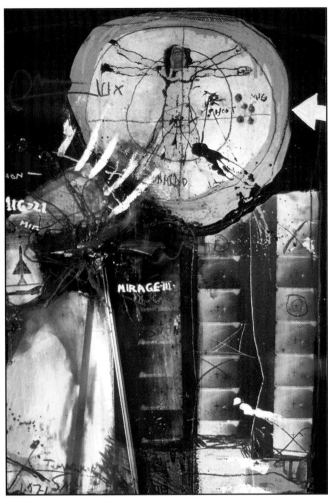

Giora Rom's varied experiences also include a short but intense period as a POW. Shot down while flying Mirage 719, he survived four months of confinement and poor medical treatment. He was finally repatriated in December 1969. His wife, Miriam, commissioned artist Igal Tumarkin to commemorate her husband's ordeal. This collage includes Rom's shootdown, and in a striking reference, the actual metal rod that his Egyptian doctors inserted in his badly injured leg. (via Giora Rom)

Even brigadier generals keep up their skills in the IAF. Some 20 years after he became the IAF's first ace, Giora Rom suits up for a flight in an F-15. (via Giora Rom)

This "Orange Tail" Phantom's crew has their canopies up. Note the F-4E's extended refueling probe. This view emphasizes the Phantom's great size and power. Israeli F-4s are relatively "smokeless," having relieved themselves of the Phantom's trademark exhaust trails that made them easy to spot from a distance. (Gil Arbel)

Above: This Phantom of No. 107 Sq. also wears the striking red fuselage arrow usually associated with the Scorpions of No. 105 Squadron, which transitioned to F-16s in the early 1980s. This F-4E is on a weapons training mission as indicated by the blue inert ordnance beneath its wings. (Gil Arbel)

Left: An F-4E from the Bat Sq. launches for a training mission. (Gil Arbel)

An F-4E of "Hapatishim," the "Hammer Squadron," lands, while an F-16A of the "First Jet Squadron" waits its turn. (Gil Arbel)

One of the first IAF pilots to transition to the Fighting Falcon, Col. Iftach Spector stands by an F-16A at Hill AFB in 1980. Spector soon commanded a wing of F-16 squadrons and helped the new fighter enter IAF service. A year later, his wing flew in the attack on the Iraqi power plant at Osirak. (via Iftach Spector)

Now-B. Gen. Amir Nahumi enjoys a little time away from the office in the cockpit of an F-16. Many senior officers still maintain their flight skills and stand alert with more younger crews. (via Amir Nahumi)

An F-16A of No. 117 Sq. slides up to the camera. The IAF has found the Falcon to be an important and tractable aircraft, capable of engaging enemy fighters, hauling a sizeable amount of ordnance a fair distance, and also able to accommodate that particular brand of Israeli innovation and modification that have stood the IAF in such good stead for nearly 50 years. (Gil Arbel)

An ace in two fighters — the F-4 and the F-16 — B.Gen. Amir Nahumi attends to paperwork. This photo shows the khaki working uniform of the IAF. Besides the IAF's shoulder flap, rank epaulets, and his pilot's wings, General Nahumi also wears three campaign ribbons from the 1967, 1973 and 1982 campaigns, as well as a blue ribbon for the E-tour Hamofet he received for his first mission in 1973 during which he shot down four attacking MiG-17s. (Gil Arbel)

M. Gen. Avihu Ben-Nun as Commander of the IAF in 1992. He wears IAF pilot's wings, three campaign ribbons, and parachute jump wings.

A fine study of an F-16A Fighting Falcon over the legendary desert fortress of Masada. The squadron badge might be that of No. 253 Sq. The IAF has made great use of the F-16, and until the 1991 Gulf War, was the only country to have taken the Falcon into combat. The IAF uses four variants of the F-16, the A, C and the two-seat B and D.

Two Kfirs of No. 144 Sq. show two different paint schemes indicating their divergent roles. No. 826, a Kfir C.2, is in air superiority gray, while No. 853, a Kfir C.7, is in desert camouflage, denoting its ground-attack mission. Note its extra hardpoints directly beneath its intakes. (Gil Arbel)

M. Gen. Avihu Ben-Nun, Commander of the IAF, returns from a flight in an F-16A of No. 117 Sq. Retiring in 1992, Ben-Nun shepherded the IAF through the 1991 Gulf War when much of northwestern Israel lay exposed to Iraqi missile attacks, and the question of Israeli reprisal raids was on everyone's lips. (Gil Arbel)

An F-15A Eagle of No. 133 Sq. armed with AIM-7 and AIM-9 missiles.

Left: A 133 Sq. F-15A Eagle in flight from the underside.

An F-15 lands past another Eagle and two waiting Mirages. This scene, probably in the late 1970s, shows the Mirages in camouflage but sporting the large black-and-orange triangles used to distinguish IAF Mirages from Arab Mirages. (Gil Arbel)

On October 11, 1989, Major Adal Bassam of the Syrian Air Force defected in his MiG-23, landing at the IAF field at Megiddo, in northern Israel, prompting a major investigation into Israeli security. The investigation, however, did not reveal any important problems, and the IAF quickly turned to studying the important new acquisition. The Flogger was soon displayed in the air with a suitable F-16D escort. (Gil Arbel)

Above: No. 133 was the first, and for several years, the only F-15 Eagle squadron. As such, its distinctive tail insignia became as well known as No. 101's Death's Head and candy-striped rudders. (Gil Arbel)

Left: F-15D No. 957 has five kill roundels, scoring its fifth over a Syrian MiG-23 on 19 Nov. 85, one of the last IAF victories. The Hebrew name is "Skyblazer". (Gil Arbel)

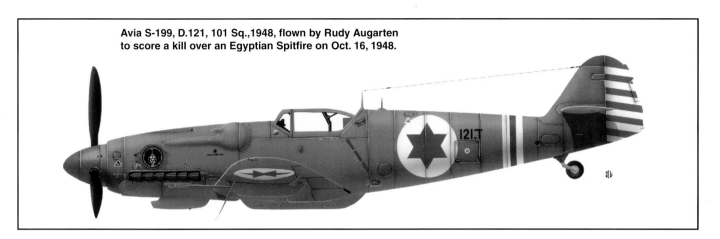

Avia S-199, D.121, 101 Sq.,1948, flown by Rudy Augarten
to score a kill over an Egyptian Spitfire on Oct. 16, 1948.

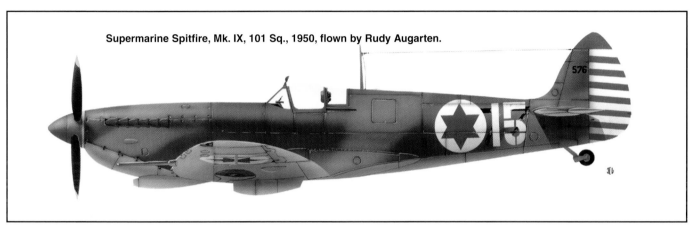

Supermarine Spitfire, Mk. IX, 101 Sq., 1950, flown by Rudy Augarten.

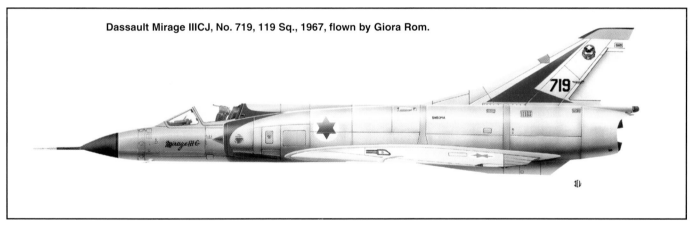

Dassault Mirage IIICJ, No. 719, 119 Sq., 1967, flown by Giora Rom.

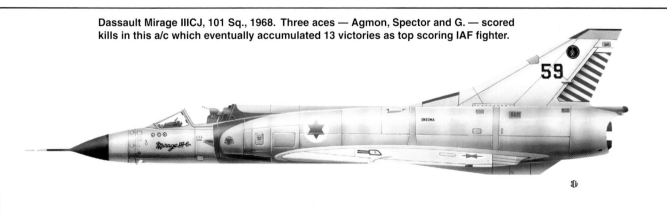

Dassault Mirage IIICJ, 101 Sq., 1968. Three aces — Agmon, Spector and G. — scored
kills in this a/c which eventually accumulated 13 victories as top scoring IAF fighter.

IAI Nesher, No. 527, 144 Sq., 1973.

McDonnell-Douglas F-4E Phantom II, 105 Sq., flown
by Ben-Ami Peri to make the last IAF Phantom kill.

General Dynamics F-16A, 110 Sq., 1982.

McDonnell-Douglas F-15D, 106 Sq, 1985. The Hebrew name means "Skyblazer."

Phantoms as the true heroes of this phase of the Arab-Israeli conflict.

It took tremendous courage to dive against the array of *tillim* (Hebrew for missiles) a few thousand feet below. No longer was the conflict solely Jew against Arab; it had widened. Although undeclared, it was a war between Israel *and the Soviet Union.* As groups of western reporters watched from their Cairo hotel rooms, IAF jets continuously blasted the SAM sites near the Suez Canal. Occasionally, the reporters saw flame and smoke blossom as a flak burst or SAM found its target and blasted another Israeli striker from the sky.

Major Shmuel Hetz, one of the first Phantom pilots and the popular CO of 201 Squadron, was killed during a raid on July 18 against missile sites west of the canal. It was a dangerous mission.

As Hetz and his navigator, Major Menahem Eini, approached their target, an SA-3 battery fired a missile that exploded 150 feet from the F-4, despite a new ECM pod under the Phantom, which the crews hoped would disorient a missile's radar system. A second missile exploded even closer.

For a few seconds it looked like Hetz' aircraft was undamaged. He turned north, back toward the canal. However, after three or four minutes, Hetz called, "Goodby. I'm wounded." He lowered the nose of his plane to gain valuable speed. Within a few minutes he could be over Israeli territory. But the situation quickly deteriorated, and Eini ejected from the dying F-4 at 600 knots, nearly 700 miles per hour. (It is not known whether Hetz command-ejected his navigator before trying to go himself, or in the terror of the moment, Eini initiated the sequence.)

Eini's chute blossomed, and he pulled out his hand-held survival radio to call for help. He watched for his pilot's chute but never saw it. Eini was too far inside Egypt to be rescued. He was captured and spent the next three years as a POW before being repatriated in November 1973, after the Yom Kippur War. Shmuel Hetz never returned.

As soon as he could after his release, Eini went into the area west of the Suez Canal, near Ismailia, which was under Israeli occupation, and, using reconnaissance photos, found the wreckage of his Phantom. His pilot was still in the cockpit. The squadron commander had never left his aircraft.

Eini and Hetz' widow visited the site a few days later and erected a simple concrete tablet that said, "Here fell Lt. Col. Shmuel Hetz on 18.7.70." They planted a border of fig trees around the site. (Hetz had been promoted posthumously, a common practice.)

Fifteen years later, Hetz' son and Eini found the site again, made sure it was clean and that the tablet was still in place. Then, they brought Shmuel Hetz home to be buried in a northern suburb of Tel Aviv, where many of his fellow IAF friends and pilots now live.

Eventually, and with heavy losses, the Israelis seemed to make a dent in the SAM umbrella. The IAF

had begun training its crew in various avoidance techniques, some of which involved flying at extremely low altitude to escape radar detection, or following commercial airliners into Egypt.

The Russians countered the latter ploy by ordering all commercial traffic to swing wide over the Mediterranean, north of the coastal town of Matruh, before turning east toward their Cairo destination. The Russians also sent more MiGs to Egypt. Some estimates put the total at ten MiG squadrons, with some 150 fighters and 300 pilots by mid-1970; more realistic guesses suggested five or six squadrons.

By the end of June, the SAM umbrella was nearly completed along the Suez Canal. The intensity of IAF attacks increased, and so did the interceptions by Soviet MiGs. On July 25, a Russian pilot launched an AA-2 Atoll air-to-air missile at an attacking Israeli Skyhawk. The missile exploded nearby, and the lucky Skyhawk pilot was able to return to his base where parts of the missile, which had imbedded themselves in the A-4, could be studied. The markings were obviously Russian, which gave Israel incontestable proof to show the world of Russian intervention. Concerned about the growing rate of encounters with Soviet pilots, the Israelis – under the instigation of Lieutenant General Chaim Bar Lev, the IDF Chief of Staff – began planning a showdown with their Soviet foes.

Tasking from Jerusalem was clear: a clear-cut victory over the Russians was the only goal, a head-to-head encounter and a decisive Israeli victory. The tactic? If it had worked in the past, it might work again – an aerial ambush.

Four Mirages faking a reconnaissance mission would be the bait. High above them more Mirages and Phantoms would wait for the Russians to engage.

After a one-day delay because of last-minute jitters in Jerusalem, the "recce" Mirages took off on July 30 and headed toward the canal. As expected, the Russians scrambled in flights of four MiG-21s, and the Israelis knew they had succeeded – so far.

Lieutenant Colonel Avihu Ben-Nun led the first two-plane section of covering Phantoms; his wingman was Captain Aviem Sella. Major Ehud Hankin, who had gotten the first kill by an Israeli Phantom the previous November, led the second section. Among the Mirage pilots were aces Captain Iftach Spector and Captain Asher Snir. The 12 "shooters" in the Mirages and Phantoms had shot down a total of 59 Arab planes.

Asher Snir was the first to score, hitting a MiG at 30,000 feet. The MiG pilot ejected at that high altitude and as he floated down he had a long time to observe the toll the Israelis were taking of his fellow MiG pilots.

"We say there is only one pilot who really knows what happened in the big dogfight," said Avihu Ben-Nun, "the pilot of the MiG that Asher Snir got. He could watch the fight from his parachute."

The hapless Russian pilot also served as a "landmark" for the IAF pilots. The featureless desert below

Having flown Mirages and Mystere IVs in combat, Avihu Ben-Nun was an experienced aviator by the time he assumed command of one of the first Israeli Phantom squadrons. Here, the young pilot stands by his Mirage before a flight in 1965. (via Avihu Ben-Nun)

was devoid of reference points. Thus, all action was referenced by the caller's position from the Soviet flier, such as, "I'm south of the parachutist."

"There were so many aircraft in the fight," Ben-Nun continued, "that we changed adversaries and almost shot at each other."

After chasing several MiGs, he and his wingman cornered one that seemed to be going much faster than published performance figures said the MiG-21 could fly. At Mach 1 at only 100 feet above the desert, Ben-Nun chased the desperate Russian pilot, accompanied by a Mirage, whose pilot had decided to tag along.

The MiG was a mile ahead of us. The only worry I had was that the Mirage pilot would shoot him down before me. He had Shafrirs, while I had Sidewinders.

I launched a missile, but because of the MiG's speed, we were at the edge of the envelope. The missile

got to the target and exploded. But it seemed to do little damage; the MiG kept on flying. He didn't even slow down.

"Let's try a Sparrow," my navigator suggested. I hadn't even thought about using an AIM-7, which was an older type that was not supposed to work at that low an altitude. My navigator was an excellent radar operator, however. I was already quite low, but then the ground dropped away as we approached the Nile, giving us a little space between our planes and the terrain.

My backseater locked onto the MiG, I launched the Sparrow and got him. I'm sure that the pilot didn't survive because he was too low.[2]

Captain Spector arrived during the last moments of the engagement. Three days before, on July 27, he had shot down two Egyptian MiG-17s that had been harassing Israeli ground troops near the canal. Like many of the dogfights in the Middle East, the Israeli Mirage chased the Arab MiGs at 100 feet over the Egyptian marshes.

"I wrote 680 knots [780 mph] in my log book," Spector noted. He gunned down the first MiG, which splashed into the marsh water, skipping like a child's stone. A Sidewinder took care of the second MiG.

Spector's Mirage section had been on the outskirts of the July 30 ambush of the Russians, but he quickly spotted missile smoke trails in the distance.

"It was like a summer's night with lightning bugs flashing on and off."

By the time he got near the fight — which actually lasted only four minutes — the Russians had had enough and were trying to disengage. Spector punched off his three big external fuel tanks and went after a MiG-21. He was flying Mirage 52, the same aircraft in which he had gotten his first kill three years earlier.

He fired at the MiG but had to break away. He was never sure if he actually got the MiG. Confirmation came only several years later. Then, the authorities would only tell him that additional information confirmed the kill.

Captain Aviem Sella, Ben-Nun's deputy commander of No. 69 Squadron, bagged a MiG-21 in a fight that went from 15,000 feet down to 2,000 feet. He fired one missile, then another, but only the first one was needed as the MiG gushed flames and its pilot ejected. As he left to rejoin his flight, Sella could see the original "parachutist" still making his slow way toward the ground, and by then, probably half-frozen at about 10,000 feet.

The free-for-all — at one time there had been perhaps as many as twenty-four MiGs from three different bases in the air — seemed to take the starch out of

In 1969, at his new F-4 squadron, Major Ben-Nun, in flight gear, briefs Israeli IDF Chief of Staff Lt. Gen. Chaim Bar-Lev. (via Avihu Ben-Nun)

the Soviets. Even the Egyptians seemed to enjoy themselves at their teachers' expense. Rumors of the humiliation of the Soviet Union's best kept newspaper writers busy. However, official Israeli confirmation took a while. Finally, during a visit to New York in October, Prime Minister Golda Meir answered the question of whether there really were Russians in Egyptian MiGs.

"How do I know there are Russian pilots in Egypt?" she said. "Very simply, because we had shot down four Soviet planes that were flown by Soviet pilots." (At the time, reports claimed four definite kills for the Israelis, against no losses. Spector's late confirmation would raise Russian losses to five.)

As if to rub salt in the Russians' wounds, an Israeli newspaper reporter writing for *The Washington Post* on October 29, wrote that Marshal Pavel Kutachov, commander of the Soviet Air Forces, had gone to Egypt after the July 30 engagement. He concluded that his pilots were too inexperienced to fight the Israeli pilots and restricted his pilots from any future engagements unless they were sure of winning – which was probably never.

The fight with the Russian pilots helped to bring about a ceasefire in the War of Attrition. A week later, on August 8, the Soviet government told the Egyptians that it could no longer guarantee the sanctity of Egyptian airspace. This admission had to be the bitterest of pills to swallow for the proud Russians. Without Soviet protection of his bases and cities, Nasser decided to accept an arrangement put together by the U.S., and agree to a ceasefire.

During the three years since the 1967 war, the Israelis claimed 113 enemy aircraft destroyed in aerial engagements, with an additional 25 downed by Israeli SAMs and antiaircraft (AA) fire. Israel's losses were unofficially estimated at 25-35 aircraft, with 16 of these specifically as a result of combat, usually surface-to-air missiles and AA.

As with most wars, the War of Attrition – in some respects the bitterest of all the Arab-Israeli confrontations – showed many visions and lessons to the interested parties. Besides what some analysts viewed as a closer relationship between the Israeli Army and Air Force, the war gave the Israelis a sharply focused picture of what aerial combat would be like in the next war.

Israeli victories could no longer be assured simply because IAF pilots were better than the Arab counterparts. The men in the cockpits had a new enemy, cold and impersonal, whose radar "eyes" could not be seen above an oxygen mask if you caught up with him and stared at him across the 40 feet of air that separated his aircraft from yours.

As American pilots were learning over Southeast Asia, Israeli pilots had discovered that the surface-to-air-missile could kill them much more efficiently than any MiG pilot. And as if to underscore the point, as well as to let everyone know he had not given up, Nasser moved his missile batteries closer to the Israeli front lines shortly after the ceasefire, in direct violation of the agreement. It was one of the last actions he took.

Sick with diabetes, which his Soviet doctors did not consider very serious, and exhausted from meetings and shuttles, Nasser died of a heart attack on September 28, 1970. In the long run, Nasser's departure allowed a more moderate leader to succeed him. However, in the period immediately following his installation as president, Anwar Sadat, a close associate of Nasser, planned the next major war with the Jewish state.

Endnotes:

1. *Newsweek* (April 6, 1970)
2. Avihu Ben-Nun, interview, Tel Aviv, November 20, 1992.

Although the rudders of these Mirage IIIs may have been retouched by the censor to hide the traditional red-and-white stripes, the red intake flash and Death's Head badge on the vertical tails identify 101 Squadron.

9

BUILDUP TO CATASTROPHE

Although Nasser's death surprised everyone on either side of the Suez Canal, the Egyptians were not leaderless for long. Granted, he did not have his predecessor's fiery charisma, but Anwar Sadat had learned much living in the shadow of his longtime friend, and had a more stable personality. He knew what he wanted for his people and although it would take some time before he could focus on contributing to peace in the region, Sadat became what some people consider the most important leader in the Middle East of the 20th century. But for the first three years of his presidency, Sadat was beset by ancient hatreds and policies. Old wounds had to be avenged, and he began planning for another major war against Israel.

At first, Sadat kept his country in the Soviet camp, enjoying the umbrella of Russian technology. The Soviets kept supplying the latest in weaponry, including late-model aircraft, such as MiG-21Js and Su-20s, a variable-geometry – or swing-wing – version of the veteran Su-7 Fitter.

They also maintained their own presence, flying patrol aircraft out over the Mediterranean against American and British task forces steaming just off the Egyptian and Lebanese coasts. They also flew high-performance MiG-23 Floggers and MiG-25 Foxbats (which, with a top speed of over Mach 3.2, or 1,860 knots at 63,000 feet, were the fastest operational production aircraft in the world, with the exception of the U.S. SR-71) on reconnaissance flights over Israel, much to the discomfort of the government in Jerusalem. IAF aircraft were hard-pressed to scramble to reach the intruders. (On October 10, 1971, for example, two Soviet-piloted Floggers eluded their IAF pursuers in F-4Es as they flew off the Israel coast between Ashdod and Ashqelon, south of Tel Aviv, before turning west toward Port Said.) For the first 18 months following Nasser's departure, Egypt and Syria were still very much Soviet client states.

Exhausted from the debilitating War of Attrition – which was, after all one of Nasser's main goals – Israel continued to modernize the IAF and to bolster existing strengths. Jerusalem pressed Washington for more F-4s and A-4s while trying to maintain dwindling numbers of tired Vautours, Mysteres, and Super Mysteres. By late 1970, Israel had received or contracted to receive 100 new A-4s – 90 A-4Hs and 10 TA-4Hs – in addition to more than 40 A-4Es that began arriving in late 1967.

New F-4Es straight off the McDonnell Douglas production line in St. Louis were also being modified for IAF service with wing leading-edge slats, which were originally developed for Federal German Phantoms and which greatly enhanced low-speed maneuverability. By October 1973, the IAF had received 122 F-4Es and six RF-4Es from existing USAF stocks and off the production line.

The two American aircraft had taken over the majority of fighter and attack missions flown by the IAF, but the veteran French aircraft were held in reserve for whenever the next war might be. Pilots still used them for advanced training.

And, of course, there was the queen of the fighters, the Mirage. Seldom has a country gotten so much for its initial purchase money. The lithe delta was still able to command the skies, especially when flown by the caliber of pilots that Israel continued to produce. But the Mirage had passed its peak, and replacement aircraft had not been available since the churlish French embargo of June 1967. Indeed, it was now only the third most important aircraft in the IAF lineup behind the Skyhawk and the Phantom.

At first, the Israelis had lived with the problem of no reserves, but the attrition of combat and training had drained the Mirage fleet over the years. Also, with a growing emphasis on ground-attack capability, the Mirage was found somewhat wanting, even though it had been, until the arrival of the F-4, the only Israeli aircraft besides the big Vautour able to tote 1,000-kg (2,200-pound) bombs.

France continued its embargo of arms to Israel after the June 1967 war, even though Israel had paid for 50 new Mirage 5Js, a ground-attack version. It was not until February 1972 that France finally agreed to refund the money along with a seven-percent interest for the four-and-half years that it had held the Israelis' money. But the French also said they would not send the new aircraft, nor any spares to cover the loss of the original aircraft. The desperate Israelis knew – indeed, they had known for a long time – that they would have to help themselves.

Accordingly, Israel began designing a new fighter, based on the Mirage but using an Israeli copy of the original French Atar engine. While a few components for the new fighter were procured over the counter, several important areas of interest were obtained beneath it. A Swiss engineer sent plans for the IIIS variant – a Mirage built for Switzerland – to Israel. He was later imprisoned.

The first prototype of the hybrid, now called Nesher (Eagle) flew for the first time in September 1969

This long-nosed Nesher rests at the IAF Museum. Heavier than its parent Mirage V, the Nesher enjoyed some success in the skilled hands of IAF aces, most of whom, however, preferred the lighter, more maneuverable Mirage III. The Israelis painted the Nesher's nose black to mislead observers into thinking there was a powerful new radar inside. However, Neshers probably flew with nothing in the radome, except perhaps a low-grade ranging radar, which most veteran Mirage pilots tended to ignore. (Author)

with an unlicensed Atar 9C copy, the same engine used in uprated Mirage IIIs.[1] Neshers entered service with Mirage squadrons in 1972, but the aircraft met with mixed reviews from some of the veteran aces. Neshers equipped portions of No. 101 and No. 117 Squadrons at Hatzor and Ramat David, respectively. No. 113 Squadron at Hatzor, and a new unit, No. 144 Squadron, flew only Neshers. No. 144 was led by Mirage ace Uri Even-Nir, and began operations in July 1972 from Etzion, a base in the southern Sinai, commanded by Yalo Shavit. Menachim Sharon relieved Even-Nir in August 1973, two months before the Yom Kippur War. By 1973, 40 Neshers had entered service. (According to one source, 50-60 were produced, including 10 two-seaters.)[2]

"We tried to make pairs of Neshers and pairs of Mirages," said G., "not to mix them because of the difference in their ranges."

Giora Rom was supposed to transition No. 113 Squadron from its veteran Ouragans to Neshers, but he was sent to command an A-4 squadron after the death of its CO in a flying accident. Rom didn't see too much difference between the Nesher and the Mirage III that he had flown for so long. He knew some purists thought the Nesher's long control column hindered their movements during dogfights; they were used to the Mirage's shorter stick which sat on top of a rubber boot and housing. He did feel that the Mirage III was more "elegant" than the heavier Nesher.

The Nesher *was* heavier than the Mirage, mainly because it included some 930 more liters (242 gallons, or 1,451 pounds) of fuel in the wings and belly, nearly a third more than the Mirage's 2,500 liters (650 gallons, or 3,900 pounds). The Nesher's landing gear was strengthened and two more underwing attachment

points were added to increase the aircraft's load-carrying capability. Its centerline station under the belly was also reinforced so that the Nesher could carry a MER (multi-ejector rack) or TER (triple-ejector rack), American-designed, underwing racks that could each carry several stores. Altogether, the Nesher more than doubled the Mirage III's bombload, but at a price.

Like any other aircraft, the Nesher's maneuverability was based on its wingloading and power. While the engine remained the same, the plane was 1.5 tons heavier than the Mirage.

G. was not thrilled with the Nesher.

"I may have been the first or second IAF pilot to fly the Nesher before it went into service," he said. "Until then, only IAI test pilots had flown it. When I first flew it, doing aerobatics and such, I liked it very much. It was like a Mirage. But the first dogfight with it, I felt like a cripple..."[3]

Major Moshe Hertz was more resigned. "I flew the Nesher in 1973. It was heavy and hard to maneuver, but it was OK."[4]

Former Vautour pilot Captain Ariel Cohen, now with No. 144 Squadron, remembered that the Nesher was "slightly inferior to the Mirage III."

This difference is significant when the other components of the air combat are equal. Frankly, I considered the differences very important when I had to face a friend in a Mirage while I flew the Nesher.

In my combat engagements, I think that the combat picture acquisition [what we might call situational awareness today], the implementation of tactics and the efficient use of weapons, were the most important things. I don't remember a crucial need for extra maneuverability in combat.[5]

A crossbreed though the Nesher might have been, it was fairly successful, accounting for nearly twenty-five percent (more than 100 victories) of the IAF's aerial kills in the 1973 Yom Kippur War.[6]

While the Arabs and Israelis continued rebuilding their air forces, the constant probing kept the political situation tense along the Suez Canal and the Golan Heights. In July 1971, now-Major Iftach Spector took command of a new F-4 unit, No. 107 Squadron.

Originally a Spitfire squadron in 1953, and later changing to Mustangs, the squadron stood down by the end of the decade. It reappeared as a Meteor squadron in 1962, only to stand down again two years later. This see-saw existence continued with the squadron flying Ouragans in 1967. After the June war, however, 107 remained active and acquired Phantoms.

Soon promoted to lieutenant colonel, Spector had to borrow F-4s from other IAF squadrons to get his men's training started since the first squadron aircraft would not arrive until February 1972. When their own aircraft arrived, Spector had the ground crews paint the Phantoms' rudders a bright orange, thereby generating the nickname "Orange Tails." As the commander, Spector availed himself of the chance to fly new Phantoms with the leading-edge wing slats. Within four months, the squadron was declared ready and started flying "red" or operational flights. Although at that time, he had perhaps only 20 hours in the Phantom, Spector brought a wealth of experience to his first command.

> I took advantage of my experience with other aircraft. We had a few months left to make the squadron operational. The base [Hatzerim] provided soldiers, but we didn't have mechanics who were trained on the Phantom. We got some from the flight school.[7]

After spending his adolescence as a member of the Gadna Youth Corps, Spector entered flight training and received his wings in July 1960. Of the fifteen pilots in the graduating class, only five survive today, ten having died in the air, some in combat and some in operational mishaps.

Spector spent a busy tour instructing in various aircraft, and occasionally made more than five, and even ten, flights a day.

"It was a very unsafe way to fly," he remembered, "but we were trying to emulate the war aces. We lost many friends in training accidents."

Transitioning to the Mirage, he soon was scrambling against Egyptian and Syrian intruders. There seemed to be no end to the action in the mid-1960s. He got his first kill, a Syrian MiG-21, on April 7, 1967.

Like most of his contemporaries, Spector flew many missions during the Six Day War, and continued the fight in the War of Attrition. By the time he took com-

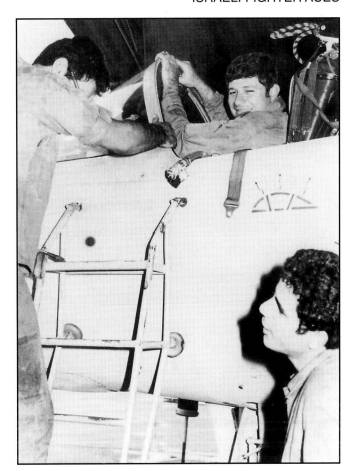

Mirage and Nesher ace Moshe Hertz is probably returning from a mission in a Mirage. (via Moshe Hertz)

mand of the new Phantom squadron, Spector was an established ace. (His score would total fifteen kills by the end of the 1973 war.) He had even participated in the legendary ambush on July 30, 1970, of the Russian MiG squadrons, gaining what turned out to be the last of the five kills by the Israeli fighters.

Although he was used to flying single-seat fighters, Spector soon began to appreciate having someone behind him in the powerful F-4. He considered every one of his navigators equal to his pilots, and treated them so in all phases of squadron life, including discipline. On one occasion, he put both the pilot and the backseater of one of his aircraft in hack for buzzing a beach. When questioned as to why he included the navigator, Spector retorted, "Because he's part of the mission. He was there."

Another thing we learned from the other squadrons," Spector recalled, "also concerned the navigators."

> When I was in charge of Mirages, I only had pilots, but now, in my Phantom squadron, I had double the manpower. We didn't know how to handle the navigators. So, we asked them.
>
> They helped us understand that they enhance the effectiveness of

The crew of this 119 Squadron F-4E taxis at the start of another mission.

our new plane, and our mission capability. We decided not to use the word "navigator," and called everyone a pilot. We sent the backseaters to flight school to teach them about flying the aircraft, and we also flew with them in Fougas. Everyone was equal.[8]

In February 1972, 107 Squadron received 24 F-4s and began returning the six Phantoms it had borrowed from other squadrons. Meanwhile, other pilots, some with experience and some without, kept watch, patrolling along Israel's boundaries, as their Arab adversaries parried and occasionally thrust into Israeli territory.

Eitan Peled had flown Super Mysteres in 1967, accumulating 16 missions in five days, five in one day. After a tour of instructing, he flew the Mystere then transitioned to the F-4 in 1969 as a member of the first Phantom class in Israel. However, an Egyptian artillery offensive in 1970 required that the new Phantom crews actually start flying missions *during* the course, an unusually intense form of on-the-job training.

Navigators were a rare breed at this early period, and new Phantom pilots like Peled flew their first few months in the rear cockpits. After perhaps 100 flights, they were allowed to move to the front seat.

In late 1970, Eitan Peled had his first aerial engagement. He was part of a 10-plane flight that ran into eight Syrian MiG-21s. The Israelis tried their Sparrow air-to-air missiles, but the Syrians were beyond the AIM-7's range.

The Phantoms were at 15,000 feet, with the enemy MiGs 5,000 feet higher. Peled's navigator locked onto a MiG, calling,"Range is OK," letting his pilot know he could fire a Sidewinder.

There were two Mirages beneath the Phantoms and two more deltas above them. Perhaps the Syrians did not yet see the F-4s, but at any rate, Peled fired an AIM-9D and bagged a MiG.

A year later, before the 1973 war, he got his second kill, an Egyptian MiG-21, again with a Sidewinder.

Commenting on the Phantom, Peled said, "I liked the Phantom a lot. I felt very comfortable in it and I liked to fly it. I liked its power and I really liked to fly with a navigator. He made sure everything was OK. I looked for MiGs and he looked out for everything else."[9]

There were several clashes between Israeli and Egyptian or Syrian fighters in 1971 and 1972. The most violent, however, occurred on September 13, 1973, when 16 Syrian MiG-21s bounced four Israeli RF-4Es that were photographing installations in northern Syria. A free-for-all developed, in which 12 MiGs were destroyed for the loss of one Mirage, whose pilot was rescued.

Avihu Ben-Nun had left No. 69 Squadron and was serving in the IAF headquarters in Tel Aviv. But he stood the customary alert and was on duty when the call came to scramble from Ramat David toward the big engagement over Syria. Along with his flight of Phantoms, four Mirages also launched.

The fight had been going on for some time when he and his navigator arrived over Tartus on the coast. Ben-Nun was concerned about beating the Mirages behind him to the MiGs.

"I spotted a MiG in a turn and I launched a Sparrow, just as the Mirage flight leader, 90 degrees to me, fired a Sidewinder. We were after the same MiG, one of the last Syrians in the enemy formation."

The MiG exploded, but no one was sure whose kill it was. With four previous kills, this shot could make Ben-Nun an ace. However, when the pilots looked at the gun-camera film of the fight, they could see that the Mirage pilot's missile had arrived at the target only 100 yards in front of the Phantom's Sparrow. Thus, Ben-Nun did not make ace. No matter. For in the larger scheme of careers and contributions, he was to attain a much higher position.

Iftach Spector was also involved in the big dog-fight on September 13. He downed two MiG-21s, his 10th and 11th kills. He used a missile to kill the first MiG. The MiG exited from the explosion engulfed in flames. It had lost a wing and its flaps were down. Spector then hit the second MiG with 20 mm cannonfire from his nose-mounted weapon.

It was obvious that the confrontation would continue until another war began. However, Israel had decided not to make another pre-emptive strike like the one on June 5, 1967. For one thing, such action would not have the support of the U.S., Israel's main source of weapons.

Israeli confidence also led to the belief that any initial strike from the Arabs could be absorbed and dealt with. Such misplaced confidence – though understandable, given the string of successes over the Arabs – allowed the Arabs to fortify their armies relatively unhindered. Egypt bolstered the thickets of surface-to-air missiles along the Suez Canal with SA-3 Goas and mobile SA-6 Gainfuls. Shoulder-launched SA-7 Grails, which had begun appearing in Vietnam, and proved effective against low-flying American helicopters, also arrived in the Middle East.

The SA-6's radar was initially hard to counter, and along with ZSU-23-4 anti-aircraft guns, provided the Egyptians with a formidable air defense that would sometimes take the measure of the IAF's bombers. The next war would not be the traditional cakewalk for Israeli aircrews.

(The visual warning for an SA-6 launch was a puff of white smoke, after which the low-altitude SAM quickly reached Mach 2.8. The ZSU was a tracked ve-hicle with four 23 mm cannon aimed by high-frequency (HF) radar and fired together, an awesome anti-air weapon.)

Following his ordeal as a POW, Giora Rom quickly returned to the cockpit of his beloved Mirage. After moving to No.113 Squadron (Ouragans), which would transition to Neshers, he received orders to No. 115 Squadron at Tel Nof, an A-4 unit whose CO had been killed in a training accident on Wednesday, October 3, 1973. He had never flown the A-4, however, and made his first flight in a two-seat TA-4H. He had little time to learn his new plane's capabilities.

Morale in the Skyhawk squadron was understandably low after the death of the previous CO, who was well liked. The funeral was Friday, October 5th, and the following day, the Yom Kippur War broke out.

"I was with a squadron, half of whose members I didn't know," Rom recalled, "and an aircraft I didn't know, either."

On the morning of the 6th, Rom had convinced his base commander to let him strip his A-4 of its bombs to make his first solo flight. He chose a young pilot to chase him. At noon, the junior pilot gave his new CO a cockpit brief, showing Rom how to start the Skyhawk's J-52 engine, and how to operate the navigational system.

Rom started up and taxied to the runway. It was the first time he had been in a plane with nosewheel steering. The Mirage used differential braking to maneuver on the ground.

Everything went fine until the two Skyhawks got to the runway. Rom couldn't close the canopy! A squadron jeep brought another pilot who scrambled onto the

These Mirage IIIs from 101 Squadron display a variety of IAF serials on their vertical tails. Originally using a two-digit identifier, the First Fighter Squadron eventually instituted a three-digit system in keeping with the other Mirage and Nesher squadrons.

Originally scheduled to lead No. 113 Squadron in its transition from its ancient Ouragans to Neshers, Giora Rom received orders instead to an A-4 squadron whose CO had just been killed in a flight accident. The fighter ace was now a light-attack pilot. (via Giora Rom)

A-4's wing and showed Rom how to operate the lever on the left console that locked and unlocked the canopy.

Ready to launch at last, Rom lined up on the runway only to have the tower call that MiGs were inbound and that he had to hurry back to a shelter. He did so, and as he was getting out of his unarmed plane, he spotted some of his pilots in flight gear. They told him they were going on a mission to the canal.

Grabbing some charts, he declared, "I'm going to be in No. 4. It's 25 minutes to the canal. I'll ask you all the questions in the air. Everything will be OK." Thus, Giora Rom's first solo flight in an A-4 was as part of a formation, carrying eight Mk-82 500-pound bombs.

It was one of several such stories that accompanied the opening of what would be the IAF's hardest war.

Endnotes:

1. Another Israeli version of the Mirage was the Barak (Lightning) – a Mirage III with an American J-79, the same engine that powered the Phantom. A few Baraks served during the 1973 war.

An improved version, now called the Kfir (Lion Cub), was based on the Mirage 5, updated avionics and the J-79, and eventually became the definitive post-Mirage III variant.

2. *World Airpower Journal*, Volume 15, Winter 1993.
3. G., interview, Tel Aviv, May 5, 1993.
4. Moshe Hertz, interview, Tel Aviv, May 5, 1993.
5. Ariel Cohen, letter to author, June 16, 1993.
6. *World Airpower Journal*, Volume 15, Winter 1993.
7. "Knights of the Orange Tail," by Sharon Geva, *Israel Air Force Magazine,* June 1992.
8. Ibid.
9. Eitan Peled, interview, Tel Aviv, May 6, 1993.

10

WAR ON THE HOLIEST DAY

Eitan Karmi sped through the streets of Tel Aviv toward Hatzor. Having flown in the 1967 war, and the War of Attrition, Karmi had left active duty in 1969, but still flew as a reservist. He was also an airline pilot for El Al. Earlier on this Saturday, October 6, 1973, he had taken a phone call at home ordering him to his Mirage squadron.

The streets were quiet not only because it was the Sabbath, but because this particular Saturday was Yom Kippur, the Day of Atonement, the holiest day of the Jewish calendar. Normally a day to be spent in prayer at one's synagogue, Yom Kippur was also a day of fasting and personal rededication.

As Karmi passed some of the more zealous individuals on the streets, perhaps on their way to synagogue, they threw stones at his car! He couldn't believe it. He was going to his squadron to protect these people, and they were throwing stones at him!

He arrived at the base at 8 am, suited up and waited. Finally, a call scrambled him and another Mirage at 2 pm. But no one was quite sure what the mission was. First, the controller sent the two planes toward Ashqelon. Then they were told to head due west, out over the Mediterranean.

"Look for a big airplane," the controller said, "maybe a Badger."

Soon, Karmi spotted a Tu-16, with an AS-5 Kelt air-to-surface missile under its wing. The flying bomb had a small jet engine and was aimed by radio beams. The Badger released the Kelt and dove for the water.

"Find the missile," the controller said.

"I see something," Karmi's wingman called. He had spotted the Kelt's smoke trail. The bomb was going down; it was out of fuel and was headed toward Tel Aviv.

"We flew toward the Kelt," Karmi said, "and I fired a Shafrir. But my missile was a heat-seeker and without an exhaust from the Kelt to guide on, it had nothing to home on."

Karmi closed to 250 meters, and began firing his cannon. He hit the Kelt's wings, which was fortunate since the bomb's 1,000-kg warhead was in the fuselage. The missile spun into the water and exploded. (During the Yom Kippur War, approximately 25 Kelts were fired against Israeli targets. Five reached their targets, Israeli fighters and defensive fire accounting for the other 20.)

*   *   *

As Eitan Karmi was scoring one of the first Israeli kills of the new war, Giora Rom was leading his A-4 squadron against Egyptian targets on the Suez Canal. It was the first time he had flown a single-seat Skyhawk. He had to make a pop-up delivery against enemy tanks. His first run didn't go well and he lined up for another. He dropped his load of 500-pound bombs and turned for home.

The flight lead, a younger, but more experienced pilot in the A-4, called for fuel states. Everyone reported that they still had 4,500 pounds. Rom, the new squadron commander, was horrified to see that his gauge showed only 700 pounds. What had happened? Some-

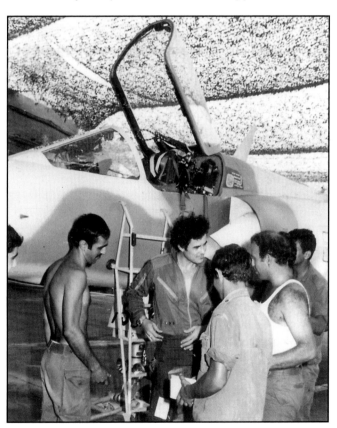

Energetic Mirage ace Eitan Karmi greets his ground crew after returning from a mission. His camouflaged aircraft is a Nesher, evidenced by the large blade antenna behind the cockpit, and the air intakes farther back on the fuselage, nearly aligned with the rear bulkhead of the cockpit. Like ground crews everywhere, Israeli mechanics fretted as "their" planes launched toward battle and strained to hear the returning pilot's every word as he described an engagement. More often than not, when returning from a successful dogfight, drained IAF pilots indulged in the traditional victory roll over their base more for their ground crews than for themselves. (via Eitan Karmi)

thing wasn't right, he knew. He couldn't be that low when everyone else had enough to get back. Then he realized that he had not activated the fuel transfer. Where was it? After a few tense minutes – during which he simply reported having the same fuel as the rest of the flight – he found the switch that said, PRESS. His fuel gauge's needle jumped and he suddenly had more gas.

Even though he had limited time in the Skyhawk, Rom knew his place was with his squadron when the first mission of the war launched.

"They didn't care that it was my first flight," he said. "They *expected* that the commander of the squadron would go. After my fifth flight, I felt more comfortable in the A-4."

It wasn't as if the Israelis had lost their zeal for their two-millennia-old dream; the love for their tiny nation-state was as strong as ever. Their watchfulness had never slackened. But it had been three full years since Nasser's death, and although the clashes with Egypt and Syria had continued, there had been a thin veil of hope for dealing with the new leaders of the two largest and most intractable enemies.

Anwar Sadat had booted the Russians out of Egypt in July 1972. He did not like being their lackey and whipping boy, and the rise and fall of the Soviet supply rate, as well as the continuing smugness of Soviet advisors grated on the collective Egyptian psyche.

In Syria, Defense Minister Lieutenant Colonel Hafez al-Assad led a coup that toppled the government in February 1969, and while he still relied heavily on Russian support and supplies, and railed against the Jewish settlements on his western borders, he seemed to be more occupied with settling old scores among his Arab brethren, especially in Lebanon. As a younger officer in the early 1950s, Assad had been a promising fighter pilot, and had flown a wide variety of foreign aircraft, including Italian Fiats, and MiG-17s and MiG-19s.

The destruction of large portions of the air forces of Egypt and Syria in 1967 presented a two-part dilemma. The first problem was easily overcome by Soviet resupply of aircraft – one of the reasons that Sadat kept the Russians in Egypt as long as he did. However, training new pilots required time and the loss of many senior pilots in 1967 left a hole at the mid-level positions.

Some Arab countries, such as Libya and Algeria, occasionally offered help, and sometimes trained with the Egyptians and the Russians. Libya had bought some 60 French Mirages 5Ds in 1971, and loaned many of them to Egypt in time for the October war. (The French denied the transfer of Libyan fighters. Newspaper reports quoted the French as saying that the news of Libyan aircraft heading for Egypt was "a joke," and that such reports were commonplace, and false.)[1] Pakistani pilots were rumored to be flying the Libyan fighters, as well as other mercenaries. The possibility of similar aircraft on the enemy's side presented recognition problems for all the combatants. Israel painted large orange (sometimes yellow) -and-black triangles on the wings and vertical tails of its Mirages.

Egypt had lost several important airfields in 1967, and embarked on a major construction program, building 20 bases complete with hardened shelters.

Egypt and Syria loved to play war games with each other, skirting the Suez Canal or the Golan Heights, perhaps testing Israeli response times, but never threatening to take their exercises any further. Besides, if Egypt and Syria were foolish enough to go to war again with Israel, they would be as soundly trounced as they had been in 1967, or even during the War of Attrition, when it was obvious that even with new Russian missiles and radar barriers, the Israelis could have destroyed them, if they wished.

However, by early 1973, Sadat had decided on another war – to revenge past defeats and transgressions, and more importantly, to establish himself as the acknowledged Arab leader. He did not have to win the war against Israel; indeed, that was something he knew he and his partners could not do. No, all he wanted was to win a few battles, show the world that the Israelis were not invincible, and that the large countries of northern Africa were worthy of international respect and understanding. From that position of strength, no matter if in the end, Israel ultimately triumphed, he could then begin his agenda of bringing peace to the Middle East, a peace with honor for the Arabs.

All these hopes and expectations rode on the shoulders of the teams of artillerymen, and on the backs of the some 8,000 commandos who scrambled into rubber boats along the west bank of the Suez Canal in the early afternoon of October 6, 1973. (The date also had religious significance for the Arabs: it was the 10th day of Ramadan, the day on which the Prophet Muhammad started preparations for the battle of Badr that later permitted him to enter the city of Mecca.)

They were preparing to unleash a massive barrage against Israeli positions, weakened, not only by the reduced readiness of the Yom Kippur holiday, but by faulty Israeli intelligence, which indicated that if the Arabs attacked, it would not be until the late afternoon or early evening. There was still time to pray and bring people to their positions.

At 5 am, Saturday, October 6, Lieutenant General David Elazar, the IDF Chief of Staff, the top military man in Israel, had called Major General Benjamin Peled, the IAF commander. Word had come that the Arabs would launch their attack at sunset. Elazar had told Peled to begin planning a pre-emptive strike against Egypt and Syria for some time after 11 am.

Shortly before 11, however, Elazar had called again. Prime Minister Meir had decided against a first strike; it was vital that the world see the Arabs as the aggressors this time.

As the French Mirage became the symbol of the IAF during the whirlwind victory of the Six Day War, so did the American Phantom symbolize ultimate success in the brutal Yom Kippur War of 1973. Here, an F-4 returns from a mission over perimeter barbed-wire.

Captain Amir Nahumi sat in his Phantom at the remote Ophir Airfield near Sharm el-Sheikh. Taken from the Egyptians in 1967, Ophir had remained an alert strip on the southernmost tip of the Sinai, guarding the Gulf of Aqaba.

Nahumi had entered the army in 1962. He had gone to flight school but had washed out. He then became a member of the crew of an AMX-13, a French light tank that featured a 75 mm gun. As the commander of one of these ubiquitous little vehicles, he saw considerable combat in 1967 in the Sinai. He had been attacked by Algerian MiG-17s, but poor aim by the MiG pilots had saved him as they overshot his position by half a kilometer.

After the war, he left active duty to attend college, but resolved to try again to become a pilot. This time, he succeeded, training on Fougas, then Ouragans, before transitioning to F-4s. Now he stood alert on the desert strip at Sharm.

As a junior captain – his wingman was also a junior pilot – he had not yet qualified as a flight leader, an important milestone. Who was to be the leader for this mission, should it come? Amir Nahumi called his squadron commander, now-Lieutenant Colonel Iftach Spector.

"What's the problem?" Spector asked.

"We don't have a flight leader."

"*You* are the flight leader," Spector came back. Just like that it was done.

"To become an *intercept* flight leader," Nahumi said, "a real milestone. Many of our leaders had kills and we really looked up to them. Now, the CO was telling me that I was a flight leader. I took the responsibility very seriously."[2]

Suddenly, the base siren sounded. The new flight leader taxied his two Phantoms toward the runway. What was happening? The controller told the F-4s to hold. MiGs were inbound and he had instructions to keep the Ophir

Phantoms on the ground. Incredible! War was coming, and Nahumi was going to meet it on the ground? Not likely!

"Are you sure?" he asked.

"To tell the truth," the controller said, "I see a whole bunch of MiGs over the sea!"

The MiGs were coming from a base way down in southern Egypt, nearly due west of Ophir. Nahumi knew that the decision not to start the war had been made at the highest levels. Action would be authorized only in retaliation for an Arab attack. Nevertheless, he told his wingman to run up his engines. The controller started shouting for the Phantoms to hold their positions.

"Shut off your radio," Nahumi told his wingman as he led the way onto the runway.

Accelerating down the runway, the F-4s rotated and clawed their way into the sky. Nahumi glanced up at the small mirrors hanging from the bow of his canopy; he could see columns of smoke on the runway's hold-short position, where they had been only moments before. The MiGs were over the field.

He caught the glare of sunlight bouncing off another aircraft some five miles away.

"You'd better punch off your externals," his navigator prompted him. As the tanks tumbled from the Phantoms, Nahumi told his wingman to separate; they would have to fight on their own.

Suddenly, he was engaged. There were MiGs everywhere he looked. Later, 28 Egyptian fighters were estimated to have attacked Ophir. On this, his first aerial combat mission, Nahumi was shooting at everything he saw. He hit MiGs, but didn't have time to watch as other MiGs would saddle in behind him. He used every weapon he had, all of his Sidewinders, and all of his cannon ammunition.

Once, he wound up in a circling contest, only 200 feet above the ground, with two MiG-17s. The Egyptians made very tight turns and the big Phantom was in danger of overshooting the camouflaged MiGs. Then, one MiG turned *into* Nahumi, who reacted automatically – even today he is not exactly sure what he did. But he wound up behind the MiG, too close to shoot a missile.

He slowed down and dropped back to 1,800 feet behind the MiG, waiting for the enemy pilot to stop turning. Nahumi shot a Sidewinder at the Egyptian fighter, the missile going right up the MiG's tailpipe before exploding.

Mesmerized, he watched as the MiG came apart.

"Forget him," his navigator cried. "Leave it!" The man behind him already had two kills, and roused from his transfixion, Nahumi climbed away.

He re-engaged, this time, becoming the filling in a "MiG sandwich," with two MiGs in front and two behind him. The ones behind him started shooting. His navigator warned him again.

"Don't bother me," Nahumi replied, "if they shoot us, we'll eject over our own territory!" He switched to his cannon.

He chased one of the MiGs in front, firing his nose gun. Suddenly, one of the Phantom's engines stalled. Power went down to 60 percent. But he would not be denied. He could see hits on the wings of the MiG, only 600 feet ahead of him. Somehow, the MiG stayed in the air.

The last go-round for Yak Nevo. The IAF's senior tactician was a colonel by the 1973 war, and had taken command of the southern Sinai base of Ophir barely an hour before the base was attacked by Egyptian MiGs. Nevo flew several missions with his old squadron, No. 105, which still operated their ageing Super Mysteres. (via the Nevo family)

Nahumi kept firing, then, boom! Were they hit? The Phantom was still flying. Nahumi looked down at his instruments, and only then realized he had been flying on one engine. He left the MiG and succeeded in getting a relight.

He tried to tell his controller, but the man on the ground was shouting and didn't hear him. He looked for his wingman and saw him chasing a MiG-21 low over the water of the Gulf. The Phantom's jetwash was sending up geysers of water. The MiG fairly jumped over the water as it escaped toward Egypt.

In the quiet that now followed, Nahumi looked around. Seven columns of smoke rose from the desert floor. He and his wingman had shot down seven MiGs – four and three, respectively.

As they neared Ophir, they could also see holes in the runway, surrounded by mounds of earth that Egyptian bombs had thrown up. The two Phantoms landed, barely avoiding the holes in the runway.

As they taxied back to their line, the four crewmen could see the ground troops gesturing wildly. One bomb had hit right in the middle of the flight line but had not exploded. It remained stuck in the ground.

Two more F-4s and four Mirages now recovered, some still with their missiles. Weapons were precious at this remote base, and the unexpended ordnance was taken from the returning fighters.

No one at the base could believe that the two junior pilots had accounted for seven enemy raiders. The two old hands, squadron commander Spector, and Colonel Yak Nevo – the IAF's shining light in the late 1950s, who had taken command of the base only an hour before the attack – took the most convincing. Lieutenant Colonel Spector had to see the gun camera films several times that evening before he believed it.

To add to the day's total, Spector's deputy, Major Shlomo Egozi, and his wingman had flown out late in the afternoon toward the canal, where they found several flights of Egyptian Mi-8 helicopters – 100 aircraft in all – transporting troops across the water. Before the two Phantom crews were through, another seven Egyptian aircraft lay on the desert floor. Egozi had batted down the last Mi-8 with his jetwash by flying over the struggling helicopter, jerking his nose up, and aiming his F-4's two powerful exhausts at the big enemy aircraft, which slammed into the ground.

Spector was grateful for his capable deputy. "Egozi complimented me. Administrative details did not interest me...but Egozi took care of them and let me see the big picture."

Arab helicopters were to suffer many times at the hands of IAF fighter pilots over the next three weeks. Twenty were lost on October 6. The Mirage and Phantom pilots turned out to be very inventive when dealing with the slower, tighter turning Egyptian and Syrian helos. Eitan Peled and G. destroyed two and one Egyptian Mi-8s, respectively, during the October 1973 war.

This camouflaged Mirage of No. 117 Squadron has two kill symbols below the cockpit.

Although the IAF maintained a standing patrol over Ophir, the Egyptians never returned. Nahumi and his flight had taken the heart out of the MiG-17 squadron. He received the E-tour Hamofet, Israel's third highest military award for this mission.

The initial Arab attacks were devastating, especially because the Israelis had so little strength to withstand them. As IDF reservists made their way to their assigned mobilization points, and IAF reservist pilots hurried to their squadrons — some from the cockpits of El Al airliners — the members of the regular defense forces coped as best they could.

For the moment, though, the Egyptians and Syrians had the advantage, and they made the most of it. Waves of Sukhois and MiGs struck Israeli bases in company with a massive thousand-gun artillery barrage. Refidim in north central Sinai, captured from Egypt in 1967, came in for special attention, while areas of the Golan Heights were subjected to furious attacks by Syrian fighter-bombers. In one raid, four Syrian Mi-8s lifted commando teams onto strategic Mount Hermon, above the Sea of Galilee, and captured the Israeli outpost. For the moment, Israel's ability to see into Syria was gone.

From the Sinai to the Golan, Arab guns, aircraft, soldiers and pilots attacked Israeli positions, but however long the Arab victories lasted, the first 24 hours of the Yom Kippur War burst the myth of Israel's invincibility, not only for the Arabs and the world, but for the Israelis, themselves.

For the IAF pilots in the A-4s and F-4s, supported by aging Super Mysteres, the worst times came as they dove against the frightening array of surface-to-air missiles. The SA-6 was an especially nasty surprise. It was not susceptible to the traditional countermeasures of chaff or flares, and was faster at lower altitudes than the SA-2 and SA-3.

Limited Israeli ECM — electronic countermeasures — and standard tactics allowed the missiles to take a heavy toll at first. Not until the IAF mounted a strategic campaign against the SAM and flak sites and devised drastic weapon-delivery techniques, was the threat from the missile-and-gun defense reduced — somewhat.

Only after suffering heavy losses against the highly mobile Gainful positions, did the IAF come up with maneuvers to defeat the missiles. But even these maneuvers, low to the ground and sometimes in incredibly complex twists and turns, required the courage and skill that had been the hallmark of the IAF since 1948. On one afternoon alone, SA-6s and ZSU-23 antiaircraft artillery claimed perhaps 30 A-4s and 10 Phantoms over the Golan Heights, 10 percent of the IAF's attack force. The Israelis stopped their attacks, which were aimed at halting a major Syrian breakthrough and reassessed the situation.

As the Syrian armored columns — 300 tanks under President Hassad's brother — pushed to within five miles of the Benot Yacov Bridge, 10 miles north of the Kinneret, the Sea of Galilee, on the Jordan River, they stopped; they had run out of fuel and ammunition. In a ground interdiction operation, the Israelis had hit them from behind in the dark on the previous night, taking out the supply convoys that followed the tanks.

IAF pilots threw themselves against the Egyptian pontoon bridges that had been quickly placed across the Suez Canal, 20 in all, to carry heavy machinery. Thousands of Egyptian soldiers had crossed the canal in rubber dinghies and attacked poorly-defended Israeli positions on the eastern side of the important waterway. Egyptian SAMs were nearly as effective against the Skyhawks and Phantoms as were the Syrian missiles on the eastern front.

In the first three days of the war, Egypt lost 113 aircraft, Syria, 149, and Iraq, 21. Defense Minister Moshe Dayan reported that in the same period, the IAF had lost 50 planes, mostly on ground attack missions, 20 percent of the IAF's strike capability.

By the end of the first week, the IAF was in desperate need of reinforcement, more aircraft. More than 80 aircraft, mostly A-4s and F-4s, had been lost. By the end of the second week, 35 more Israeli planes had been destroyed.

However, only after sending two SR-71 high-speed, high-altitude reconnaissance planes over the battle zone on October 13, did the U.S. decide to cover Israel's losses by sending in supplies by huge Air Force C-5 transports, and beginning shuttle flights of Navy and Air Force Phantoms and Skyhawks. The Soviets muttered rather loudly about this effort from Washington, but they were really not in a position to complain.

Navy and Marine Corps pilots flew in Skyhawks, drawn from fleet squadrons, and staging out of Norfolk, Virginia. Wending their way across the Atlantic, meeting USAF KC-135 tankers, the American aviators recovered aboard aircraft carriers in the Mediterranean. Then, they would launch toward Cyprus, refuel, and take off again, this time to be picked up in the air by orbiting Israeli Mirages, which led the Americans into IAF bases near Tel Aviv.

The Americans had not realized how frantic the situation was until they got out of their aircraft. Their planes were quickly surrounded by IAF technicians, and as the American pilots watched, the Israelis painted over the U.S. insignia with the blue Star of David. A-4s that had arrived perhaps only an hour before were already taxiing to the runway, bombs beneath their wings, headed for their first mission for the IAF. There was no time to repaint the Skyhawks in the three-toned IAF camouflage. The little bombers looked odd in their U.S. Navy gray with the incongruous blue-star-in-a-circle markings of Israel. Many A-4s only arrived by the third week of the war, some making barely four sorties before the ceasefire, but their value as replacements was vital.

These ferry flights were not the first such intense operations. In October 1970, as well as during other periods of Israeli need, U.S. pilots — many of them reservists, themselves on extended weekend duty — had flown Phantoms and Skyhawks to Israel within three days. The Americans each received $1,000-$2,000 for their work, as well as a one-way ticket home on El Al.

As the war raged around them, the IAF pilots kept flying, grabbing painfully short catnaps whenever they could, sprawling out in their ready rooms in their flight gear. The scenes were strikingly reminiscent of RAF crews during the Battle of Britain in 1940, more than thirty years before.

Moshe Hertz flew even though he was sick, with a temperature of 101. Sometimes, he even ate in his plane between missions. He finally went to the doctor, hoping to get some medicine. The doctor said that he could relieve the young pilot's symptoms but that the medicine was strong and Hertz would have to come off flight status. There were no options at this point; he had to keep flying, and refused the medication. Finally, as the reserve pilots began to appear in numbers from their El Al cockpits, the regulars like Moshe Hertz could enjoy longer rest periods. He tumbled into bed and slept for six hours, a real luxury.

By October 10, both sides were worn out. The Syrians, by some estimates, had lost 867 tanks, including some new T-62s. After a strong early showing, Syrian columns had been shoved back to their starting points by the resolute Israeli army. But both sides were tired. Some IDF members had been fighting since October 6, and their ammunition was gone.

Aircraft losses were heavy and replacements were unavailable at least until the U.S. agreed to send A-4s and F-4s, and that effort would need time to gather momentum.

The Arabs had no such supply-replacement problems. Their Soviet quartermasters were on the job, and new aircraft and more ammunition flowed into Egypt and Syria. New SAMs came direct from Red Army stocks!

On October 10, the IDF began its offensive on the Syrian front. By the 12th, Israeli tanks had smashed through Syrian, Iraqi, and Moroccan positions and were well on their way to Damascus. The Syrian Air Force tried to fight, but the IAF destroyed twenty-nine Syrian aircraft in two days.

On October 13, Amir Nahumi flew a mission over Syria, where he engaged MiGs after dropping his bombs. One of the other crewmen shouted, "MiGs!" and Nahumi saw a Syrian fighter closing on a Phantom.

"Four, break! Four, break!" he screamed, but the endangered Phantom was really No. 2. Nahumi drove for the MiG, going up into a scissors turn. The Syrian was aggressive but wasted most of his energy, ending up almost "parked" in midair.

Nahumi shot a missile at 600 knots, and the MiG exploded, its pilot ejecting. The Israeli Phantom flew close by the enemy pilot now hanging in his chute. From perhaps 100 meters, Nahumi looked at the pilot of his fifth kill.

The following day, the 14th, the targets for 107 Squadron were in Egypt. Inbound, Nahumi's flight was bounced by MiGs. He was leading a flight of two F-4s, flying very low and fast.

"The air was full of insects," he recalled, "and they covered my windscreen. I tried everything to clear my vision forward, without success. I was preoccupied with this problem and I was worried that I wouldn't be able to aim properly."

He looked at his wingman. There was a MiG-21 1,200 feet behind the other Phantom, and the Egyptian was firing. Nahumi called for a break and the wingman turned into his leader. The Egyptian MiG followed, also turning into Nahumi's fighter. Quickly saddling in behind the enemy plane, he fired a missile and the Egyptian disintegrated.

The two F-4s rejoined to refuel from one of the few IAF tankers in service. Suddenly, Nahumi saw another MiG-21 about half a mile away, coming in on a quarter attack.

"OK," the wingman called after Nahumi told him of the threat, "fly low very fast."

Nahumi pushed his control stick forward and quickly reached 600 knots. The MiG overshot, then re-attacked. The second try resulted in another overshoot. After three tries, Nahumi decided to engage the Egyptian.

He broke away from his wingman and lost sight of his No. 2. They rendezvoused. Nahumi didn't want to be alone at this point. About 20 miles after the Phantoms crossed the coast, he realized that he was low on fuel, having used his afterburner so much. As he was looking at his fuel gauge, he heard a bang and look back to see a MiG-21 coming in fast.

I pulled the stick into my stomach and went vertical. The Egyptian fighter passed me at 150 feet. I could see that he was wearing a cloth helmet, not a jet helmet. He looked back at me, and then he was gone.

I knew he was going to come back at me and I had to decide what to do. I cheated. At 220 knots, I pushed the nose over and went down. The aggressive MiG pilot also went with me. I waited, waited, then pulled up at about 250 knots. I went into the vertical, but the MiG just sank, spiraling down. I followed him.

"Watch your altitude," my navigator warned, as I started shooting. The MiG just went into the sea. I'm not sure I got him, or if he simply flew into the water. We flew over the sea at 500 feet. We had about 1,500 pounds of fuel.

Nahumi knew there were two emergency landing fields nearby, but he didn't know which one was available. One strip already had another aircraft on it that had run out of fuel. El Arish was available, and he headed for that.

He climbed to 35,000 feet as his wingman joined to escort him the 80 miles to El Arish. He throttled back to idle, thinking he could cover the distance at this altitude on both engines. He made it, but rolled out with only 150 pounds (barely 25 gallons) on the gauge. That was the good news. The bad news was that they had to stay at the remote field for a week because there were no technicians or fuel. He had also used his drag chute and there was no one there to repack it.

The October 1973 War saw the maturing of several of the young fighter pilots of 1967. Not only had they progressed in rank, and in some cases, achieved the status of squadron commanders, but they had also gained considerable experience in the air. (Iftach Spector's squadron had shot down 18 MiG-21s, seven MiG-17s, and seven Mi-8s.)

There were also the younger pilots, those who had gotten their wings after the Six Day War. A few had fought in the War of Attrition, while many saw their first combat in 1973. Russian-born Moshe Hertz had flown Mirages in 101 Squadron. In July 1970, he had shot

While retaining assignment with his Mirage squadron, Moshe Hertz was an instructor with an A-4 training squadron. Here, he gets into A-4 No. 846 before a mission in the early 1970s. (via Moshe Hertz)

down a Egyptian MiG-21, in the War of Attrition flying out of Refidim during the free-for-all "Texas" days.

Hertz got his second kill on October 13, while flying Neshers with 101 Squadron. By now he was the deputy squadron commander and was leading the Nesher escort for Phantoms on a mission to Damascus when his No. 4 spotted MiG-21s coming from behind the Israeli formation. The junior pilot called for everyone to break, but in his excitement used his *own* name, creating considerable confusion. The Neshers kept on flying. The tail-end charlie finally collected himself and called for the break again.

Hertz and his escorts reversed and saw the threat just as the MiGs began shooting missiles. The Syrian pilots were surprised at the Israeli maneuver and flew under the Neshers. Hertz dove after the MiGs and shot a Shafrir. The MiG exploded.

"We didn't have enough experienced pilots," Hertz commented. "We put the junior pilots on the easy missions. On one patrol on October 22, I took one of these younger pilots with me. As we flew along toward the canal, we heard on the radio that there were some engagements in progress, but that we were being held in reserve."

Hertz finally made out two dots some 20 miles away. He headed toward them, and as he and his wingman got closer, he could make out MiG-21s. It was

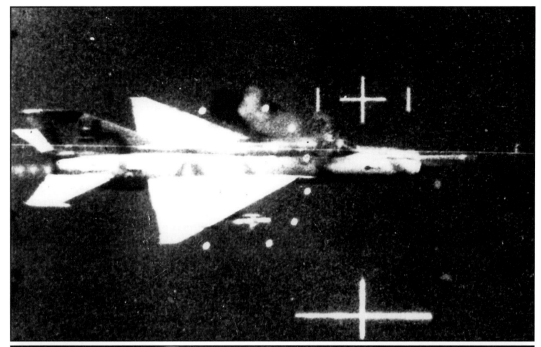

A MiG-21D erupts in flames after being hit by cannonfire from an Israeli Nesher during the Yom Kippur War. The Nesher's compass is reflected in the fighter's gunsight, an early version of a heads-up display (HUD). This display was carried only in the Nesher and not its predecessor Mirage. Some pilots questioned the need for the compass, which was not only distracting, but perhaps the least important instrument in a dogfight.

getting dark and to the west, the two Israeli pilots could see the usual brown and yellow of a desert sunset. Hertz began to worry about his wingman as they approached the enemy fighters.

"We started to maneuver with the MiGs, and got down to low altitude and low speed." Egyptian pilots had been trained to fly low and slow as a means of defending against the more aggressive Israelis, and it was in this regime that many of the Arab-Israeli dogfights occurred.

I got into some hard turns with the leader. As we turned I called my No. 2. I saw that the second MiG was escaping to the west. My wingman wanted to pursue him.

I didn't agree and told him to come back. At first he didn't want to, and I finally had to *order* him to return. I kept turning with my MiG so that he couldn't run away. The Egyptian pilot was getting nervous because I was higher and he probably knew he was alone. Every time he saw me, he started shooting even though he couldn't get me in his sights. I could see him looking up at me as he shot at the empty air.

By this time my wingman had returned. I told him to maneuver behind the MiG slowly and take him. He came in at high speed and couldn't make the

98

shot. He passed us – the MiG and me.
I told him to slow down and try again.
This time, he shot a missile and got the
MiG.[4]

Hertz's official score was 6.5, although he personally counts 7.5. He engaged one Syrian MiG-21 on October 17, and after dogfighting with the enemy plane, got behind him and put down the trigger – the trigger was always up and the pilot had to push it down when he was going to shoot. As he lined up the brand-new MiG-21, resplendent in green-and-brown camouflage, its pilot ejected. As was common practice, the kill was credited to the squadron but not to Hertz since he had not actually *shot* the MiG down with missiles or guns.

He shared another kill on October 18 with another Mirage pilot. Hertz had found the MiG-21 and hit it. But although the MiG sent out considerable smoke, it kept flying. Another Israeli pilot found it and fired. The MiG remained in the air. It wasn't until later confirmation came in that the kill was split between the two pilots.

On another mission, Hertz was leading four Neshers on the west side of the canal when they saw four MiGs high above them. Hertz took his flight up, but felt his plane shake from ground fire and had to turn back. Black smoke poured from the wing, and he thought he might have to eject.

There had been a lot of ground fighting near the canal and the Israelis had reportedly captured the Egyptian air base at Fayid. With smoke trailing behind his plane, and a fire light in his cockpit, Hertz wondered if he could make it there. His ground controller could not confirm that Fayid was actually in Israeli hands.

"Wait!" he warned Hertz, but the Nesher pilot was quickly running out of time. He took a chance and headed for Fayid. He touched down at 150 mph, higher than normal. To make matters worse, the runway was full of holes and he had to maneuver around them as he rolled out. As he finally stopped and raised the canopy, he was glad to see Israeli faces smiling at him. A Cessna flew him back to Hatzor. His fighter was repaired in two days and returned to service.

By the end of the first day of fighting, the IDF commanders decided that the most critical area was the Golan Heights. The Sinai front was manageable, especially since it involved such large expanses of uninhabited desert. The Heights, however, overlooked important agricultural areas, with major Israeli towns and farms. Two-thirds of the overall sorties for the next two days were against Syria. The A-4s continued to take terrible beatings from the Syrian SAM and flak batteries. Everyone in the Mirage/Nesher squadrons lost close friends in the light-bomber squadrons. Some of the Skyhawk pilots ejected into captivity, toward what at times seemed to be a dubious survival.

The pilots of the Phantoms and Mirages also had their share of losses. Perhaps the loss most felt by everyone was that of 101's commander, Lieutenant Colonel Avi Lanir. The popular CO had led two Mirages on a mission on October 13 over the Golan Heights.

"Number One hit," was all the ground controllers heard, and soon afterward, Lanir punched out. Israeli soldiers on the ground followed the pilot with their binoculars as he drifted down under his parachute behind enemy lines. They watched as a Syrian jeep approached Lanir and captured him. He was never seen alive again. The IAF mourned the loss of the 33-year-old commander, although no one was sure of his specific fate. Was he alive or dead?

Even after the war ended, and lists of POWs were exchanged, Lanir, the highest-ranking Israeli officer to fall into enemy hands, was not on them. Only one other Israeli reported seeing Lanir while both were in a Syrian hospital. Lanir confided that he was badly hurt and not doing well.

Finally, Lanir's remains were returned in June 1974, but the cause of his death was never publicly released, if indeed, it was ever truly discovered. His final score was two kills.

Lieutenant Colonel Herzl Bodinger, with two MiG kills himself, took over command. He would rise to command Ramat David during the 1982 Lebanon War, and ultimately, to relieve Avihu Ben-Nun as Commander of the Israel Air Force in January 1992.[5]

Lanir had been on the flight on the third day of the war, October 8, when the Nesher got its first kill. He led four Neshers from Hatzor on a patrol over the Hula Valley. An air battle was developing over the Golan and

Lt. Col. Avi Lanir was a rising star in the IAF, destined for higher rank when he was shot down and captured in the Yom Kippur War. A popular CO with his pilots and ground troops, Lanir would probably have become an ace during some of the hectic dogfights of the war if fate had not intervened. His remains were returned to Israel from Syria in 1974.

Lanir's flight could see the bursts of smoke far ahead of them. They would not be able to get to the engagement before it probably ended. As they approached the area, IAF Phantoms flashed past them on their way home.

Syrian MiGs were still around, however, and Lanir and his pilots scanned the skies. Their fuel was nearly down to where they would have to turn for home.

Then they spotted several MiGs and although, low on fuel, Lanir decided to engage the enemy planes, who would, he reasoned, surely attack the Neshers if the Israelis turned away.

The MiGs were high above the Neshers, but Lanir pointed his flight toward the enemy force. Soon, a rather slow-moving tail-chase developed and one of the Nesher pilots, a Captain Y., closed on the rear pair of MiG-21s. He would soon have to break off and turn for home, but he kept pushing, hoping for the right moment as the growl from his missiles buzzed in his headphones. Finally, Captain Y. fired a missile, and split-essed back around. The missile hit the MiG, which threw smoke as it headed for the ground. Captain Y.'s wingman confirmed the hit, but not the actual kill. It was not until the evening that the kill was confirmed, and the Nesher had its first score.

The first few days of the war belonged to the Arabs, particularly on the ground. The Israelis found themselves desperately trying to catch their breath. Former Tu-16 Badger pilot, Air Marshal Husni Mubarrak, now the commander of the Egyptian Air Force, praised the visual reporting stations on the Mediterranean coast. The observers warned of incoming Israeli strikes, allowing MiG interceptors time to scramble and meet the threat. Mubarrak also said that the EAF had been doing much better than in 1967. Indeed, unlike the Six Day War, Egyptian fighters would fly throughout the conflict.

Like many of the first generation of aces, now-Colonel Oded Marom was a senior pilot assigned to staff duty in Tel Aviv's IDF/IAF headquarters complex.

"It was a mess," he said, recalling the first reports on October 6, "very confused. I had my driver take me to Hatzor where I saw two Mirages taking off, while two more waited near the runway." Marom went to the operations office where he saw his name was last on the flight schedule. Since he was at headquarters, no one thought he would come.

The squadron commander, a good friend, asked him to stand by while he made a head call. Marom obliged. As soon as the CO left, the sirens began to wail and Marom dashed for the alert fighters. He was still current in the Mirage, and knew exactly what to do.

"I pushed the starter button, the engine spooled up, and I ran through the pre-taxi checks. I soon found myself on the runway, although I didn't know who my wingman was. We hadn't briefed, but I knew he was well trained."

The two Mirages launched and were directed toward Syria, 12 minutes flying time. Their position was northeast of the Golan Heights and the controller ordered them up to 20,000 feet to run north and south, or to "iron the air," as the IAF pilots referred to this method of patrolling.

However, Marom and his No. 2 never got to 20,000 feet; the controller issued new orders. There were four MiG-17s nearby.

"MiG-17s were my *pleasure*," Marom smiled. "I spotted them in a line-astern formation, beginning to close a circle, a wagon-wheel, a Lufberry."[6] The MiGs saw the Israeli fighters coming nose on and began shooting. But their red tracers were ineffective, "very beautiful," as Marom recalled. Two of the MiGs fell to the guns of the Mirages – Marom got one – and the two survivors ran for it.

When Marom and his wingman returned with two kills, his friend, the CO, was furious. Marom laughed. "But, everyone got their MiG during the war; everyone had a chance."

The Egyptians and Syrians occasionally flew their aircraft with an aggressiveness that surprised the IAF pilots. Oded Marom was again standing alert on the second day of the war, October 7. The senior pilot would be the wingman for the young pilot in the second Mirage. After taking off, they were sent to the western Sinai along the road to Qantara. Egyptian MiGs used to come before sunset to strike Israeli troops. Ten minutes after the sun went down, the MiGs felt safe. It was during this time of lowering light that Marom and his squadronmate began their patrol near the Suez Canal.

"The controller told us that four aircraft were coming from the south. We saw four black – perhaps brown, but very dark-colored – Hunters, Iraqi fighters." A dozen Iraqi Hawker Hunters – elegant, single-engine jets made in England – were known to have been stationed in southern Egypt, and thus formed the first Iraqi force in the war. In the dusk, Marom had to make sure of the type of on-coming aircraft. From frontal aspects, the Hunter looked a little like the veteran Super Mysteres still in IAF use. As the two formations closed, however, he knew for sure.

At first the Iraqis fighters didn't see the two Mirages. The Hunters flew very low, then pulled up to enter a strafing pattern against the Israeli troops below. As the Hunters turned left, Marom and his leader were right behind them. Then, the Iraqis saw the threat and broke off their strafing runs.

Marom told himself, "Well, at least we've accomplished our main mission to protect the men on the ground."

The Mirage pilots chased the Hunters northwest, a course of 300, at 50 feet above the desert. The Iraqis were trying to go through the Nile delta, which is a very level area, surrounded by hills and low mountains. The two Mirage pilots split up, each taking on one Iraqi. The remaining two Hawkers had disappeared.

Marom was now low on fuel, and in the reduced light of the setting sun, he knew he would not have many chances to shoot down the enemy fighter. They were also heading straight into Egypt, into a nest of SAM sites. He stopped talking to his wingmate and concentrated on the plane in front of him.

The Hunter pilot knew that his life depended on his ability to go lower and lower and making the Mirage pilot behind him give up. Marom pressed the attack, flying barely 600 feet behind the dark Iraqi fighter, which was *very* low now. The Hunter's jetwash bounced the Mirage around as the two fighters skirted the Egyptian plain.

Marom decided to shoot a Sidewinder. The sun was going down almost directly in front of them. Perhaps the Iraqi pilot considered this as he twisted and jinked trying to throw Marom's aim off, or have the Israeli's missiles lock onto the sun, instead of his Hunter's tailpipe.

At first, the Iraqi pilot was successful and stayed alive. Marom struggled to get a steady tone from his Sidewinder as it searched for a target. Everything was moving so quickly. Finally, Marom pushed the button, but the first 'winder hit the ground. "It was a bad moment."

The sun was nearly gone, and the canal was getting closer. There was no more time. Marom put his sight higher, got another tone and fired the second missile. What would happen? Would the missile make a ballistic arc and fall ineffectively to earth?

Instead, the Sidewinder struck the Iraqi's dorsal fuselage and exploded; the Hunter disappeared.

"Maybe I closed my eyes," Marom wonders. "I don't know. He was gone."

Pieces of the shattered Hawker flew back and broke Marom's windscreen, wounding him slightly in the face. Out of the corner of one eye, he saw what he thought was the orange flash of an aircraft exploding on the desert floor. He broke left at very low altitude and checked his fuel. The gauge was close to zero and he recovered at Bir Gafgafa (Refidim).

"What was the orange explosion I saw?" he asked his friends.

"Don't you know?" they replied. "It was an SA-3." The Goa was still a relatively new missile, much smaller than the telephone-pole-size SA-2. The deep orange of the explosion was a big surprise.

Lieutenant Colonel Iftach Spector, commanding No. 107 Squadron, had been in on the early fighting. On October 10, he got an Egyptian MiG-21 in a hard-fought engagement, made worse by bad weather. Egyptian fighters bounced the IAF attackers, forcing the Phantoms to break off their attack. One of the Phantoms was hit but was able to get home.

As the F-4s broke, Spector found himself alone and under attack. Undaunted, the Israeli ace began maneuvering his big fighter against the lithe Egyptian MiG. The maneuvers became harder as the two opposing fighters fought their fight alone.

They were very low, so low that their exhausts created columns of sand as they twisted and turned above the desert. The MiG pilot suddenly lost control and spun in.

Spector scored again on October 14 and October 15, eventually gaining four kills during the October war to bring his final total to 15. But like most IAF Phantom pilots during the war, he flew most of his missions – 42 in all – against ground targets, and into the terrifying missile barrages sent up by the Egyptians and Syrians. One such mission was the one on October 8, which sent Spector and his squadron against Syrian missile batteries on the Golan Heights.

The mission was supposed to be against Egyptian air bases, but the intensity and success of the Syrian missiles altered Israeli objectives. There was little time for in-depth planning and the flight crews picked up their charts and briefings on the run. Indeed, so immediate were the requirements that Spector was ordered to hold at the runway, the two other aircraft in his flight behind him, while a jeep rushed up with new target information.

After takeoff, struggling to keep his place in the bustling formation of Phantoms and Skyhawks, Spector waited for his navigator to assimilate the new information and headings as they sped on to the northeast.

Flying as low as they dared, the Israelis crossed into Jordan and then Syria. It was hard navigating at such low heights and high speeds, but they found their targets, perhaps with the help of the missiles that the Syrians fired at them.

Spector eventually arrived over his specific target, climbed, and rolled over to begin his delivery. The Syrians fired volleys of SAMs at the diving Phantom, but Spector concentrated on releasing his bombs on target. Lighter without its bombs, his Phantom gathered speed as he ran for home.

Major Asher Snir, also flew several attack sorties during the war. He had been on instructor duty at the flight school and was recalled to his old squadron. On October 15, he was part of a 50-plane raid on the big Egyptian air base at Tanta Airfield. He was flying with his close friend, Aharon Katz, later killed over Lebanon in June 1982. As usual, the briefings were hurried as the crews ran to make their launch times.

The route took them over the northern Sinai coast, then south into Egypt, checking all the while for the whereabouts of SA-2 and SA-3 batteries along the Suez Canal. Flying the mission like so many others, low and fast, Snir's formation searched for their target. Pilotage – navigating by landmarks – was hard because of the generally featureless marshland below. Fortunately, they hit the marks on schedule and prepared to attack.

Snir pushed his throttles forward. His flight followed, and the speed accelerated to 570 knots. He could now see the first columns of smoke from fast-rising SAMs, as his formation rushed on, barely 100 feet above the ground.

A missile found its mark and one of the F-4s left the formation. Eventually the pilot and navigator were forced to eject, but the backseater was apparently badly wounded, if not already dead when his seat left the cockpit.

Snir turned his attention back to the attack as Tanta appeared. Using all his concentration, Snir flew through the mass of SAMs and anti-aircraft fire.

The three remaining Phantoms delivered their weapons and beat a hasty retreat only to be confronted by two Egyptian MiG-21s. As the defenders lined up behind Snir's wingman, Snir rushed in, afterburners blazing. With Katz behind him clearing his rear quarter, Snir closed the distance to the lead MiG, now threatening the hard-jinking Phantom in front of him.

Finally, after hour-long seconds, Snir fired his cannon, and the MiG disintegrated, its pilot ejecting.

Surprisingly, the second MiG returned to the fight and launched an Atoll missile at Snir's aircraft. But he was too far away, and the missile ran out of fuel and fell away. At this point, the MiG retreated, leaving the three F-4s to fly home, their crews exhausted, but not too tired to indulge in the traditional victory roll over their base. It was necessary, not only for them but for the hard-working troops on the ground.

This photo shows now-Maj. Asher Snir during the 1973 War, with Aharon Katz, one of the IAF's most capable and respected Phantom navigators, to his left. Snir and Katz flew many missions during the war. But while Snir rose through the ranks, eventually commanding an air base as a brigadier general, Katz continued flying combat missions and was shot down and killed over Lebanon in June 1982. Snir did not survive his faithful backseater much longer, dying of cancer in 1986. (via the Snir family)

Endnotes:

1. *Washington Post, April 11, 1973*
2. Amir Nahumi, interview, Tel Aviv, November 19, 1992.
3. "Knights of the Orange Tail," by Sharon Geva, *Israel Air Force Magazine, June 1992.*
4. Moshe Hertz, interview, Tel Aviv, May 2, 1993.
5. *Israel Air Force Magazine, August 1991.*
6. This circling formation, designed for each plane to protect the tail of the plane in front, was named after an American fighter pilot of World War I who flew with the famed Lafayette Escadrille, Major Raoul Lufberry.

The pilot of a 117 Squadron Mirage taxis out for another mission. Mirages flew in both natural metal and camouflage schemes in the 1973 war. All Neshers were camouflaged.

11

RECOVERING FROM THE WAKE-UP CALL

The alarm took three weeks to shut off. In the end more than 2,400 Israeli soldiers and airmen lost their lives. Until the end of the first week, the outcome was seriously in doubt, and Israel's survival was questionable. As the world watched, the Egyptians and Syrians, aided by other Arab countries – such as Libya, Algeria and Jordan – as well as their Soviet benefactors, engaged their ancient enemy on the plains of Sinai and on the rolling hills of the Golan. Huge tank battles – the like of which had not been seen since the massive engagements on the Russian steppes between Hitler's Panzers and Soviet armored divisions in 1943 – decimated both sides.

In the air, while Israeli quality kept the situation from deteriorating to the extent it had on the ground, the first week's losses placed the IAF in great difficulty. Replacing aircraft and flight crews was a hardship. The pilots of the single-seat A-4s and few remaining Super Mysteres battled with grim determination every day, seldom grabbing the international headlines that seemed to follow the fighter crews in the Mirage/Nesher and Phantom squadrons.

The Phantom squadrons, in particular, struggled to fly their primary ground-attack missions, and to be always prepared to engage whatever MiG force rose to do battle. Eitan Peled had shot down two MiG-21s – one Syrian and one Egyptian – before the war. In the Yom Kippur War, he destroyed two Mi-8s as they crossed the Suez Canal in a formation of five helicopters headed into the Sinai. One of the kills came as Peled began shooting from 3,000 feet away. As he closed to 1,800 feet, his Phantom's cannon shells found their mark and the Egyptian helicopter went down.

Although most of his missions in 1973 were ground attack, Peled also gained his fifth kill over an Egyptian MiG-21, using a Sidewinder. On another occasion, he chased another Egyptian MiG-21, which, typically, dove for the ground to escape the Israeli Phantom. As the desert rushed up, Peled realized that he was running out of room and pulled up, at the same time rolling over to find his target. The MiG had crashed near some trees, leaving Peled to bottom out before heading for home. Following standard practice, this kill was credited to the squadron rather than to the pursuing pilot.

Peled felt comfortable in the F-4. He liked the big fighter's power and having a backseater.

"The navigator made sure everything was OK," he said. "I looked for MiGs, and he looked out for everything else. It worked very, very well."

Junior Nesher pilot Ariel Cohen was flying with No. 144 Squadron at Etzion in the southern Sinai. A Sabra, his family was an interesting mix of Jews from Egypt, Turkey, Italy and Tunisia. Entering flight school in 1967, he got his wings two years later, and flew Mysteres and Vautours. He flew the big French Vautour for eight months and accumulated thilrty-one missions against targets – mostly bridges – in Egypt, Syria and Jordan before the Yom Kippur War.

He transitioned to the Mirage, spending his time standing alert and flying patrols. To gain an assignment to a Mirage squadron, Cohen had to extend his period of active service, and wound up instructing in Fougas and Piper Cubs. The Yom Kippur War began eight months before his instructor tour was to end, and he returned to standing alerts. Although he had a few exciting moments, he had little to show for the first missions.

However, during a patrol on October 8, along the Syrian border, he met with his first success. No. 144 Squadron's Neshers usually toted three big fuel tanks and two Shafrir II missiles, making the Mirage variant even heavier. (It should be remembered that Israel is only 300 miles north to south, and it was not unusual for squadrons based in the south to be sent to patrol the Golan Heights in the north.)

The Neshers flew low until their controller told them to head north toward the Israeli border town of Metulla, along the line with Lebanon. Four Syrian Su-20s – export versions of the Su-17 swing-wing Fitter – were approaching.

The Nesher pilots punched off their tanks and started maneuvering against the Syrian planes. While Cohen's leader engaged one Sukhoi, he closed on another. After one-and-a-half turns, the Syrian turned east toward home. He raised his nose, fired all his air-to-ground rockets, and kept flying straight-and-level, the flame from his afterburner burning brightly.

Cohen completed his turn and saddled in behind the fleeing enemy fighter. At half a mile, he fired one of his Shafrirs; the distance was really at the end of the missile's range. The Israeli missile struck the Fitter and exploded, but the Syrian came out of the fireball. The Fitter pilot cycled his wings forward and aft a few times, probably checking his plane's controllability, and flew on, still in afterburner.

An unusual view of a Fitter H's underside. Export versions of the swing-wing version of Sukhoi's Su-7 of the late 1950s can also be counted in many air forces. Although a dedicated ground-attack weapon, Fitters also carry air-to-air missiles as does this Libyan aircraft. Close inspection of the metal work reveals typical heavy-handed Soviet technique, with prominent rivets and occasionally ill-fitting seams. However, as with most Soviet designs, the Fitter family is tough. Many Arab pilots owe their lives to the big Sukhoi's tough construction.

With its large wings swept aft, the big Sukhoi was very fast and Ariel Cohen realized he was dropping behind. He fired his second missile but this time, the range was too great and the Shafrir fell away. The young Nesher pilot pursued the Syrian fighter toward the border, which was full of Syrian flak and missile batteries. Reluctantly, Cohen turned for home, thinking that he had lost the kill.

However, confirmation came in later. Intelligence reported that the Sukhoi had not returned to its base. Apparently, Cohen's first missile had done more damage than he thought, and the Fitter pilot eventually had to eject. Cohen had his first kill.

His next kills came during the middle part of the war. On October 16, Cohen claimed an Egyptian MiG-17 over Dwer Swar Airfield, near the Suez Canal. On October 19, he scored a double, two Egyptian MiG-21s in the same general area. It was at the time the Israelis called "the MiG hour," around three in the afternoon. The sun was already beginning to set by this time, giving the Egyptians a perfect backdrop from which to attack.

Flying as No. 4, Cohen saw MiGs attacking Israeli positions in the distance. Soon, the Neshers were on the enemy fighters. One of the delta-winged MiGs broke toward Cohen, and he closed the angles in a very tight turn. He fired his cannon and the MiG disappeared in a huge explosion even before the Israeli pilot could lift his finger from the trigger. The Egyptian pilot punched out and Cohen flew past him.

Before the Neshers were able to rejoin, another group of MiGs appeared. The Egyptians flew their typical tactics and dove for the ground with the IAF fighters in hot pursuit. Cohen completed a split-s, about 3,000 feet behind one MiG-21 whose wingman seemed to have disappeared. Actually, the second MiG had made a wide turn, and the third Nesher's pilot had shot it down.

Cohen lined up his MiG and fired another missile, hitting the enemy fighter, slamming it into the desert. The Egyptian pilot had no chance to escape. As they rejoined to fly back to Etzion, Cohen reflected that his four-plane formation had engaged two enemy groups of four planes each, and had shot down six MiGs without loss to themselves. Cohen and the flight leader had each gotten two, while the pilots of the third and fourth Neshers had each scored once.

The pilot of the third Nesher had fought his first aerial engagement. He chased one of the MiGs, firing his cannon from 1,800 feet, "very good range for a missile," Cohen observed, "but not for guns."

Cohen's fifth and last kill came on October 23, one day before the war ended.

The Etzion Neshers flew a patrol across the canal near Jabal Ataqa looking for a flight of MiG-21s that the controller said was headed their way. The two flights soon engaged, and Cohen's leader got one of the Egyptians. Cohen dutifully followed his No.1 through a left turn as a shout in his earphones warned, "Mirage heading north, break!" He thought the call was for him and he responded, racking into a tight turn.

About 3,000 feet behind him, he saw two aircraft, which he was sure were his flight's No. 3 and No. 4. He looked again and now saw that the oncoming planes were a MiG followed by a Nesher whose pilot had shouted the warning to Cohen. As he broke, Cohen saw the Nesher shoot a missile at the MiG. Cohen jinked right, then left as he climbed away from the fight. But the other two aircraft were close and he could see the Nesher's bullets hitting the MiG.

"I didn't know if I was glad or not they were so close," he recalled.

The fight ended with nothing for either side to show for it. However, another call from the Israeli controller warned of MiG-17s. Sure enough, the Neshers engaged the slower, but more maneuverable enemy fighters. This time, Cohen was in a better position than his leader. He lined up on a MiG and fired a missile. Just like his first engagement with the Su-20 over the Golan, this MiG was enveloped by the missile's fireball only to stagger out of the explosion. The MiG pilot climbed and Cohen knew he was in danger of overshooting his target.

"The MiG-17 is a good dogfighter, and it is very dangerous to maneuver tightly with one. I looked all around and saw two more MiG-17s coming in from behind at low level. It was a difficult situation. If I stayed with the first MiG, I'd be involved in a close dogfight with his reinforcements."

He could not chance it and disengaged. He had the height and speed, and escaped before the other two MiG pilots had apparently seen him.

Later, also like before, Cohen learned that the pilot of the first MiG, the plane he had hit with a missile, had ejected. The pilots of the third and fourth Neshers confirmed the kill.

The IAF launched continuous campaigns against Arab airfields, but results were somewhat indecisive – perhaps because of the Egyptian's intense pre-war construction building of hardened aircraft shelters, a defense they had considered after the Israelis' devastating first strike of the June 1967 war.

Israel also attacked the bridges that the Egyptians had thrown across the canal, claiming most destroyed by late October 8. IAF bombers managed to destroy 14 bridges for the loss of three aircraft, thereby halting a critical crossing of the canal by Egyptian armored units. Indeed, the destruction created massive traffic jams along the approaches to the bridges on the Egyptian side of the canal.

By the end of the hectic first day, it was clear that the expanses of the Sinai were not as immediately vital as were the more concentrated hills of the Golan Heights, where a massive Syrian tank offensive was building. Moshe Dayan directed General Peled to hit the Heights' missile screen at dawn on October 7.

Capt. Ariel Cohen relaxes between missions in 1973. Like Oded Marom, Cohen was a former Vautour pilot, and had flown many missions in the big attack bombers during the War of Attrition before assignment to the Nesher squadron at Etzion in the southern Sinai. (via Ariel Cohen)

Former IAF commander Moti Hod had become a reservist after handing over the reins to Benny Peled shortly before the war. Hod was now serving in a special capacity as air advisor to the Northern Front Commander. As he watched the war's progress, Hod was awed by the huge swath of Syrian SAMs – sometimes 50 missiles at once – that rose to greet the Skyhawks and Phantoms. Clearly, something had to be done to counter such a catastrophic defense.

Hod sent waves of IAF strikers against the Heights in an effort to keep the Syrians shooting, and eventually deplete their missile stocks. By noon on Monday, October 8, the Syrians had, in fact, stopped firing; they had run out of missiles.

The IAF went after the Syrian and Egyptian SAM batteries on October 8, using Shrike anti-radiation missiles. These American-made missiles worked against the SA-2 and SA-3, but the SA-6's more active transmitter could avoid sending a homing signal for the Shrike. Bombing the Gainful sites with traditional iron bombs seemed to be the most successful method of attack – *if* the Skyhawk or Phantom crews could avoid the deadly missiles in the first place. They paid a heavy price in men and aircraft for the moderate success they achieved. Official figures will probably never be released, but reports of the decimation of Israeli attack formations occasionally said that 60 percent to 80 percent of the force was lost to SAMs and the ZSU-23-4 flak systems.

After the war, at an IAF open house, IAF commander Benny Peled remarked, "Anyone who puts too much faith in ground-to-air missiles will lose."[1] But it was hard to dismiss the fact that of the 105 aircraft that Israel *admits* to losing during the war, ninety-nine were shot down by Arab missiles and guns. With the missile threat reduced – for the time being – the Israelis could send strikes against other targets unimpeded.

Yoram Agmon had downed the first MiG-21 in July 1966 while a member of No. 101 Squadron. He had been among the first group of IAF pilots to transition to the F-4 in 1969 during training with the U.S. Air Force. Now, in 1973, as the commander of an F-4 squadron out of Ramat David, he was on an attack mission against Syrian positions east of the Golan Heights. Leading three other Phantoms, each carrying eleven 500-kg bombs, as well as a full load of air-to-air missiles and 20 mm ammunition, he ordered a combat spread as they hit their last checkpoint.

"The Phantom was the only plane that could carry such a heavy load. Although we could feel how heavy the planes were as we climbed through the mountains, we felt good."[2]

Suddenly, off to the right side of the formation, far away and very low, Agmon spotted two silhouettes flying parallel to his flight. He told everyone to watch the suspicious shadows but not to do anything. He was not sure if the Syrians had seen his Phantoms, but he later found out that the Syrian controller in the area had, in fact, alerted Syrian interceptors to the oncoming enemy aircraft.

The bandits were MiG-17s, whose pilots quickly turned toward the Phantoms, splitting the Israelis into two 2-plane sections. Agmon was still not sure whether the MiG pilots realized that there were four F-4s, or perhaps just two. Finally, the squadron commander decided that the Syrians had only seen his No.3 and No. 4, a distinct advantage. He ordered his flight to drop their bombs as he turned to meet the threat.

The two MiGs broke with the other two Phantoms, while Agmon maneuvered behind the enemy section. He was nearly astern of one MiG and began firing his cannon. The Syrian went down under the onslaught, however, his No. 2 had disappeared. While the Syrians had lost one aircraft, they had done their job by preventing the Israeli Phantoms from bringing their bombs to the target.

Yoram Agmon also downed three MiG-21s during the war, to bring his overall score to six. During one mission over the Golan Heights, he heard of a battle involving another Phantom squadron. Agmon asked his controller about it, but the controller told the Phantom skipper to continue his particular patrol.

Suddenly, on the emergency guard channel, a pilot called that he had ejected and was in his chute with a MiG-17 shooting at him. Agmon called but did not get a reply. He headed toward the fight.

Sure enough, he saw the smoke of the downed Phantom in an area well known for its dense SAM and AAA concentrations. Flying at 17,000 feet, he could see the red-and-yellow parachute of the Israeli crewman. He could also see the MiG which was, indeed, shooting at the helpless pilot as he floated down.

"All I wanted to do was, as soon as I could, show the MiG pilot that he was not alone — only that."

Agmon put his plane's nose down and rolled. He did not take time to aim. He only wanted to send a spray of tracer fire toward the MiG. The MiG's pilot was surprised as he saw the Phantom's bullets surround his aircraft. He made a high-G turn and ran.

By this time, Agmon was down to 3,000 feet and found that one of his engines had stalled after ingesting the cannon's smoke, a common problem. Agmon was in a spot, with flak and SA-7s flying around him. His training took over. The main thing was not to try to re-start the engine. Procedures called for actually shutting the engine off before trying for a relight. But at this point, he was not sure which engine was affected. If he shut down the wrong engine, it would certainly be catastrophic at so low a height.

Flying toward Mount Hermon, he realized that his starboard engine was actually the stalled side and got a relight.

Eitan Karmi got two MiGs over the Egyptian city of Port Said during the October war. However, he finished the engagement at a very low height and was hit by flak. He kept going until he began losing altitude. All his engine oil, which also lubricated the operating controls for the Mirage's Atar engine, was gone. The engine soon heated up and seized. Karmi was lucky to be able to retain some measure of control as he prepared to eject.

He bailed out at 1,000 feet at low speed, getting perhaps one swing in his chute, before landing on a small beach. He landed hard, right on his tailbone, and broke it. Soon, however, a helicopter picked him up and flew him back to Hatzor, where after two days recuperation, he was back in the cockpit — sitting on a big cushion!

Karmi's last victory — his ninth — was a Syrian MiG-21, shot down near Damascus during a big dogfight. The engagement began at 6,000 feet and Karmi used a missile. The area was ringed with enemy flak sites and the Syrian batteries filled the skies with antiaircraft fire.

"They shot everything at us," Karmi said, "at their own airplanes, *everything*. Not only flak, but SAM-6s. Jewish airplanes, Syrian airplanes. I was lucky to escape between the mountains around Mt. Hermon before landing back at Hatzor."

G. was rattling around the inner sanctums of the IDF headquarters in the middle of Tel Aviv when the Yom Kippur War started. He had left his post as the deputy commander of 101 Squadron and joined Avihu Ben-Nun's operations branch. As did every other senior pilot, G. kept current by standing alerts at least once a week with his old squadron, but it was not the same as a regular assignment.

Most sensible people knew that the Egyptian-Syrian coalition would eventually start shooting again, and many even knew that the date would be October 6.

Cannonfire from a Mirage disables a MiG-21. The Arab fighter's flaps are down, and its pilot has probably pulled the face curtain to eject.

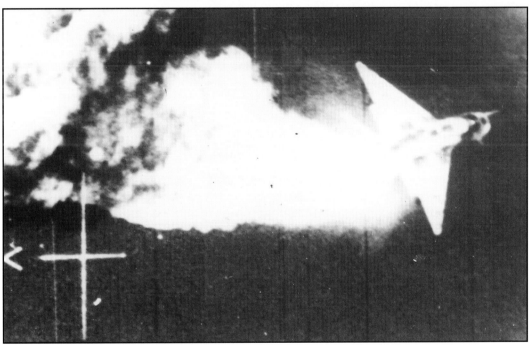

The time of the opening barrage was what was open to debate.

His base commander called G. on Friday afternoon, October 5.

"There's going to be a war tomorrow," he said.

"No kidding," G. replied, unimpressed with this bit of news.

G. went into his office on Saturday, even though it was Yom Kippur. He had orders to fly a Mirage that had been ferried in to a local airfield by another pilot back to Hatzor. At about 11 am, G. flew a Cessna back to Tel Aviv, returned to his office, and waited. When the Arabs attacked at 2 pm, the city's streets were empty; people were in synagogues.

For the first week, G. spent most of his time underground in the headquarters. He managed to get away and stand a few alerts, even scrambling a few times, but he did not have any engagements. The war was passing him by it seemed. However, on October 18, he gained permission to fly a few more missions during a two-day posting at 101.

"All my friends were shooting down MiGs," he said, "dropping bombs, and I wasn't doing anything, except signing all the orders for missions for everyone else.

"There were enough pilots who weren't flying any more. They could come to HQ and I could go to the squadron." The energetic ace's logic was irrefutable, and he made his way to Hatzor. The next two days were to be busy ones for him.

Picking up a fighter, G. flew west toward Refidim on the early evening of October 18. He heard on the radio that several Egyptian Mi-8 helicopters were rolling out canisters of napalm on Israeli positions near bridges on the Suez Canal. Spotting one of the big helos in the lowering light, he attacked, destroying the Egyptian aircraft. He then landed at Refidim, a place he knew well.

The Egyptian ground forces had been pushing eastward, behind a thousand-gun artillery barrage, toward Refidim and its vital airfield. In the biggest tank battle since 1943, 700 Israeli tanks met 1,000 Egyptian tanks. Anti-tank missiles, air-to-ground rockets, and shells from 100-mm turret guns blasted across the desert.

Until now, the Egyptians had kept their fighters close to their bases and did not send them out on sweeps, preferring to protect their positions with rings of surface-to-air missiles. There was something to be said for relying on the robot defenders; the SA-3 and especially the SA-6 had been particularly effective against the IAF. For instance, on October 7, IAF strikers encountered some 60 Egyptian MiG-21s as they waded through the SAM belt on their way to their targets. The MiGs followed the raiders even though the intense groundfire claimed several of the defenders.

On the 15th, IDF commandos crossed the canal behind 25 tanks to attack SAM sites. Eventually, some 20,000 Israeli troops and 300 tanks were in Egypt. On the 16th, Israeli ground troops had waded through concentrations of Egyptian tanks and troops and begun cleaning up Egyptian missile positions on the west bank of the waterway, using tanks as spearheads.

The Egyptians started sending MiGs out to protect their missiles, an incredible reversal. There was nothing between Israeli forces and Cairo! Up to this time, aerial engagements between Israeli and Egyptian fighters had only occurred over Egyptian bases, now the dogfights were above the canal as the Egyptians tried to fend off the Israeli drive west. Between 16-22 October, the Egyptian Air Force reported flying 2,500 sorties and fighting the IAF in 18 separate engagements.

The situation had flip-flopped: now the Egyptians were on the defensive. Now the fight was for air superiority over the desert. During this period, the Egyptians lost 150 aircraft, while the Israelis lost fifteen.

At midday on October 19, G. and his flight took off to provide support for IDF ground troops near Deversoir. Five Su-7s were preparing to dive on the Israelis as G.'s Mirages appeared.

He dropped one Fitter with a Shafrir II missile, then lit out in hot pursuit of another Sukhoi flight that had dropped its bombs and was high-tailing it for home. G. caught up with the second Su-7 and fired another missile. This Fitter also went down.

Another scramble in the late afternoon sent G. back up against a new enemy force, this time swing-wing Su-20s. He added two more kills to his growing tally.

He scrambled twice on the morning of October 20, but without seeing any action. Normally, the Egyptians attacked twice a day – once when the sun was high, around 1030, and then again in the late afternoon to take advantage of the setting sun.

G. was on a break for the early afternoon, but launched again as the Egyptians sent their late-afternoon attackers in. Near a small mountain, where, to some estimates, Israeli fighter pilots had dispatched some 200 Egyptian aircraft over the years, he spotted two MiG-21s. The MiGs tried to lure the Israeli pilots into Egypt. It was obviously a trap. The formation was a mix of Mirages and Neshers. G. was in Nesher No. 61.

There was even a two-seat Mirage IIIB, a trainer that had been, in typical Israeli fashion, reconfigured with cannon. The trainer's second seat had also been removed to accommodate the fighter's radios. These alterations were common, and presented little trouble to the ground crews, who could make the changes in two to four hours. G. remarked:

> Everything was prepared [for the war]. We always used two-seaters in combat; it's what we had. We didn't have enough single-seaters. We are very capable of doing things very fast.[3]

On the late afternoon of October 20, the four Neshers and Mirages of 101 Squadron engaged a large formation of MiGs; G. estimated "ten couples of MiG-21s." He fired one Shafrir at the first MiGs, the decoys. The second MiG exploded. As he lined up on the remaining enemy fighter, G. saw the main force as it climbed toward the Israelis at 25,000 feet.

The Egyptians were eager, but untried, and by the time they got to the Israelis' height, they were out of steam and slow. A big dogfight began, and G. went after the lone MiG from the first pair.

"After a few minutes, he was flying like a *meshigene*, as we say – a crazy nut! He did things with his airplane that – while they didn't threaten me – didn't allow me to get him. Maneuvers like split-esses from 3,000 feet. The dust rose from the ground as he passed."

Meanwhile, the other three Mirages went after the other MiGs. One 101 pilot shot down an Egyptian fighter, but then turned for home because he was 10 miles away from the main fight. A second Israeli pilot launched missiles but was having trouble with his engine. G. told him to leave. The third plane, the two-seater, was low on fuel. The pilot shot down one MiG and turned for home, too. That left G. by himself. He had shot down a second MiG and was now surrounded by a dozen MiG-21s.

The lone Israeli and the 12 Egyptian pilots maneuvered for five minutes, from ground level to 10,000 feet. Whenever G. tried to escape, he was set upon. There were missiles flying everywhere; the frustrated Egyptian pilots often fired from too far away. G. finally got a good tone and launched another missile, scoring his third kill of the mission.

A Libyan Su-7 Fitter H in cruise configuration. Large and surprisingly fast, swing-wing Fitters could occasionally outrun pursuing IAF fighters if their lead was great enough. The IAF rarely engaged aircraft from Arab countries other than Egypt and Syria. Iraqi and Jordanian pilots occasionally entered dogfights, while other countries lent surrogate pilots to fly usually Egyptian planes. Libyan pilots seldom, if ever, flew their own aircraft against the Israelis. However, these photos, taken by U.S. Navy fighter crews off the Libyan coast, show the same fighters used by Egypt and Syria in 1973.

The MiG force had dwindled considerably — some had been destroyed, and others, probably low on fuel, had left the fight. Only two MiGs remained, and G. chased them at 10,000 feet, destroying the leader for his fourth kill. The wingman fled.

> I still had fuel, and about thirty rounds in each cannon. I asked the controller if he had any more MiGs on his scope, but he said no. I headed back to Refidim. When I landed and taxied back, I couldn't get out of the cockpit. My legs shook and the crew had to pull me out.

The mission had lasted barely twenty-five minutes, and the Israelis had shot down seven MiGs. G. took a call from Benny Peled, commander of the IAF.

"All right, have you had enough? Come back. We need you."

G. returned to Tel Aviv and spent the next four days at headquarters. He returned to Refidim on October 24, in time to participate in the last, and one of the biggest dogfights of the war, with ten Mirages and Neshers engaging some twenty MiGs.

Flying a two-seater Mirage, G. accounted for three more MiG-21s — two with AIM-9D Sidewinders and one with cannons. He had shot down twelve Egyptian aircraft during the conflict, bringing his final total to seventeen.

Israel lost 103 fighters and fighter-bombers, and six helicopters during the October war, including forty aircraft from direct SAM hits. Thirty-one aircrewmen were killed in action, while a further fourteen were captured after bailing out over Syria, and approximately ten IAF POWs were in Egypt. A further thirty-one Israeli aircraft were lost to flak — No. 69 Squadron *reportedly* lost *six* Phantoms on October 7 (while flying some 600 ground attack missions during the war) — but only six

in aerial engagements. The IAF claimed 277-334 (depending on the source) Arab aircraft in air-to-air combat, thirteen by SAMs and thirty by anti-aircraft artillery. Selected squadron kill totals show a dramatic increase from the Six Day War. No. 117 (Mirages and Neshers) was the top scorer with fifty-five victories, while 101 (Mirages and Neshers) claimed forty-eight, and 113 (Neshers) scored twenty-five kills. No. 144 (Neshers) claimed forty-two to forty-four Arab planes shot down. Two of the F-4 squadrons, No. 69 and 107, posted totals of twenty and thirty-two, respectively.[4] The remaining two F-4 squadrons, No. 119 and No. 201, have yet to have their numbers broken out with any degree of confidence, although the reader can tell that these two important units had their share of successful aerial engagements.

The Yom Kippur War was nothing like the Six Day War; rather, it was a outgrowth of the later stages of the War of Attrition, which saw the appearance of surface-to-air missile batteries as the primary defense against air attack. While the relative quality of Arab pilots remained as it had for the previous 25 years — predictable and uninspired — the initial successes on the ground prompted the MiG pilots to be more aggressive, thereby compensating, to an extent, for their lack of experience.

The Israelis had fallen victim — understandably — to the overconfidence they developed after the 1967 war, and certainly after the conflict of 1969-1970 where, no matter how individual engagements might appear initially, the overall outcome was never in doubt; aerial kill ratios remained overwhelmingly in favor of the IAF.

The Arab Pilots as Adversaries

By and large, Israeli fighter pilots curried a disdainful view of their Arab opponents. Disregarding Arab superiority in numbers, the Mirage and Phantom pilots

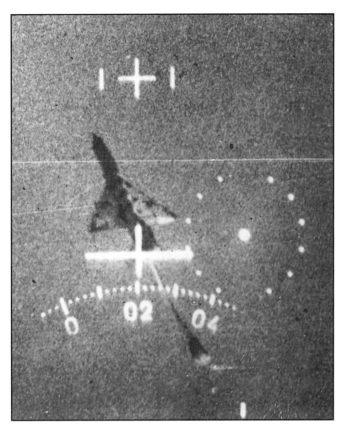

An unusual pair of frames from a Nesher's gun camera showing a chocolate-brown-and-tan-striped MiG under attack. The Nesher's cannonfire hit the chute's bullet housing, forcing the Egyptian fighter's brake chute to deploy.

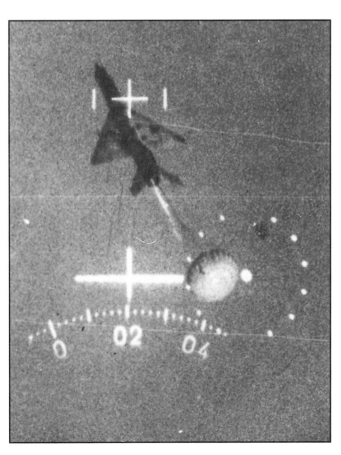

knew they were, man for man, far better trained than their counterparts in the MiGs and Sukhois. If the Israeli could get his Mirage behind the MiG, or within the range of his Shafrir or cannon, the Arab was going down – clear and simple. And if the Phantom's missiles or cannon did not actually hit the MiG, the poorly trained Egyptian or Syrian pilot might fly into the ground, anyway. The result was the same: one less enemy plane.

It was not that the MiG pilots lacked courage; they simply could not fly their planes in combat with the likes of the Israel Air Force. Most IAF aces are somewhat quizzical about discussing their successes, viewing their engagements as sequential: "I saw the MiG, I maneuvered behind him, and I shot him down. That's all there is to the story."

Modesty is usually becoming, and sometimes even promotes the individual's heroic qualities. Perhaps it *was* easier to shoot down Arab fighters than those of other countries. But the intensity of the relatively confined Arab-Israeli conflicts negated any lack of difficulty in plane-to-plane engagements for the Israelis. And besides, there was always the chance that the target MiG's wingman might come around and pump an Atoll into the Israeli Mirage.

Viewed from the vantage point of 20 years, the capabilities of their opponents meld into one basic description for most Israeli aces: The Egyptians and Syrians in the cockpits of the MiGs and Sukhois could fly well enough, but they lacked imagination and understanding to truly wield their weapons effectively.

Some IAF aces gave limited praise, while others shrugged to indicate there was little to distinguish one Arab pilot from another in the way he flew his aircraft. One or two were fairly complimentary, and noted a few enemy pilots that had caused them some anxious moments. For the most part, however, the Egyptians and Syrians fell into one area, while several IAF aces commented on how well the RAF-trained Jordanians flew. As Yoram Agmon recalled, "The Jordanians were the best pilots; they had western training."

Ariel Cohen remarked, "At points in the engagements where I had been trained to turn and face the enemy, they simply turned away, which turned out to be fatal. I don't think they had a 'picture' of the battle..."

Eitan Karmi opined:

> I don't think that the Egyptian
> or Syrian pilots I met were well trained.
> They knew how to fly their airplanes but
> not how to fight with them. To fly and
> fight are not the same.

Now-Brigadier General Amir Nahumi remembered one engagement.

> I saw one Syrian pilot diving on
> a Phantom, shooting, his bullets hitting
> the ground. The Syrian was probably so
> preoccupied with the target that he just
> flew into the ground. The Egyptians
> might be aggressive, but...

One man shot his missile but probably didn't wait for a tone, and he missed. Still, he was very consistent, pointing the nose directly at me and shooting.

Maybe you would occasionally see one Arab pilot who was something different...That one Egyptian who was really mixing it with me until I went vertical, he was different. *He* put his nose in the vertical.

Avihu Ben-Nun, who had met the Russian surrogates over Egypt in 1970, considered his Soviet opponents.

I thought the Russians flew very nice maneuvers. It was even surprising what they could do with an airplane, but they couldn't fly effectively to shoot something down. That was their lack of combat experience. They were good pilots, but not in a tactical sense. They were fairly predictable.

As for any personalities on the other side, Giora Rom observed, "We did not know too much about the

Lt. Col. Amir Nahumi poses in his flight gear for a quick post-mission photo. IAF pilots wear the European style of G-suit, which incorporates two kneeboards, instead of the American version of a separate board that is strapped to the pilot's leg.

Arab pilots as individuals. We knew our side of the business and that was enough."

Oded Marom remembered the time before the 1967 war.

At the beginning, around 1962, the Egyptians didn't know how to fly, except straight and level. They made us laugh whenever they tried to maneuver. But, if you fly two or three fights a day, you have to learn, and *we* were their instructors! And I have to say that they learned very well. During the War of Attrition, they were excellent pilots. Maybe they had a new generation, better than their predecessors.

In my ready room, we had a saying, "The enemy pilot is the best pilot in the world. Prove that he is not!"

Yoram Agmon climbs the boarding ladder to his F-4E. (via Yoram Agmon)

Asher Snir confers with his CO, Lt. Col. Eliezer Prigat during the Yom Kippur War. Prigat flew Mirages with the Bat Squadron during the 1967 war. (via the Snir family)

Iftach Spector summed up the discussion.

I have been asked many times what makes a good pilot. We were on a higher level because of much better training than our opponents. But they could fly very well; it was sometimes very hard to catch them.

They always had superior numbers and sometimes we were in a lot of danger. We were always short of fuel, while they were always close to their bases, but we had the training to manage it.

For several aces, the final assessment of their enemy and the collective experience of aerial combat in the Middle East came from Asher Snir's description of a single dogfight in May 1970. During the War of Attrition, Snir and his commanding officer, then-Major Amos Amir, encountered a Syrian MiG-17 pilot, who engaged the two Mirage aces with skilled abandon, holding them at bay over Mount Hermon for eight-and-a-half minutes, a long time during a dogfight.

Snir admired the lone MiG pilot's ability, and while he finally caught the Syrian with a Sidewinder in a valley, he was saddened by the death of such an unexpectedly worthy adversary.

Endnotes:

1. *Air International, September 1974.*
2. Yoram Agmon, interview, Tel Aviv, May 5, 1993.
3. G., interview, Tel Aviv, May 5, 1993.
4. *The Small Air Forces Observer, October 1992 and June 1993.*

Nemesis of aviators around the world, the SA-2 Guideline surface-to-air missile, and its improved relative, the SA-3 Goa, probably caused IAF flight crews more concern than any Arab defensive weapon. This unit was captured by the IDF and wound up at the IAF Museum. (Author)

12

NEW AIRCRAFT, SAME MISSION

The half-decade after the Yom Kippur War was a period of intense soul-searching for a nation that is already introspective. Usually exhibiting a cautiously happy outlook on life in general, Israel was beset with self-doubt and recrimination. Investigations yielded little solid, treatable reasons for the success of the initial Arab assault, and political in-fighting affected many of the committees established to discover the causes of the debacle. Perhaps the most heartbreaking result of the postwar self-flagellation was the resignation of Prime Minister Golda Meir in April 1974.

Besides government turmoil, the continued attacks by Palestinian guerrillas in the northern border areas made life dangerous and tenuous at best for the hardy settlers and farmers of the towns and kibbutzim that faced southern Lebanon and the Golan Heights. All the fighting since 1948 had given Israel very few periods of peace. There seemed to be no solution except to remain strong and vigilant.

In late November 1974, Syria flew a series of air patrols over Damascus with MiG-21s and MiG-23s. While sending MiG-25 Foxbat intruders on high-altitude, high-speed snooper runs over Israel to monitor Israeli troop buildups in the Golan Heights. The buildups were in response to Syrian troop movements near strategic Mount Hermon.

As it did after the 1967 war, the Soviet Union re-supplied its Egyptian and Syrian clients, beginning right after the October 24 ceasefire. Huge An-22 Cock and An-12 Cub transports ran shuttle flights, bringing new equipment to Cairo and Damascus.

American uneasiness about Russian activities raised tensions, creating the threat of a direct confrontation between the two superpowers. The possibility of a renewed Soviet presence was intolerable for the Nixon administration, now beginning to fight for its own life in the growing Watergate scandal.

A detachment of reconnaissance MiG-25 Foxbats, along with their Soviet pilots, arrived at Cairo West Airport in March 1975, and the March 10 edition of the weekly *Aviation Week & Space Technology* also reported that North Korean, Cuban, and Pakistani pilots were "augmenting Arab fighter units."

Concern over the success of Egyptian and Syrian surface-to-air missiles also made the Israelis reconsider their traditionally nonchalant (at least officially) attitude toward the robot defenders. Studies and inquiries about current and future electronic counter-measures (ECM) began to bolster Israeli knowledge of how to deal with the arrays of Arab SAMs and ZSU anti-aircraft cannon that would surely face IAF Phantoms and Skyhawks again.

The IAF also looked at boosting its modest aerial refueling capability. The ageing fleet of piston-engined Boeing KC-97s – long-since retired from the USAF – were hard-pressed to keep up with newer Israeli fighters and attack bombers. A-4s and KC-130s afforded limited IFR services, but a larger, faster platform was needed.

With typical ingenuity, the state-associated development firm Israel Aircraft Industries (IAI) modified several surplus Boeing 707 airliners, in effect rendering a home-grown version of the highly capable KC-135 Stratotanker, again another long-serving member of the USAF, and the French Armee de l'Air as well.

One of the F-16's regular victims in 1982 was the MiG-23 Flogger. This photo of Libyan Floggers shows the swing-wing MiGs, which first appeared publicly in 1967, with their wings extended to cruise position.

IAF air-to-air missiles were also under further development. Developed by the Rafael Armament Development Authority − Israel's main military research-and-development organization − the Shafrir II had done well in the October war, overshadowing the American Sidewinder and Sparrow. If a Shafrir II struck a MiG-21, it usually obliterated the Fishbed, with little chance for the pilot to eject. Sidewinders, while lethal, had a smaller warhead than the Shafrir and thus did not immediately destroy the target. A Sidewinder hit usually made the MiG or Sukhoi erupt in flames, which allowed the Arab pilot time to eject.

Besides the Shafrir II, Rafael was developing another AIM, the Python 3, which ultimately saw combat service in 1982 over Lebanon. Ze'ev Bonen, then managing director of Rafael, discussed the new missile in an article in The New York Times.

"With the Python, pilots can get into firing positions more easily, launch their missiles and shoot down enemy planes with less risk."[1]

It was in the areas of air-superiority and ground attack, however, that the IAF sought specific improvements, in the form of new aircraft. Except for a few examples of veteran Super Mysteres, upgraded with American Pratt & Whitney J-52 engines, Vautours, the seemingly ageless Fouga trainer, and assorted small transport aircraft, the IAF was totally committed to American equipment, both fixed-wing and rotary-wing. While the Super Mystere and Vautour soon left service after the October war, the dainty, little Fouga continues to introduce neophyte IAF pilots to the wonders of jet flight.

The Phantom enjoyed a rebirth with the IAF. Typically never satisfied with the status quo, the energetic Israelis had constantly upgraded, modified, and revised their premier fighter-attack aircraft almost from the time it arrived in 1969. A major revision of the redoubtable Phantom became the Kurnass (Sledgehammer) Phantom 2000.

The Phantom and Skyhawk had proved themselves time and again, and American resupplies of these aircraft kept IAF squadrons well stocked. (By the mid-1980s, the Skyhawk had been relegated to advanced training duties, although it still stands alerts at desert bases, bombed up and ready to launch.) However, both designs were of 1950s vintage, decidedly dated, especially when compared to newer Russian types as the later MiG-23/27 Floggers and soon-to-come MiG-29 Fulcrum. Also, the Mirage, and its Israeli-designed derivative, the Nesher, were approaching obsolescence, at least in their air-to-air role. Several Neshers were sold to Argentina, which called them Daggers, after the Yom Kippur War. They participated in the 1982 Falklands Conflict with Great Britain, but with very limited success against Royal Navy Sea Harriers.

Israel's next generation of jet fighters had to be top of the line, specifically, the McDonnell Douglas F-15 Eagle and the General Dynamics F-16 Fighting Falcon. By the end of the 1970s, three new Israeli jets −

one of indigenous design, the Kfir − would join the IAF, but the change would take a lot of work.

Development of the basic Mirage III had continued since its arrival in the early 1960s. The aircraft's original Atar 9B engine was replaced with the 9C, and the disappointing Cyrano nose radar was eventually removed. Besides the moderately successful Nesher, another IAF Mirage variant was the abortive Barak (Lightning), a Nesher with an American GE J-79, the same engine that powered the F-4. A small number of Baraks was reported to have seen limited action during the 1973 war.

The Barak's control and maneuverability were disappointing, and after considerable redesign, another derivative, the Kfir (Lion Cub) C-1 entered service with No. 101 Squadron in April 1975. Improvements resulted in the C-2 model, which featured distinctive canards, horizontal surfaces behind the air intakes that gave better low-speed control. Another squadron (possibly a re-formed No. 144) also formed on the Kfir at Hatzor. (Five squadrons eventually flew the Kfir.)

The C-2 also included greatly improved avionics, which made the Kfir a vastly improved ground-attack aircraft. Further upgrades resulted in the Kfir C-7, which entered service in 1984. At the start of the 1990s, the C-7 was still the main close air support (CAS) IAF fighter.

Long taken for granted by Soviet and Warsaw Pact, and western air forces, especially by the U.S., which included the specifically dedicated CAS mentality of Marine Corps Harrier, Hornet, and Cobra squadrons, CAS had enjoyed barely secondary consideration by the IAF until the 1973 war. In 1975, the IDF Chief of Staff, Lieutenant General David Elazar said, "Even before 1973 I considered the subject of close air support the last priority task of the [Israel] Air Force."[2] Thus, the luxury of having a specific CAS aircraft − even though it was a hand-me-down variant of a decidedly otherwise intended platform − was an important development for the IAF.

Several experienced Mirage and Nesher aces served out their last flying assignments as Kfir pilots, either as regular IAF members, or as reservist pilots. Several found themselves in the their third war in June 1982, flying over the dangerous Lebanese hills. By the end of the 1980s, according to one report, reservists filled 70 percent of Kfir squadron billets.[3]

The Eagle and the Falcon

Unlike the mid-1960s, when Ezer Weizman tried to pry F-4 Phantoms from the Johnson administration, Israel had little trouble obtaining shipments of the Phantom's successor almost as soon as it arrived in USAF squadrons.

The McDonnell Douglas F-15A Eagle was another huge fighter from St. Louis. Like the Phantom, the Eagle's physical size also indicated the breadth of its

Skyhawks line up with Kfirs at the base at Ovda before a training mission. Skyhawk pilots delight in the chance for air-to-air engagements, and if flown well, the A-4 frequently comes out the winner.

capability. Committed to American equipment, and largely Air Force types – the IAF apparently considered the equally massive Grumman F-14, but decided against it – Israel sent four pilots and one navigator to evaluate the F-15 in 1974. Within 16 months, the first Eagles arrived in Israel, although their arrival precipitated a government crisis. The IAF's newest fighters had come during the sacred Saturday sabbath. Orthodox members of the government were appalled, and the government of the long-ruling Labor Party fell.

After the political uproar subsided, and the Eagle – which the Israelis renamed "Baz" (Falcon) – quickly became part of the IAF, equipping No. 133 Squadron at Tel Nof.[4] The big fighter's size did cause some concern among some Israeli pilots. Such concern had also been voiced by American Eagle pilots, who had to put up with constant jibes from their fellow jet pilots of smaller aircraft.

"I don't want to be the biggest target in the sky," one IAF pilot said. "The biggest target draws all the fire first."[5]

The second new American fighter that entered IAF service after the 1973 war was the General Dynamics F-16 Fighting Falcon, which initially equipped squadrons 101, 105, 110, 117 starting in 1980.

Intended as the next-generation ground attack aircraft – somewhere between the much larger F-4 and the smaller Kfir – the F-16 quickly established itself as a good air-to-air fighter, and assignment to a Falcon squadron was certainly nothing to be ashamed of. Indeed, top ace G. – now a reservist – looks forward to standing alerts in an F-16. As with previously mentioned reserve Kfir units, F-15 and F-16 squadrons count on participation by their reservists.

When he saw his first F-16, now-Colonel Yoram Agmon, who had gained the first kill for the Mirage in 1966, and had flown Phantoms during the War of Attrition and the Yom Kippur War, thought, "Here comes the Mirage of the '90s; it has the same classic qualities."

Rounding out the influx of new American types was the Grumman E-2C Hawkeye, an airborne early warning aircraft that had been serving U.S. Navy squadrons since the early 1960s. Although not a glamorous jet fighter to be flown by aces, the E-2 quickly became part of the overall fighter operation.

Thus, by the 1980s, the IAF had completed a large part of its modernization program.

Besides the modernization of the IAF, Israel was also involved with the continuous search for a peaceful solution to the political conflict, which, after all, was always at the heart of any military considerations in the Middle East. President Sadat had traveled to Jerusalem in November 1977 to address the Israeli Knesset, and Prime Minister Begin reciprocated with a trip to Cairo.

The well-meaning, but decidedly ineffective U.S. president, Jimmy Carter – a one-term governor of the southern state of Georgia, and ultimately one-term president, with a Bible Belt understanding of the Moslem-Jewish confrontation – had decided to place the power of his office behind designing some form of long-lasting treaty between Israel and Egypt, perhaps the most moderate of the four or five Arab states.

With great fanfare, President Carter hammered out a surprising understanding between Cairo and Jerusalem, then invited Prime Minister Begin and President Sadat to the presidential retreat at Camp David, Maryland, for the signing ceremonies in September 1978. With the stroke of the ceremonial pens, the ages-old conflict between the Egyptians and Jews was put to rest. Israel could now relax its guard to the west, and no longer have to look at the Suez Canal as a launching ground for a new Egyptian attack, or a bloody boundary against which Israeli soldiers and airmen would throw themselves.

The treaty was not without cost to the IDF, however. Israel gave up its hard-won territory in the vast Sinai, including strategic air bases at Bir Gafgafa and Etzion. The U.S. helped offset these losses by helping to build two new complexes in the Negev – Ovda and

Ramon. Thus, along with the training base of Hatzerim, the new fields in the ancient biblical land south of Jerusalem formed a triangle of above- and below-ground complexes for the new airplanes that Israel bought from America.

While the treaty with the Egyptians took a firm hold, there was still reason for concern. In October 1981, on the eighth anniversary of the 1973 War, Anwar Sadat was assassinated by right-wing extremists, while he reviewed a parade, bringing to a violent end the hope that he had begun a trend. General Husni Mubarak, chief of the Egyptian Air Force during the 1973 war, and former Tu-16 Badger pilot, assumed the presidency.

Perhaps the worst aspect of the postwar period was the continuing conflict between the Palestine Liberation Organization (PLO) and Israel. Basically landless and without a central government, the itinerant arabs that wandered between Jordan, Lebanon, and Israel clamored for their own country. Finally organized – after a fashion – under one of the most unique characters in the Middle East, Yasir Arafat, the PLO began a far-ranging program of terrorism, sponsored by the more aggressive Arab states, especially Syria, which had simply refused to sit down at the bargaining table with Israel.

In March 1978, terrorists attacked the highway between Tel Aviv and Haifa, capturing a tour bus, killing 34 people, and injuring many more. Two weeks later, IAF planes and ground units attacked targets in Lebanon to roust the PLO terrorists from their training facilities. The Israelis reported that more than 300 terrorists were killed in this six-day campaign called Operation Litani.

Unfortunately, Litani did nothing but generate reprisals and more raids by the PLO guerrillas. Besides continuing ground action, there were several engagements between Israeli and Syrian planes. In a period that recalled the months immediately before the wars in 1967 and 1973, 13 Syrian aircraft were shot down between June 1979 and February 1981. The first engagement after Operation Litani on June 27, 1979, opened the scorecards for the F-15 and Kfir.

Realizing that it had to send aircraft to defend its PLO clients against continuing IAF attacks, Syria dispatched a force of MiG-21Js to intercept an incoming raid of Skyhawks escorted by Eagles and Kfirs From their vantage point of 20,000 feet, 5,000 feet above the Syrian MiGs, the escort pilots quickly began maneuvering to meet the threat.

One of the Eagle pilots was Major M., already an ace with six kills. While on a visit to St. Louis to watch the IAF's newest fighter being built, he brashly – but characteristically enthusiastic for an Israeli – told his hosts that he would be the pilot to make the first kill in an F-15. The Americans laughed for it was a proud boast.

When he returned to Israel, Major M. took assignments that seemed to place him far away from anything but an occasional flight in the Eagle. But, on the early morning of June 27, 1979, his squadron commander, Lieutenant Colonel Eitan Ben-Eliyahu,[6] called to invite him on a mission that seemed to hold great promise. (Ben-Eliyahu would become IAF commander in 1996. He also scored one of the first F-15 kills during this fight, his fourth and final kill to add to kills in 1969, one Syrian MiG-21, and two in 1973, one Egyptian MiG-17 and MiG-21.)

Arriving at the squadron, M suited up and launched, heading toward the Lebanese town of Sidon. The ground controllers called two four-plane formations of MiGs approaching the Israelis. Two Syrians crossed M's nose, eventually turning toward the IAF fighters. He lined up a MiG and launched a missile, which quickly blasted the Syrian fighter into two pieces. Soon after this kill, four other MiGs were spiraling down in flames. One of them was the first kill by a Kfir pilot.

Captain S. and his flight, of two Kfirs from 101 Squadron, were at 12,000 feet, considerably below the F-15s and MiGs. The Eagles got to the Syrians first, but S. saddled in behind a pair of MiGs and launched a missile, which exploded close by a MiG. The Syrian fighter began throwing smoke as S. rocketed past. He swung his Kfir back toward the MiG and soon saw that its pilot had, in fact, ejected.

Thus, in one engagement, two of the IAF's newest fighters had scored their first kills, and Major M. (he is now a brigadier general) had made good on his promise. As if rubbing salt in Syrian wounds, *Newsweek* reported that the "Syrian MiG-21s were hopelessly outclassed...high overhead a flight of four U.S.-built F-15s – the world's most sophisticated fighters – had been flying protective cover...the Israelis pounced on the slower enemy with a barrage of air-to-air missiles..."[7]

Even with the surface success of the Camp David Accords between Egypt and Israel, there was much to be accomplished, not the least of which was vacating the Sinai and the strategic air bases. The date for the Israelis to finish their evacuation was 1982; until then, the desert base at Etzion remained in IAF hands as an outlying field, for emergency and training purposes.

In the meantime, occasional aerial engagements between Syrian and Israeli pilots through April 1981 kept the skies over Lebanon at a low boil. Two months after the F-15 and Kfir gained their first kills, four more MiG-21s went down. A year followed before another MiG-21 fell, and in December 1980, two more Fishbeds were shot down. In February 1981, a MiG-25 Foxbat was shot down, by an F-15, the first time that one of Russia's superfighters had been destroyed in aerial combat. The Eagle pilot, the squadron commander, used an AIM-7F Sparrow. A second Foxbat fell to another F-15 on July 29, 1981. The F-15 claimed yet another MiG-25 on August 31, 1982, after the height of the Lebanon invasion.

On April 28, 1981, even while Israel and Syria were trying to start some form of high-level discussion, an F-16 pilot from No. 110 Squadron, at Ramat David, scrambled with his CO, now Lieutenant Colonel Amir

Nahumi, to intercept Syrian aircraft somewhere over the Mediterranean, off Beirut. The controller told the two Falcon pilots that their quarry was a flight of helicopters, Mi-8s Hips. After some anxious moments, the IAF pilots spotted the helicopters. The junior pilot launched a missile, which failed to guide properly. As he flashed over his lucky target, he could see his CO taking target practice with his plane's cannon. At first, the Syrian Hip pilot evaded the fire from the Israeli fighter.

As the controller called to disengage because of inbound MiGs (no doubt the hard-pressed helicopter pilots had screamed for help), the junior Israeli pilot armed his cannon. He fired a long burst that sent the Hip diving into the ground, trailing a long plume of smoke.

While most pilots say that a kill is a kill (several IAF aces included Arab helicopters in their scores) – and certainly the F-16 pilots had some difficulties dealing with their slower quarry flying at low level – shooting a helicopter did not have the same glamour, or final level of difficulty and danger, as scoring a kill against another fighter. Thus, it remained for the Falcon to get its first fixed-wing score.

The chance came to Lieutenant Colonel Nahumi, who as a Phantom pilot, had shot down four Egyptian MiGs on his first combat mission during the opening strikes of the Yom Kippur War.

On July 14, 1981 – exactly 15 years after Yoram Agmon had scored the first kill for the Mirage over a Syrian MiG-21 – Syrian fighters launched to intercept a flight of Israeli A-4s near Tyre. The Arab pilots tried to sneak up on the IAF formation from low altitude in the late afternoon's retreating light.

Nahumi maneuvered behind an airplane. He was about to shoot when he stopped. Where was his wingman? It was hard to see in the rapidly falling darkness. Suddenly, the pilot of the plane in front lit his afterburner, and in the glow of the flames, Nahumi could plainly see the huge vertical tail of a MiG-21. There was no doubt of the bogey's identity now, and he launched a Sidewinder at the Syrian fighter. The MiG exploded. With the first F-16 MiG kill, Nahumi looked at his fuel. At the beginning of the engagement he had 2,500 pounds of fuel. When he landed, he had 1,200 pounds.

Nahumi seemed to enjoy flying his fighters to the boundaries of the endurance. He had a chance to test his F-16's endurance to the maximum a month before, flying as part of the strike force against the Iraqi nuclear reactor at Tuwaitha, just west of the capital of Baghdad.

Uneasy over Iraqi nuclear development – could Hussein be planning a nuclear Holocaust for the Jewish state? – Jerusalem began considering a quick, surgical strike on the Osiris reactor, which was being supported by French technology.

Iraq had also begun what would be a long, bloody war with its neighbor, Iran, which was still going through an equally bloody revolution following the overthrow of the Shah. It was truly a jittery time in the ancient land of the Fertile Crescent.

Having just returned from a flight, Lt. Col. Amir Nahumi poses with the ground crew of his F-16A in 1982. The enthusiastic, young enlisted men are proud to stand with their CO by "their" Falcon. The F-16's cannonport is directly above Nahumi. (via Amir Nahumi)

The IAF plan included flights from two squadrons of F-16s – eight bombers – escorted by six F-15s. A team of pilots trained for this important mission, which was originally set for May 10, 1981. However, even as the pilots began heading for their aircraft, word came to scrub the mission, because Jerusalem was concerned of a security leak.

Finally, on June 7, the strike force launched in the late afternoon from Etzion, still in Israeli hands. It was a long flight from the southern Sinai as the force drove north. Yet, for all the time in fearful silence, the IAF pilots evoked no Arab response as they sped over Jordan, Saudi Arabia, and finally into Iraq. The 2,500 kilometers (1,550 miles) flowed beneath the wings of the Eagles and Falcons flying at low altitude to avoid radar detection.

Finally, near the target, at a little past 5:30 pm, the strike lead sent the F-15 escorts up to 25,000 feet, while he and the other F-16 pilots began their pop-up deliveries from 8,000 feet. Accelerating to 600 knots in afterburner, the F-16s rolled over one by one, sighting in on the Iraqi facility. At 3,500 feet, the camouflaged Falcons each released their 1,000-kilogram bombs.

Now, the Iraqi defenses were awake and firing, but it was too late. The eight Falcons were already speeding back in the early evening darkness toward the Euphrates River and home. All the strikers checked in safe and sound, and the leader called the anxious command post in Israel: mission accomplished, no losses. For the time being, Iraq's nuclear program lay in the bombed-out ruins of the Osiris reactor.

The strike, which the Israelis had named Operation Babylon (ancient Babylon was in what was now Iraq), was the first major military operation for the U.S.-manufactured F-16, and the startling success of the mission was both a source of pride and embarrassment for the newly-installed administration of President Ronald Reagan. For the time being, additional shipments of F-16s were put on hold — probably to soothe the furious Iraqis and other Arab states like Syria. However, there was little the Iraqis could do militarily. The Syrians were relatively powerless as well. Instead, they increased their aid to the struggling PLO in embattled Lebanon, and by the first anniversary of the Osiris raid, IAF pilots would find themselves embroiled in another short, but intense conflict. Nahumi would be there, too.

The week-long operation by IDF forces that centered around the embattled Lebanese capital of Beirut evokes bitter memories for all Israelis. To many of the younger generation and members of the more liberal factions, the massive invasion constituted an Israeli Vietnam or Afghanistan. Street demonstrations fought for media coverage along with that of the actual military confrontations.

Even after more than a decade, official IDF sources discourage anything more than a general discussion of the engagements on the ground and in the air. Indeed, an official IDF publication devotes no more than two paragraphs to the fighting in Lebanon, saying only in a chapter on the history of the IAF that "Operation Peace for Galilee provided proof that the new mix of fixed wing aircraft with smart munitions and electronic countermeasures and helicopter gunships was an effective force."[8] Though this statement is certainly true, the limited exposure that Israel gives to this operation, which generated considerable international outcry against Israel (as well as internal strife), illustrates how sensitive the Jewish state remains to the events of 1982.

Criticism and home-grown demonstrations not withstanding, however, by June 1982, Israel had reached the end of her patience in absorbing continuing guerrilla attacks from southern Lebanon, whose low mountains offered considerable sanctuary to PLO rocket squads. Syrian-supplied, Soviet-built Katyusha rockets — little changed from the days of their more noble use against invading Nazi armies in 1941 — rained down on northern Israeli towns and settlements, recalling the dangerous days of 1967 and 1973 when Syrian gunners shelled Israeli farmers in their tractors.

The once-beautiful city of Beirut — the "Paris of the Middle East" — had begun its backslide into a shattered collection of bombed-out apartments and rubble-strewn streets. There was little for young Arabs in Beirut to do but blame Israel for their hardship and lack of future prospects.

Besides continuing PLO activity, two major events finally sparked IDF action. Syria had moved SAM batteries into the Bakaa Valley in eastern Lebanon to defend against Israeli air strikes on PLO facilities and camps. And on June 3, 1982, a PLO hit squad tried to assassinate the Israeli ambassador to England. Shlomo Argov was badly wounded but survived. However, enough was enough; some action was required and IDF ground forces crossed into Lebanon on June 6 behind massive IAF strikes. It was the beginning of a week of intense ground and air action the like of which had not been seen since the first desperate week of the October 1973 war.

While Israeli army units thrust deep into Lebanon, battling Syrian and PLO troops every inch of the way, Israel Air Force squadrons fought their Syrian counterparts in a sharp, but incredibly successful five-day campaign.

Israeli security prohibits publishing any but the barest official assessment, particularly of the aerial action. The stunning, lop-sided tally of Israeli victories varies considerably from a low of 85 to a high of 97, depending on the source, even those sources with some official standing. Whatever the actual numbers, it is clear that the IAF shot down at least 80-90 Syrian MiGs — MiG-21s, MiG-23s and MiG-25s — without the loss of a single IAF fighter in air-to-air combat. Two fixed-wing fighters and a single helicopter were shot down by flak and missiles.

Since most of the pilots of the 1982 campaign are still actively flying, the normal Israeli policy is in effect of not permitting anything but an initial — which can be from the first or last name — to identify pilots.

One man who was already an ace with eight kills from the 1973 war and the first MiG kill by a Falcon in 1981 was Lieutenant Colonel Amir Nahumi, commanding No. 110 Squadron.

"During the 1982 Lebanon War," he recalled, "most of our missions were patrols, and we engaged MiG-21s and MiG-23s in bunches. Since these were not my first engagements, I was not as excited and I was much more in control."[9]

The enemy flew poorly. They were falling in clumps — 35 in one day, 38 the next. It had to be working on them when they looked around their squadron and there were a lot of missing faces. You go out in an airplane and come back in a *truck*. I imagine that toward the end, they were flying in fear.

By the end of the campaign, Nahumi had scored six kills, three in one mission, two in another, and one in another fight. His total was now fourteen.

"The F-16 performed," he remarked. "It is very friendly toward its pilot, and I am still flying it."

On June 9, the IAF went after the Syrian missiles in the Bakaa. Phantoms from No. 201 Squadron and No. 105 Squadron (which soon transitioned to F-16s) bombed and rocketed the Arab positions for three days, destroying 17 of 19 batteries of SA-2 Guideline, SA-3 Goa and SA-6 Gainful SAMs.

During the furious attacks, IAF fighters also engaged swarms of MiGs, now in the uniquely absurd position of having to defend their defenders. With E-2C Hawkeye airborne early warning aircraft controlling the actual engagements for the IAF Eagles and Falcons, the Syrian pilots were overwhelmed. Again, the great difference in quality and training far outweighed any numerical or "home town" advantage the Arabs might have enjoyed.

On June 9 on a dawn patrol, four Eagle pilots found a lone MiG-23 Flogger southeast of Beirut. The Syrian, apparently oblivious to the Israelis' presence, passed beneath the F-15s. Then, probably alerted by his ground controller, the MiG pilot punched in his afterburner in an effort to escape.

One of the Eagle pilots, Major R, fired two missiles. The first seemed to disappear into the clouds, but then returned to hit the Flogger, followed by the second missile. The Syrian went down, the pilot ejecting in full view of a foreign television crew, which filmed the engagement.

Major R. flew a noontime patrol with three other Eagle pilots. They found two MiG-21s, which promptly, and inexplicably, dove into the surrounding mountains, kills for the squadron but not the pilots.

Flying his third mission of a long day, Major R. next launched on a late afternoon escort for strikers on an attack against Syrian SAM batteries. The sun was setting as the force flew toward the Bakaa Valley, and the glaring light was right in the Israelis' eyes. However, their radar caught a pair of MiG-21s, and Major R. and his wingman launched missiles as flak and missiles started coming up from the mountains below. Although the wingman's missile downed one MiG, Major R. couldn't see what his missile had accomplished. Instead he quickly became involved in a twisting engagement with another MiG, whose pilot wrapped his fighter into a tight 8.5-G turn. Major R. could see the Syrian's white helmet as he tried to follow the MiG through the turn.

The Syrian was slowly gaining a tail position on the big F-15, and Major R. fired two missiles, one of which struck the MiG's tail. The enemy fighter crashed, but Major R's aircraft was suddenly also hit by a missile, probably a SAM.

Resolved not to bail out over enemy territory, he fought to keep control of his aircraft as he struggled over the Lebanese mountains. Finally, flying on only one engine, and with his tail still on fire, he landed at Ramat David in northern Israel.

"Landing was a tricky business," he recalled, "but somehow I got through it safely...I had always known that the F-15 was a dependable plane, but I never realized quite to what extent."[10]

The Eagle had indeed proved itself able to bring its pilot home despite extensive battle damage. Major R.'s F-15 had suffered at least 400 bullet strikes (probably from groundfire), its tail was completely burnt, and the starboard engine had been destroyed. Along with a massive fuel leak, it was a wonder that he was able to fly 20 minutes to safety.

"If I had been flying any other plane," he concluded, "I don't think I would have come out of this alive."

During the massive encounters, and even during the normal patrols, the potential for Israeli victories was constant. On one end of the experience spectrum were the junior pilots, who were in their first conflict, and on the other end were several experienced aces.

One F-16 pilot's story is typical. Although he had seen combat during the Yom Kippur War, he had flown ground attack missions in Super Mysteres. Now, in a flight of four Falcons, nine years later, he spotted a Syrian MiG on his radar. Anxious to score a kill, he left his formation to chase the target. But the Syrian pilot, perhaps alerted by his own ground control, sped away at 600 miles per hour, headed toward Damascus.

The disappointed Israeli pilot had to give up the chase and rejoin his comrades. His flight leader had begun calling. The errant would-be MiG killer replied that he was only a few miles in trail and would soon rejoin the flight.

One older F-16 pilot was much more successful. An accomplished ace, Lieutenant Colonel Uri Gil engaged a MiG over the Bekaa Valley, firing his F-16's cannon while in a turn of more than eight G's. Gil had a lot of experience to call upon and kept his eyes outside the cockpit instead of following current training that dictated using the fighter's radar. He got the MiG.

Semi-official totals for the two American fighters – the F-15 and the F-16 – give the Eagle a score of 40 Syrian aircraft downed, and the Falcon, 44 kills. By 1983, according to a report from McDonnell Douglas, Israeli F-15s had scored 54.5 kills, including 23.5 MiG-21s, three MiG-23s and three MiG-25s. Two more MiG-23s were added to the list in November 1985. One F-15C, number 840, nicknamed "Commando," is the top scorer with six kills. Another Eagle, number 975, named "Skyblazer," has five kills, which is remarkable since this aircraft collided with an A-4 in May 1983, sustaining heavy damage. Its pilot managed to return to base, however, and the fighter was repaired and returned to service.[11]

Typically, the Israelis were not impressed with their opponents. One F-16 pilot remarked

The Syrian pilots in some instances showed greater boldness than usual, and even tried to fight. We achieved superiority and shot them down. In such cases, their boldness was their undoing.

One should bear in mind that the Syrians had combat experience from some battles they fought with us in the past, and they did apply some of the things they had learned, but the gap is still wide...[12]

On June 11th, an F-4E shot down a MiG-21 over the Bekaa with a Python 3 missile. It was the 116th and final kill for IAF Phantoms. The pilot, Lieutenant Colonel Ben-Ami Peri of 105 Squadron, became an ace with this victory, scoring his squadron's only F-4 kill, the only IAF Phantom kill over Lebanon. (The Scorpions had traded their veteran Super Mysteres for Phantoms in 1974.) He had claimed four kills during the Yom Kippur War. Leading another F-4 on a patrol, Peri received a warning from his controller of a flight of MiGs to the west. As he headed toward the Syrians, he found himself in a race with two F-15s headed for the same targets over Lake Qir'awn on the Litani River.[13]

The Eagles got there first, and one F-15 pilot shot down one of the MiG-21s. The second MiG disappeared, perhaps initially diving for a ground-level dash to escape. Lieutenant Colonel Peri spotted the MiG about seven miles to the north but turning back to the fight. The Syrian pilot fired a missile at the F-15s, who evaded it. Peri was able to get behind the MiG, whose pilot was apparently concentrating on the F-15s, and fire. His missile flew straight up the MiG's exhaust.

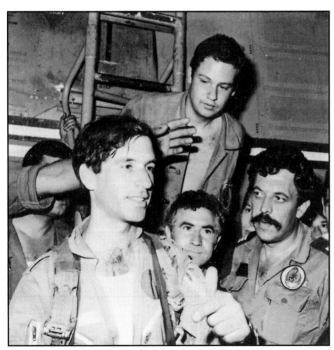

Ben-Ami Peri gestures as he recounts his MiG kill, the last for IAF Phantoms, planeside for his squadronmates. The victory was the fifth for Peri, making him an ace, the last in the F-4. (via the Peri family)

By June 12, both sides had accepted a ceasefire, under great international pressure. However, IAF operations continued. On July 24, an F-4E was shot down by an SA-6 as the Phantom made a reconnaissance run over the Bekaa Valley. The navigator was one of the IAF's most experienced backseaters, Major Aharon Katz. Tall, slim, and calm in battle, he had flown behind Asher Snir many times during the Yom Kippur War when they flew with No. 119 Squadron. His pilot, Captain Gil Fogel, was taken prisoner and did not return to Israel until June 28, 1984, two years after being shot down.

Shortly before his own death, now-Brigadier General Snir had described the mission he and Aharon Katz had flown to the big Egyptian base at Tanta on October 15, 1973. At the end of the account, as he returned to the present to finally say goodby to his faithful navigator, Snir wrote, "And so, Katz, my boy, this still holds with me. Rest in peace in the meantime. If it really gets tough we'll call you. And you'll come."[14] It was a sad, even wistful farewell to a friend and fellow warrior.

The ceasefire did not end the fighting, and eventually, a multi-national force (MNF) made up largely of units from the U.S., England and France, began patrolling in the eastern Mediterranean off Beirut. This rather indecisive campaign saw a few minor attacks on PLO positions, but the worst single attack came when a suicidal truck driver rammed his vehicle into the U.S. Marine Corps barracks on October 23, 1983, killing 241 Marines and Navy personnel. Another attack killed fifty-eight French troops in their barracks.

On December 3, after PLO gunners had fired at F-14 reconnaissance flights, a poorly-executed (because of meddling by higher echelons in Washington) attack by the two air wings from the carriers *Kennedy* and *Independence*, did little to quel rebel activities. U.S. losses were an A-7E and A-6E. The Corsair pilot – a wing commander and strike leader – ejected and eventually returned to his ship. The A-6 crewmen were not as fortunate. The pilot died on the ground of wounds, and his bombardier-navigator (BN) was interned for a month before being released.

With these poor results, and high number of deaths, the MNF soon left Lebanon to its fate, and the Israelis – who had been monitoring the activities of the MNF – continued their occasional attacks against PLO and Syrian positions.

The end of the Yom Kippur War did not mean the end of their service for the aces of the IAF. Military service in Israel is a constant companion until the citizen reaches fifty-five. While many aces, as did many of their less well-known compatriots, left active service to seek their fortunes in other, perhaps less dangerous occupations, they still were part of the overall IDF. Many remained in the cockpit, flying with their regular squadrons as reservists, maintaining their proficiency in the Mirage and Kfir, Phantom or F-16.

McDonnell Douglas F-15A Eagles joined the IAF in the late 1970s. The big fighters gained their first kills in 1979. At this time there was only one Eagle squadron, No. 133. A second unit, 106, was not formed until after the 1982 Lebanon War. This 133 Squadron aircraft is fully armed with AIM-7 and AIM-9 missiles and already carries four victory symbols.

Age was not a limiting factor, and several experienced IAF pilots remained in a fast-jet cockpit into their late forties or even fifties. Indeed, G., thin and wiry, looks forward to sitting weekend alerts in his F-16, if he's not in an El Al cockpit. At fifty-eight, he is looking for his 18th kill.

Others still fly as instructors. Iftach Spector, a brigadier general in the reserves, is a primary instructor in Tzukits at Hatzerim, offering his unique outlook and vast experience to the new pilots of his grandchildren's generation.

Some aces chose to leave flying; a few had medical problems brought on by wounds suffered in combat or perhaps during ejection. Surviving three wars and a decade of aerial combat does not always mean you remain the same, physically, and certainly not mentally.

Moshe Hertz and Ariel Cohen remained in the reserves. Hertz is in R & D, while Cohen works for IAI, and also instructs in Super Cubs. His last flying assignment was in Kfirs in 1987.

Eitan Peled and Amir Nahumi chose to stay in the active IAF. Avihu Ben-Nun became the IAF Commander in 1987, serving until his retirement in 1992. His son, a recent graduate of Hatzerim, proudly proclaims himself "an A-4 pilot!" Tradition is very strong in Israel.

Eitan Karmi, trim and athletic, enjoys wind surfing on the azure Mediterranean, and sometimes shares El Al cockpits with G.

Amos Amir is in private industry, while Yoram Agmon has also gone into private business after a final tour as IAF Attache in Washington.

Oded Marom found that he enjoyed writing and channels his activities into children's books, or writing for IAF publications.

Not all the early aces and pioneers survived into middle age, however. Yak Nevo left active service after the 1973 war, with a final score of three kills, and tried several experiments in private business. He attained a measure of success, however, he became ill and deteriorated quickly. His friends remembered how dignified and alert he remained until he died on September 4, 1989.

Asher Snir, with 13.5 kills, rising to brigadier general, had remained busy, shuttling back and forth in the early 1980s between America and Israel, determined to keep his air force the best. People remembered his piercing blue eyes and strong, no-nonsense manner. But cancer overtook him. His long-time squadronmates gathered at his house to reminisce and say farewell. Weak, but alert, Snir recalled for everyone the glory days of the Six Day War, the War of Attrition and the Yom Kippur War. He died on October 5, 1986.

Amos Amir remembered, "Asher Snir was quite a character, a gentleman, and the best pilot I ever knew."

Giora Rom retired as a major general in 1995 after serving in several high-level assignments. He served as deputy IAF commander, and then as the Israel Defense Attache in Washington 1991-95. His last combat mission was the October 1985 long-range strike against PLO headquarters in Tunis.

Following the tactically successful, but politically disastrous invasion of Lebanon in 1982, Israel continued fighting incursions by PLO guerrillas. Emboldened by Syrian sponsorship, as well as a growing international acceptance of at least the aims if not the methods of PLO Chairman Yasir Arafat, the guerrillas intruded as often as they could. They came by rubber boat, and even ultralight aircraft. They attacked Israeli citizens and tourists, rocketing, shooting, wounding and killing. Something had to be done to show that Israel could and would deal with the threat. What more dramatic show of force could be planned than a long-range air strike against the PLO headquarters supposedly safely esconced in Tunis, Tunisia, 1,300 miles from Israel, and three hours flying time.

Ten F-15s (six F-15B/Ds, and four F-15A/Cs) of No. 106 Squadron would make the flight; eight aircraft would actually attack, while two Eagles would be airborne reserves. It was a complex, dangerous mission, but if successful, it would put the PLO on notice that even their headquarters was not immune from Israeli retribution.

Giora Rom, then a brigadier general in command of Tel Nof Air Base, gained permission to fly the mission.[15]

Taking advantage of increased in-flight refueling capabilities, as well as the experience of the 1981 attack on the Iraqi reactor, the pilots practiced their mission to Tunis, and by October 1, 1985, they were ready.

Launching just after 7 am, the Eagles refueled three times before reaching their target area by 11 am. (After the first refueling, the two airborne spares returned home.) The attack force's bombs destroyed several buildings, including Arafat's command center, although he was not in the area.

The Israelis encountered no defensive fire; no interceptors rose to meet them. They made their attack and headed for home, landing at 1:30 pm to the happy reception of their ground crews.

There have been few aerial engagements since the 1982 contest over Lebanon, but IDF units have met Arab enemies more constantly on the ground, supported by the IAF. Young pilots, barely started in their flight training in 1982, have accumulated several combat missions flying against PLO positions in retaliation for continued raids, intrusions and shellings.

For the time being, however, it seems that the time of sustained aerial combat in the Middle East – as elsewhere in the world – has passed. Thus, the aces of the Israel Air Force will probably remain at their present number (at least 39) for some time. Through the Yom Kippur War of 1973, 33 Israeli pilots officially became aces, with seven attaining scores of 10 or more kills.

Also, despite the large number of IAF kills in 1982, only a few – perhaps no more than six – Israeli pilots became aces over Lebanon.

One captain, who had transitioned from F-4s, became the last, and *youngest* Israeli ace while flying F-16s during the 1982 war. Now a reserve major, he still flies and therefore, his name is withheld for security reasons. (He might be – at least for the foreseeable future – the last fighter ace in the world.)

There were so many F-15s and F-16s (some sources report nearly 40 Eagles and 70 Falcons) in action that several pilots probably scored 2-3 kills, which would account for the high overall number. One source gives the F-15s 36.5 kills, less than half of the admittedly flexible range of total kills. (The Eagles were all assigned to No. 133 Squadron. No. 106's establishment was delayed until after the war.)

One engagement included approximately 100 IAF fighters and a similar number of Syrian MiGs. Nothing as big had been seen since the free-for-alls over Germany nearly 40 years before. (Similarly, during the Persian Gulf War of 1991, while American and Saudi Arabian F-15s shot down more than 30 Iraqi aircraft, no one pilot got five. Two had three kills and eight had double victories.)

While proud of their achievements, the aces of Israel have had little exposure, especially outside their own country. Besides the sometimes overwhelming IDF security, the main reason for this relative anonymity is the sense of being part of the greater team.

As noted earlier, while many IAF pilots have received the first two individual awards – the E-tour HaMofet and E-tour HaOz – none (except one pilot in the 1948 conflict) has received Israel's highest award, the E-tour HaGevora, because there are so many candidates. The official feeling is that awarding the high honor to a select few would destroy this vital team spirit.

Although each pilot knows all or most of his fellow aviators, and each ace is well acquainted with the successes of his comrades, they are imbued with the feeling that their efforts are all for the continued existence of the Jewish state. Most military organizations, particularly the more glamorous air forces, put a lot of time into indoctrinating recruits with this sense of teamwork. However, it is with the IAF that this sense of community purpose has reached its zenith.

Whether discussing the latest development for their aircraft, criticizing a friend's shooting scores, or mounting a major rescue effort, the classic dictum of "One for all, and all for one" finds its greatest proponent in the squadrons of the IAF.

Major General Avihu Ben-Nun, IAF commander from 1987 to 1992, remarked

> Even as commander of the IAF, I was flying with the young pilots, competing with them, briefing whatever mission they were flying that day, not just a special mission for me. Our phi-

losophy is to keep in touch with the lowest levels of the squadron. You know how people are thinking; they know who *you* are. They fly with you, talk with you freely, discuss things with you. And when you make the tough decisions, you know how people will be affected.[16]

It is this aura, this network of performing for the greater good of their country — always at the heart of any successful military organization, but somehow more finely tuned in the IAF — that enabled the young air force to grow from a struggling conglomeration of foreign and native volunteers to the compact, aggressive, well-equipped instrument of national policy and defense it is today. And spearheading this history of dedication and performance are Israel's air aces.

Endnotes:

1. *The New York Times, February 27, 1983.*
2. Benjamin Franklin Cooling, *Case Studies in the Development of Close Air Support* (Washington, D.C., 1990), p. 527.
3. "Israel facing pilot selection dilemma," *Jane's Defence Weekly,* 17 June 1989.
4. *Aerofax News, Vol.4, No.1*, page 4. Aerofax, Arlington, Texas 76006.
5. *Aviation Week & Space Technology, March 10, 1975.*
6. *Air Forces Monthly, October 1992.*
7. *Newsweek, July 9, 1979.*
8. Lt. Col. (Res) Louis Williams, *The Israel Defense Forces: A People's Army* (Tel Aviv, 1989), p. 117.
9. Amir Nahumi, interview, Tel Aviv, November 19, 1992.
10. "My F-15 Was on Fire," by Guy Rimon, *Israel Air Force Magazine, October 1988,* pp 16-17.
11. "The Fighting Baz," by Shlomo Aloni, *Air Forces Monthly, October 1992.*
12. "The Magic Formula of the F-16 Pilots," by Zvi Gutman. Israel *Air Force Magazine, July 1982.*
13. *Israel Air Force Magazine, February 1983.*
14. Merav Halperin & Aharon Lapidot. G-Suit: Combat Reports from Israel's Air War (London, 1990). "With Katz to Tanta," by Asher Snir.
15. *Airforces Monthly, October 1992.* "The Fighting Baz" by Shlomo Aloni.
16. Avihu Ben-Nun, interview, Tel Aviv, November 19, 1992.

A change of command ceremony at Tel Nof finds B. Gen. Amos Amir (left) relieving B. Gen. Avihu Ben-Nun (center). M. Gen. David Ivri (right), IAF commander, made appropriate remarks. Amir was an ace.

B. Gen. Eitan Ben-Eliyahu, the first IAF F-15 squadron commander and the IAF commander at the time of writing, strides toward his F-15. Acknowledged as a good "stick," he scored all of his four kills using his cannon instead of missiles. (IAF magazine)

Appendix A
Aerial Order of Battle, May 1948

Egypt:
40 fighters (Spitfire/ Macchi)
10 bombers (converted Dakota)

Iraq:
5 fighters (Hawker Fury)
4 bombers (converted AT-6 trainers)

Syria:
0 fighters
15 bombers (converted AT-6 trainers)

Israel:
25 fighters (Avia S-199 [101 Squadron])
19 observation (Auster AOP 5/PA-18 Piper Cub)
 2 bombers (converted De Havilland Dragon Rapide/ Noorduyn
Norseman)

By October 1948, the new IAF had also acquired several Spitfire IXs, P-51D Mustangs, and B-17Gs from various sources, mainly from the U.S., and France and Sweden. Other aircraft included such former RAF types as the Bristol Beaufighter, De Havilland Mosquito, and Lockheed Hudson. Six Curtiss C-46 Commandos and five Douglas Dakotas made up the vital transport section.

N.B. These orders of battle are drawn from several open sources published in Israel, the U.S., and England, including:
From the War of Independence to Operation Kadesh, 1949-1956
(Israel Air Force History Department, Israel, 1990)
Shield of David: An Illustrated History of the Israeli Air Force
(Prentice-Hall, 1978)
Air Wars and Aircraft: A Detailed Record of Air Combat, 1945 to the Present **(Facts on File, NY, 1990)**
The Small Air Forces Observer **(Small Air Forces Clearing House, CA, 1992-1993)**

Appendix B
Aerial Order of Battle, October 1956

Egypt:
90 fighters (Meteor F.8s, MiG-15s/MiG-17s)
15 light attack (Vampire FB. 52)
40 bombers (Il-28)

Israel:
80 fighters: 30 P-51Ds [105 Squadron, 116 Squadron]
         10 Meteor FR 9s (117 Squadron, 119 Squadron [3 NF. 13])
         16 Mystere IVA (101 Squadron)
20 bombers/light attack: Ouragan (110 Squadron, 113 Squadron)
2 bombers (B-17G [69 Squadron])

As in the War of Independence, both sides also included several examples of other aircraft that filled in for various transport, liaison, and miscellaneous missions. Egypt operated squadrons of C-46, C-47 and Il-14 transports, while Israel still flew aging Mosquitos and C-47s, alongside newer Nord Noratlases. C-47s of No. 103 Squadron dropped paratroops near the Mitla Pass on October 29, 1956, in one of the major Israeli offensive operations of the war.

Unlike any other war of the Arab-Israeli confrontation, Israel received direct support from two major European countries, Britain and France, whose aircraft and troops participated in attack missions and offensives against the Egyptians.

Appendix C
Aerial Order of Battle, June 1967

Egypt:
380 fighters (MiG-15, MiG-17, MiG-19, MiG-21, Su-7)
40 bombers (Il-28)
30 bombers (Tu-16)

Jordan:
34 fighters (Vampire, Hunter, F-104A Starfighter)

Syria:
136 fighters (MiG-15, MiG-17, MiG-21)
6 bombers (Il-28)

Iraq:
88 fighters (MiG-17, MiG-19, MiG-21, Hunter)
10 bombers (Il-28)
12 bombers (Tu-16)

Lebanon:
12 fighters (Hunter)

Israel:
196 fighters (Ouragan [No. 113 Squadron, No. 115 Squadron], Mystere IVA [No. 107 Squadron, No. 109 Squadron], Super Mystere [No. 105 Squadron], Mirage [No. 101 Squadron, No. 117 Squadron, No. 119 Squadron])
25 Vautour bombers [No. 110 Squadron]
76 Fouga trainers, with limited ground attack capability
   [Seconded from the flight school at Hatzerim]

The overall ratio of the combined Arab air forces to the IAF was roughly three to one. Egypt and Syria, in particular, had been the happy recipients of a flood of Soviet aid since 1956, including several squadrons of top-of-the-line MiG and Sukhoi fighters and fighter-bombers. On paper, at least, the Egyptian and Syrian air forces should have been able to steamroll right over every Israeli ground force, and every aerial strike force.

However, with less than 70 Mirage IIICJs in three squadrons, and six squadrons of aging Ouragan, Mystere and Super Mystere fighter-bombers, the IAF accomplished the impossible, nailing the Arab air forces to the ground in a brilliant air strike on June 5, 1967. By the time the Arabs had collected themselves and begun flying a limited number of operational missions, the Israelis were well on their way toward the Suez Canal, and Damascus.

Appendix D
Aerial Order of Battle, 1968-70

Egypt:
400 fighters (MiG-15, MiG-17, MiG-21)
90 light-attack bombers (Su-7)
24 light bombers (Il-28)
27 bombers (Tu-16)

Israel:
55 fighters (Mirage III [No. 101 Squadron, No. 117 Squadron, No. 119 Squadron]
32 medium-attack (by December 1969), (F-4E Phantom [No. 69 Squadron, No. 119 Squadron No. 201 Squadron])
33 light-attack (Mystere IV [No. 107 Squadron, No. 116 Squadron], Super Mystere [No. 105 Squadron])
85 light attack (A-4E/F [No. 102, 109, 110, 115 Squadrons])

The War of Attrition was a period of transition for both sides. While the Egyptians continued receiving Soviet supplies, they also modernized their defenses, eventually gaining a sophisticated surface-to-air missile umbrella that broke the blase confidence of the IAF.

Israel during this time moved away from their French benefactors and actively sought the newest American designs, specifically, the F-4 Phantom, and the older A-4 Skyhawk, which were much in demand by U.S. squadrons Southeast Asia.

Both aircraft offered greatly increased capabilities, which the IAF desperately needed. The A-4 was simple and rugged, while the F-4 was also tough but breathtakingly powerful, able to carry heavy loads, and also engage Arab MiGs with great confidence.

Appendix E
Aerial Order of Battle, October 1973

Egypt:
350 fighters (MiG-17, MiG-19, MiG-21)
120 fighter-bombers (Su-7)
18 bombers (Tu-16)
5 light bombers (Il-28)

Syria:
120 fighters (MiG-21)
100 fighter-bombers (MiG-17)
45 fighter-bombers (Su-7, Su-20)

Israel:
90 fighters (Mirage IIICJ and Nesher [in mixed squadrons, No. 101 and No. 117 Squadrons; No. 113 and No. 144 Squadrons operated Neshers only]
130 fighter-bombers (F-4Es [in No. 69, 107, 119, and 201 Squadrons])
25 fighter-bombers (Super Mysteres [No. 105 Squadron])
135 light-attack (A-4E/F, A-4H [six squadrons, including No. 102, 109, 110, 115, 116 Squadrons])

After getting through the initial shock of the Egyptian attack in the early afternoon of October 6, sustaining heavy losses in its A-4 and F-4 squadrons, the IAF fought back on two fronts, countering Egyptian and Syrian aerial attacks, as well as intense surface-to-air missile barrages.

The combined Mirage/Nesher squadrons gave good accounts of themselves against late-model MiGs, and also engaged swing-wing Su-20 Fitters, the first combat use of variable-geometry aircraft.

The heaviest IAF losses were in the A-4 squadrons, whose pilots waded into the vast thickets of SAM and AAA defenses each time they flew close air support or interdiction missions along the Suez Canal or over the Golan Heights.

Appendix F
Scores of Selected IAF Aces, 1967-1982

	Aircraft	Score	Notes
Col. G. (Res)*	Mirage/Nesher	17	1,2,3
Brig. Gen. (Res) Iftach Spector	Mirage/F-4	15	1*,2,3
Brig. Gen. Amir Nahumi	F-4/F-16	14	3,4*
Brig. Gen. Ashir Snir	Mirage/F-4	13.5	1,2,3
Col. Abraham Shalmon	Mirage	13.5	1,2,3*
Col. Ya'akov Richter	Mirage	11.5	2,3
Col. (Res) Oded Marom	Mirage	11	1,2,3
Brig. Gen. Israel Baharab	Mirage	11	1,2,3
LtCol. Eitan Karmi	Mirage/Nesher	9	1,2,3

Appendix F (cont)

	Aircraft	Score	Notes
LtCol. Shlomo Levi	Mirage	9	
Col. Yehuda Koren	Mirage	9	1+,2,3
Col. Ilan Gonen	Mirage/Nesher	8	1,2,3
Brig. Gen. Shlomo Egozi	F-4	8	3
Brig. Gen. M.	F-4/F-15	7.5	3+
Col. (Res) Uri Gill	Mirage/F-16	7.5	1,3,4
Brig. Gen. Amos Amir	Mirage	7	1,2
Brig. Gen. Ran Ronen	Mirage	7	1,2,3
LtCol. Yirmiahu Kadar	Nesher	7	1,3
LtCol. Moshe Hertz	Mirage/Nesher	6.5	2,3
Col. Uri Even-Nir	Mirage	6	1,2,3
Brig. Gen. Yoram Agmon	Mirage/F-4	6	1@2,3
LtCol. Eitan Peled	F-4	5	2,3
LtCol. Ariel Cohen	Nesher	5	3
Maj. Gen. Giora Rom	Mirage	5	1#
LtCol. Ben-Ami Peri	F-4	5	3,4#
Maj. Itamar Noiner	Mirage	5	2,3

Notes:

1. 1967, 2. War of Attrition, 1967-1970 3. 1973, 4. Lebanon War, 1982. These numbers indicate only the conflicts in which the ace scored kills, but should not be taken to mean he fought *only* in these wars.

*(Res) = reserve. These individuals have left active duty but remain part of the IDF/IAF as reservists.

1* Spector got a kill in 1966.
4* Nahumi is an ace in two aircraft, as well as being the first F-16 ace.
3* Shalmon scored two kills over Syrian MiG-21s on April 19,1974, when eight MiGs intercepted his flight of four Mirages over Lebanon during an attack on an SA-6 battery.
1+ Koren got a kill in 1966.
3+ M. got the first kill with an F-15 in 1979.
1@ Agmon got the first kill for the Mirage in 1966.
1# Rom is the first IAF ace.
4# Peri is the last F-4 ace.

Bibliographic Essay

Considering the strict Israeli security, there is a surprisingly large amount of published material on the Israel Air Force (IAF), although most of it deals with the period before the 1982 Lebanon incursion. As noted in the text, Israeli officials are still sensitive about that operation, primarily because of the international outcry it generated. Also, many of the pilots who flew during the war—codenamed Peace for Galilee—are still flying, or are in important senior military positions. For a country that has never really known but a few years of relative peace with its neighbors—and, until recent current events changed national postures with Jordan and the PLO, considers itself in a state of war with most of them—Israel jealously guards the security and identities of its military members.

The IDF Ministry of Defense maintains an active press and periodically releases histories of various subjects of interest, primarily for Israeli consumption, particularly the younger members of the IDF and those teenagers about to reach conscription age. While most of these releases are in Hebrew, some of these publications are reprinted in English, or have portions of the Hebrew editions translated into English. Some of the more pertinent government histories are:

From the War of Independence to Operation Kadesh, 1949-1956 (published 1990, The Israel Air Force History Department, in Hebrew)

The Israel Defence Forces: A People's Army, by Lieutenant Colonel (Res) Louis Williams (1989, English)

Open Skies: the IAF at 40 years, Aharon Lapidot, editor (1988, Hebrew/English)

Israel Air Force, Colonel (Res) Oded Marom, editor (1982, Hebrew/English)

In the popular, commercial press, six books can be recommended for good overall descriptions of the development of the IAF; four appeared from 1970 to 1988, while the last two are even more recent.

The Israeli Air Force Story by Paul Jackson (Tom Stacy Ltd, 1970) and *Shield of David: An Illustrated History of the Israeli Air Force* by Murray Rubenstein and Richard Goldman (Prentice-Hall, 1978) are good, short histories. There is good information on the IAF's early history as well as decent photographic folios.

Ezer Weizman's autobiography *On Eagles' Wings* (Macmillan, 1976) is a short, toughly worded memoir by one of the IAF's first fighter pilots who is now Israel's president. Weizman is often quoted by people writing articles and treatises on the IAF (and this author is no exception). Weizman was there at the beginning of the IAF—many would say he was its midwife—and therefore, what he has to say is important, whether or not you liked his methods or personality.

Lon Nordeen's *Fighters Over Israel* (Orion, 1990) is the only one of the first four that is still in print. The author has made Middle East military aviation a subject of personal interest, and thus, his relatively short book has several items of detailed interest.

It was not, however, until 1993 that a popular history of the IAF appeared. *No Margin For Error*—a somewhat dramatic but vague title—by Ehud Yonay (Pantheon, New York, 1993) includes a lively text by an author who by his own admission knows very little about aviation. The knowledgeable reader will immediately spot major errors in aviation terminology. But there is no denying that at times the author is uncovering new details or restating old ones in a vitally fresh manner.

However, he seems to borrow heavily from an earlier autobiography that was published in Israel in Hebrew, but did not appear in a U.S. edition until nearly a year afterward. *Israel's Best Defense* (Orion, 1993), is a bright, knowledgeable autobiography by one of the IAF's early pilots, and one of its first helicopter pilots, Eliezer "Cheetah" Cohen, who has as colorful a personality as Ezer Weizman. These books make a highly readable two-volume history of the IAF through 1992.

G-Suit: Combat Reports from Israel's Air War (London, 1990) is a small paperback that has enjoyed some popularity, possibly because it was the first book with specific names and experiences of several of IAF pilots, as well as including first-person accounts by these aviators. The book is largely a collection of stories that have appeared in the *Israel Air Force Magazine*, and is edited by two of the magazine's editors, Merav Halperin and Aharon Lapidot.

Turning to the aircraft that, after all, formed the inanimate, but decidedly colorful, part of the fighter-ace team, there are numerous books, long and short, and countless magazine articles, dealing with every aircraft mentioned in the text. The Spitfire and Mustang are probably the most described fighter aircraft in history, and they have benefitted from several authoritative biographies. The F-4 Phantom, and even the more modern F-15 Eagle and F-16 Fighting Falcon, have also generated a great deal of print, periodical and book-length. The reader should consult the various endnotes in the main text, which list such aircraft books and magazine articles.

Two large-format books, separated by seven years, also provide well-illustrated overviews of the IDF, with dedicated sections on the IAF. *Modern Military Powers: Israel* (Stan Morse, general editor, 1984), and *Shield of Zion: the Israel Defense Force* (Carlos Lorch and Netanel Lorch, 1991) discuss the general history of the Middle East conflict, using generous amounts of photos and drawings, as well as informed text. *Shield of Zion* provides more of a look at the IDF as a history, however, and gives unique glimpses into daily life and organization, accompanied by fine color photography.

One last book that should be mentioned is *Air Wars and Aircraft: A detailed record of air combat, 1945 to the present* (Victor Flintham, 1990), a tour de force of research and persistance. The book describes aerial combat around the world since the Second World War, and includes several fact-filled sections on the Middle East, including aerial orders of battle.

While a commercial publication, the previously-noted popular monthly journal *Israel Air Force Magazine* has strong ties to the IDF, and indeed, could not exist without the great color photography by IAF cameramen. Unfortunately, the magazine has stopped printing the short English translations of selected stories in each issue, a decision made in 1990. This lack of English thus renders the magazine a considerable challenge to readers unable to read Hebrew, much like the Japanese magazine *Kokufan*, which also has great aviation photography, but limited English translation.

One Israeli magazine with an English edition is the *IDF Journal,* a semi-official quarterly, with articles on various aspects of life in the IDF, as well as on historical topics.

Index

IAF SQUADRONS

No. 69 Sq., 59, 82, 88,109
No. 101 Sq., 17, 10, 12, **14, 15,** 21, 25, 30-32, 41, 46, 47, 51, 56, 57, 61, **68, 69,79, 84, 89,** 86, 97, 99, 106-109, 115
No. 103 Sq., 22
No. 105 Sq., **16,** 25, 43,115, 118
No. 106 Sq., 122
No. 107 Sq., 60, **73,** 87, 88, 96, 101, 109
No. 109 Sq., 17
No. 110 Sq., 18, 43, 50, 115, 118
No. 113 Sq., 18, 21, 86, 89, 109
No. 115 Sq., 89
No. 116 Sq., **65**
No. 117 Sq., 21, 30, 41, 51, 61-62, **68, 74, 76,** 86, **95,** 109,115
No. 119 Sq., 51, **88**
No. 119 Sq., **23,** 30, 41, 44, 46, 51, 56, 61, 109, 120
No. 133 Sq., **77, 79, 121**
No. 144 Sq., **76,** 86, 103, 109
No. 201 Sq., 62, 81, 109, 118
No. 208 Sq., 15
No. 253 Sq., **75**
Hapatishim (Hammer Squadron), **74**

AIRCRAFT

Avia S-199, **10,** 11, **15, 79, 97,**
Bell X-1, 15
Canadair Sabres, 17
Dassault Mirage, **15, 27, 28,** 27-31, **31, 35,** 38, **42,** 41-43, **44, 45,** 50-51, 53-54, 56, **58,** 60, 61, **68, 69, 70,** 77, **79,** 81, **82, 84,** 85-86, **87, 89, 95,** 100, 103, 106, **107,** 109, 110, 114, 115, 120
Dassault Mirage cockpit, **29**
Dassault Mystere, 17, **23, 26,** 43, 48, 54, 85, 103
Dassault Ouragan, 18, **19, 22,** 41, 42, 86
Dassault Super Mystere, 18, 19, 25, **28,** 32, **34,** 38, 41, 43, 48, **52,** 88, 104, 114, 119, 120
De Havilland Mosquitos, 15, 17
Douglas Dakota, 12, 14
Fiat G.55, 14
Fouga Magister trainers, **39,** 42, 43, 103
General Dynamics F-16 Fighting Falcon, 30, 35, 36, 39, **74, 75, 76, 80,** 114, 115, **117** 118-120, 122
Gloster Meteor, **17, 21, 23**
Grumman A-6, 120
Grumman F-14, 120
Hawker Hunters, 32, 50, 100, 101
IAI Nesher, **69, 80,** 85, **86,** 87, 89, **91,** 99, 104, 109, 114
IAI Kfir, **76,** 114, **115,** 116, 120
Macchi C. 205V, 14
McDonnell Douglas A-4 Skyhawk, 39, 55 **59,** 81, 85, 86, 89-91, 95, 96, 101, 103 , 105, 114, **115,** 116
McDonnell Douglas F-4E Phantom, 18, 30, 38, 39, 59-62, **61, 65, 70, 71, 72, 73, 74, 80,** 81, 85, 87, 88, **93,** 94-96, 101-103, 105-106, 109, **111,** 114, 120
McDonnell Douglas RF-4E, 59, 85
McDonnell Douglas F-15 Eagle, 39, **77, 79, 80,** 114, 116, 117, 119, 120, **121,** 122
Messerschmitt Bf. 109, 10
MiG-15, 17
MiG-17, 45, 56, 57, 92, 93, 95, 104, 105, 106
MiG-19, 19, 27, 33, 49, 51, 92
MiG-21, 27, 28, 30, **33, 40,** 42, 44, 46, 51, 53, 54, 60, 61, 62, 63, 64, **69,** 82, 85, 88, 94, 96, 97, **98,** 99, 100, 103, 104, 106, **107,** 108, 113, 116-119
MiG-23, 85, 113, 114, 118, 119, **113**
MiG-25, 85, 113, 116, 118, 119
MiG-29, 114
North American P-51 Mustang, 14, 15, **20, 65**
North American F-100 Super Sabre, 19
Piper Cub, 103
Sud-Ouest Vautour, 18, **19,** 41, 43 50, 51, 85, 103
Supermarine Spitfire, 13, 15, **16,** 17, **65, 79,** 87
Sukhoi Su-7, 44, 46, 47, 54, 57, 85, **104,** 108, **109**
Sukhoi Su-17, 103
Sukhoi Su-20, 108
Sukhoi Su-20s, 85
TA-4H, 59, 85
Tupolev, 16 64

Agmon, Yoram, **31,** 31-32, 53, 60-61, 63-64, **71,** 106, 110, **111,** 115
Aharon, Major Yoeli, 21
Ahikar, Eyal, 61, **71**
al-Assad, Hafez, 92
Alon, Joe, **21**
Alon, Modi, **11,** 12, 14, 15, 45
Amir, Amos, 30, 31, 50, 56, 112, 121, **123**
Arab-Israeli War, 25
Arafat, Yasir, 122
Argov, Shlomo, 118
Augarten, Rudolph, **13, 14, 16,** 17, **20,** 45

Bar Lev, Chaim, 81, **82**
Barzilay, Yitzhak, 47
Bassam, Adal, 79
Ben-Eliyahu, Eitan **70,**116
Ben-Gurion, David, 60
Ben-Nun, Avihu, 30, 48, 54, 55, 59, **71, 75, 76,** 81, **82, 83,** 88, 99, 106, 111, 121, 122, **123**
Ben-Shahar, Tibi, **16**
Beurling, George "Screwball", 12
Bevin, Ernest, 15
Bodinger, Herzl, 99
Boyington, Greg (Pappy), **13**

Chel Ha'Avir, 10, 15, 20
Close, Sergeant Pilot, 15
Cohen, Ariel, 19, 86, 103, 104, **105,** 110, 121
Cohen, Eddie, 11

Cohen, Sid, 17
Cooper, G.S., 15

Dangutt, Dan, **16**, 17
Dayan, Moshe, 60, 95
Doyle, John Joseph, 13, 15

E-tour HaGevora, 122
E-tour HaMofet, 95, 122
E-tour HaOz, 122
Egozi, Shlomo, 94
Egozi, Yeshayahu, 23
Eini, Menahem, **71**, 81
Ekron, 11
El Arish, 97
Elazar, David, 92, 114
Eshkol, Levi, 43, 59
Etzion, 103, 104
Even-Nir, Uri, 62, 86

Fogel, Gil, 120

"G", 36-38, 46, 51, 57, 62, 86, 94, 106-109
Gazit, Yeshayahu, **16**
Goodlin, Slick , 15

Hankin, Ehud, 60, 61, **71**, 81
HaPatishim, 59
Harpaz, Rami, **71**
Hatzor, 30, 32, 60, 91, 99, 106, 107, 108
Hertz, Moshe, 61, 86, **87**, 96, **97**, 99, 121
Hetz, Shmuel, 59, 62, **71**, 81
Hod, Moti, **16**,17, **37**, 43, 62, 105

Ivri, David, **123**

Jacobs., Sandy, 17

Karmi, Eitan, 30, 36, **42**, 44, **91**, 106, 110, 121
Katz, Aharon, 101, **102**
Kelt, 91
Kishon, Lieutenant David, 22
Koren, Yehuda, 50, 62

Lanir, Avi , 33, **99**
Lapidot, Amos, 46, 56
Lenart, Lou, **11**
Levi, Shaul, **71**

Mahal volunteers, 14
Marom, Oded, 19, 30, **49**, 56, **69**, 100, 101, 111, 121
Masada, **75**
McElroy, John F. , 12, 15
Magee, Chris, **13**
Meir, Golda, 60, 92
Moshe Hertz, 61
Mubarrak, Husni, 100, 116

Nahumi, Amir, **74**, **75**, 93, 94, 95, 96, 97, 110, **111**, 116, **117**, 118, 121
Nasser, 17, 22, 30, 33, 42, 53, 55, 56, 57, 63, 84, 85, 92
Nevo, Yak, **21**, 23, 24, **26**, 43, **48**, **94**, 121

Ophir Airfield, 93, 94, 95

Peer, Yitzhak, **71**
Peled, Benjamin, 25, 92, 105, 109
Peled, Eitan, 48, **49**, 88, 94, 103, 121
Peri, Ben-Ami, **120**
Pick, Wayne, **20**
Prigat, Eliezer, 44, **112**

Qastina, 17

Ramat David, 9, 14, 15, 18, 30, 32, 99, 106
Reagan, Ronald, 118
Refidim, **55**, 56, 95, 97, 101, 108, 109
Rom, Giora, 28, **29**, **35**, 41, 42, 44, **45**, 46, 57, **58**, **72**, 86, 89, **90**, 91, 92,111, 121, 122
Ronen, Ran, 32, **34**, 44, 46, 51
Rubenfeld, Milton, 11

SA-2, **112**
SA-3, **112**
Sadat, Anwar, 85, 92, 115, 116
Sayers, Sergeant Pilot, 15
Sella, Aviem, 81, 82
Shafrir (air to air missile), 28, 29, 31, 61, 62, 91, 97, 103, 104, 108
Shafrir I, 47, 62
Shafrir II, 62, 114
Shapira, Danny, **16**, **21**, 27, **49**
Sharon, Menachim, 86
Shaul, Levi, 61
Shavit, Aharon, ("Yalo"), **52**, 86
Sherut Avir, 9
Sidewinder (air to air missile), 28, 56, 57, 61, 62, 93, 94, 101, 103, 109, 114
Sidon, Yoash, 21
Simbal Win, 58
Six Day War, 9
Snir, Asher, **44**, **46**, 81, 101, **102**, **112**, 120,121
Spector, Iftach, 26, 33, **49**, 51, 57, 60, 61, **70**, **74**, 81, 87, 89, 93, 94, 97, 101, 112, 120

Tel Nof, 30
Tsuk, Yosef, 23, **49**

Weintraub, Shlomo, 62
Weizman, Ezer, 10, 11, 12, 13, **14**, 17, 18, 23, 27, 30, 32, 37, 59
Weizmann, Chaim, 11

Yair, David, **71**
Yeager, Chuck, 15
Yoeli, Aharon, **21**

Zohar, Ben-Zion, 50